Praise for
Some New Kind of Kick

"They should build Kid Congo Powers his own personal hall of fame. *Some New Kind of Kick* is an instant classic of sex, drugs, and punk rock by one of underground music's most legendary kings of cool."

—MARK LANEGAN, Screaming Trees, author of
Sing Backwards and Weep and *Devil in a Coma*

"Do you have any fucking guts? Kid Congo's got 'em all. Who else comes out of the closet when they're fifteen years old in 1974, embraces Glam, then Punk, when you would still get your ass beat for it, forms one of the most important rock bands in history before he ever played a note, then lays down the timeless tracks from the depths of his heart that last forever? I'm blown away by the courage organically flowing through him. This book is dripping with all the sadness and beauty in the world. Smell it, taste it, see it. Its pages are stained with my Angeleno tears; it demolished me. A crucial document. Thank you, Kid; you rule."

—FLEA, Red Hot Chili Peppers, author of *Acid for the Children*

"Like the man himself, bursting with humor, heart, and good grace. A gem."

—NICK CAVE, Nick Cave and the Bad Seeds, author of
And the Ass Saw the Angel and *The Death of Bunny Munro*

"I first met Kid Congo as he was babysitting a vintage store in New York City for a friend while Meg White and I perused the vintage clothes. He recognized US! (The White Stripes) at a time when nobody knew us, which was not lost on us. Meg and I walked away beaming that we'd just met a member of the Gun Club. A serene and kind soul in an ocean of scratchy, angry artists, Kid brings a cool and spiritual presence to whatever musical project he is a part of, and he is part of some of the best of all time."

—JACK WHITE III, The White Stripes, Raconteurs,
The Dead Weather, founder of Third Man Records/Third Man
Books, author of *We're Going to Be Friends*

"Kid Congo has wonderfully articulated his flamboyant adventures as a musical vagabond from teenage glam guttersnipe on the streets of Hollywood to globetrotting guitar slinger. *Some New Kind of Kick* is hilarious, heartbreaking, and historically juicy. I devoured it."

—LYDIA LUNCH, No Wave icon, performance and spoken
word artist, author of *Paradoxia* and *The Need to Feed*

"Kid Congo writes from the heart in a pure and unadorned way. This is a beautiful book about rock and roll and friendship. Read and be blessed."

—Bobby Gillespie, Primal Scream, author of *Tenement Kid*

"Kid Congo Powers is the perfect person to write an autobiography. Besides being in the Cramps, the Gun Club, Nick Cave and the Bad Seeds, not to forget his excellent solo work with the Pink Monkey Birds, he's got an unending amount of source material. What makes *Some New Kind of Kick* so much more than an anecdotal checklist is Kid's approach to his story. He goes at it with such beautiful openness, humor, and humility the reader is with him from the first page. These qualities are the very stuff of the man. There are some people you hope will one day make the time to put their life into a book because it's obvious they've taken some less commonly walked paths. Kid is one of those guys and he did it. The results are standalone and really cool. I'm a multi-decade fan and so happy he did this."

—HENRY ROLLINS, Black Flag, Rollins Band,
author of *Get in the Van*

Some New Kind of Kick

A MEMOIR

Kid Congo Powers
with Chris Campion

hachette
BOOKS

NEW YORK

Hachette Books
Hachette Book Group
1290 Avenue of the Americas
New York, NY 10104
HachetteBooks.com
Twitter.com/HachetteBooks
Instagram.com/HachetteBooks

First Edition: October 2022

Published by Hachette Books, an imprint of Perseus Books, LLC, a subsidiary
of Hachette Book Group, Inc. The Hachette Books name and logo is a
trademark of the Hachette Book Group.

The Hachette Speakers Bureau provides a wide range of authors for
speaking events.

To find out more, go to www.hachettespeakersbureau.com or call
(866) 376-6591.

The publisher is not responsible for websites (or their content) that are
not owned by the publisher.

Library of Congress Control Number: 2022940628

ISBNs: 9780306828027 (hardcover); 9780306828041 (ebook);
9780306831430 (signed edition); 9780306831447 (B&N.com signed edition);
9780306831454 (B&N Black Friday signed edition)

Printed in the United States of America

LSC-C

Printing 1, 2022

*For Ryan, who inspires me every second of every day
with his endless love and encouragement*

Life is short
Filled with stuff
Don't know what for
I ain't had enough
I want some new kind of kick

—LUX INTERIOR

Contents

Introduction by JON SAVAGE   xi

I

1   The Feminine Bridge   3
2   The Enjoyment of Fear   21
3   Theresa   35

II

4   The Prez   49
5   From the Closet to the Needle   67
6   Lysergic Acid Delinquents   91
7   Preachin' Blues   109
8   Acquiring Congo Powers   129

III

9   The Las Vegas Story   157
10 On the Ledge   177

11   Bad Seed   195

12   Good Son   219

13   This Way to the End, My Friend   237

14   He Walked In   251

Acknowledgments   *255*

Introduction

BY JON SAVAGE

K id Congo Powers is cool. At the age of fourteen, when he was
still Brian Tristan, he got to see the New York Dolls in their
first pomp. At the age of fifteen he became a regular at Rodney's
infamous glam slam English Disco. In 1976, when he was seventeen,
he rushed out to buy the Ramones album on the day of release: they
were, as he writes, "a dream fulfilled." Later that year, just after his
cousin Theresa was killed by unknown assailants, he started the West
Coast branch of their fan club and found his own tribe of outcasts.

By 1977 he was an insider in that extraordinary, lost youth
subculture—the Los Angeles Punk Scene—becoming the fan club
president for that most hermetic and futuristic of groups, the
Screamers. After setting up the Gun Club with Jeffrey Pierce, he was
asked to join the Cramps, with whom he stayed for three years—
playing on their definitive second album, *Psychedelic Jungle*. When he
left the group's "proscriptive" world, it felt like escaping "a cult."

Jumping from the frying pan into the fire, he then joined Nick Cave and the Bad Seeds.

Kid Congo Powers is gay. Like many of us, he was liberated by the arrival of David Bowie in 1972: "There could hardly have been a more perfect fantasy figure and foil for a gay teenager at the time than David Bowie. He was a rock star, of course, but androgynous to the extreme; both asexual and openly hedonistic. He was like an alien from outer space, which was exactly the experience of a gay teenager at the time—dispossessed on a hostile planet far from home."

This was something that wasn't much talked about in the late seventies Punk world. People did it, people had sex, but they didn't join the mainstream gay world of Disco, with its more open approach to the topic: "We wanted to scare the hell out of everyone and shake up the status quo. For us gay kids, that meant the homosexual status quo. we did not fit into the 'clone' or 'disco!' mentality of late '70s gay culture, nor did we want to. As first wave punk rock gays, we weren't interested in being 'out' either."

There was a ready-made, affirmative gay world out there, but punks rejected it. Perhaps it was, in a strange way, too mainstream, too regimented—too straight. Or perhaps punk was the perfect place for those who were not ready to address their sexuality, who were happy to subsume themselves into a wider weirdness that could cloak who they really were. Whichever way, punk was not an ideal place to explore a sexuality that was still ill-understood, still taboo— particularly once the jocks and the skinheads arrived. Gay punks were double outsiders.

Like many teens at that time, Brian Tristan took a trip into the dark side, dabbling with heroin, living in a succession of 24/7 party houses, "fuelled by a never-ending diet of drugs and alcohol." Renamed Kid Congo Powers by the Cramps in 1980, he embarked on a twenty-year trip of drunkenness and heroin addiction, recovery and relapse, before a series of tragedies—the death of his father, of several friends from AIDS, of his musical partner and soul mate, Jeffrey Pierce—brought him to the naked lunch at the end of that particular fork.

Unprocessed grief and denial of his sexuality had brought him to this point: "In London, I would go to gay bars and pick up people. I didn't have relationships. I was getting blackout drunk and sleeping with people." He writes: "Intimacy was alien to me. Not physical intimacy, emotional intimacy. I didn't realize until then how much I'd suppressed my true self as a heroin addict, contorting myself into this asexual posture that was very unnatural and extremely silly."

Kid Congo Powers is a survivor. Even in the darkest debauch, he is saved by some kind of innocence, a self-starter get-up-and-go, and, perhaps, simple sheer luck. The book ends in 1997, with his final release from heroin, but I suspect and hope that he has entered his sixties as a happy man—having, like many of us again, finally escaped the self-hatred and self-denial that being born gay in the 1950s engendered. What he had to go through to get to this point is in this book.

The Feminine Bridge

They say some people are born under a bad sign. I was born under a bad bridge. Well, not bad, just mixed up . . . and wrong. A bridge that couldn't decide whether it was male or female.

I grew up in La Puente, California, a largely Hispanic suburb, east of Los Angeles. Whoever named the town must have flunked first-grade Spanish, simply misheard what someone else said, or maybe didn't even speak a word, because a bridge is always, without fail, male. But we were named *La* Puente. Ours was female. Was it bisexual? Transsexual? Pansexual? Gender-fluid?

And where was this bridge? There was no bridge that I knew of in La Puente, not even a river to cross. But that wasn't the only neighborhood misnomer causing me confusion as a child.

A few blocks from my home was the City of Industry, the next town along from La Puente. Only, it didn't smell like oil and dust, but tomato ketchup and strawberry jam that wafted out of the Kern's factory abutting the train tracks at the end of East Temple Avenue.

An invisible, fragrant cloud hung over the entire area inducing an olfactory schizophrenia in the local population. On strawberry jam days, life was sweet, without a care in the world. On tomato ketchup days, for some reason, people were crabbier. Perhaps it was made from a deadly nightshade.

My sister Barbara worked down the road from Kern's, at the Mattel toy factory. Now, *there* was my kind of industry! In my imagination, she worked on the production line in a Willy Wonka wonderland alongside green-haired troll dolls, tinkering away making toys galore. In reality, the Mattel factory was your run-of-the-mill urban sweatshop. "I hate my job" was a common refrain from my big sis when she got home from work, exhausted by the mundane daily drudgery. I happily ignored her reality check for my fantasy, because she would often bring home discarded seconds and broken or misshapen Hot Wheels cars so much the rage for little boys at the time. "They were going to throw these in the garbage," she'd tell me. "I work too hard to see them trashed. I figured you might be able to play with them anyway."

Given that most of the muscle cars I was gifted usually had no more than three wheels and were so banged up they had doors or interiors missing, it was difficult to play with them in the way Mattel intended. I created my own entertainment. Those broken-up vehicles just happened to be perfect for playing "demolition derby." I would smash them together and send them careening over the end of a table to some terrible demise. I think I was probably inspired by my love for the commercials I used to see on TV for the nearby Irwindale Speedway, where supercharged customized hot rods raced along the strip every weekend. The commercials were a riot of noise and a real turn-on, motors revving, cars colliding, and the announcer screaming his lungs out on top of it all. Barb also used to bring me tons of warped pieces of plastic tracks with hairpin twists and turns, which afforded me hours of fun creating endless roads to nowhere—my favorite destination.

La Puente's road to nowhere arched north to a freeway overpass, the closest thing we had to a genderless bridge, and landed right in the middle of Hell Town. At least, that's what my mother told me they used to call Baldwin Park in the '50s, because it was the place you went to partake in any sinful activity involving drugs, prostitutes, and guns. Thanks for the tip, Mom! If you were lucky enough to crawl out of Hell Town on your hands and knees back to the overpass, a meditative respite awaited you. Just two blocks from our family abode was a solemn-looking redbrick building with a perfectly manicured lawn outside. You never ever saw anybody going in or out of its front doors. This was the Burroughs Corporation building. A nightmare-inducing *Twilight Zone* episode to some, the Burroughs Corporation was a Zen garden to me, radiating coldness and endless mystery while striking fear into the population at large, the public's minds focused on a fear of the unknown. If visitors from other planets were already here on Earth, I imagined they probably worked in that building. It was only in my adulthood that I would put two and two together and realize the company was founded by the grandfather of my favorite author, William S. Burroughs.

Adding further to the fractured collective psyche of this town, La Puente had two drive-in theaters mere blocks away that projected movies in direct moral conflict with each other. To the south, the Vineland played family-oriented first-run fare, like Disney's *The Love Bug*. The most subversive movie to play there may have been Jerry Lewis in *The Nutty Professor*. A quick hop to the west was the Edgewood Drive-In, whose stock-in-trade was almost exclusively sexploitation and horror movies, like *Psych-Out*, *Spider Baby*, and *The Gruesome*

Twosome. You could say the Edgewood was really on edge! Every parent in La Puente was presented with a moral dilemma when it came to a night out; it was like you *had* to choose between good and evil. The kids on our block were lucky ducks because all we had to do was crawl onto the roofs of our parents' houses to see both screens clear as day, and even better if you swiped your dad's binoculars. Guess which was the more popular drive-in? In craning our necks to sneak a peek at all the skin and sin we could, we bratty kids coined the term "the West is the best" long before Madison Avenue or Jim Morrison.

This was my entire frame of reference as a kid growing up in La Puente: a sexually ambiguous bridge, sweet-and-sour air, disjointed toys, morally exempt celluloid, Hell Town, and mysterious, creepy buildings. As I look back on it, my fate was set to never look at anything without an eye askew.

On weekends, we often made the three-block jaunt to the Edgewood as a family in our snot-green Nash, fondly referred to as the "Booger Bus." Mom and Dad would pack us kids up with blankets, pillows, homemade popcorn, and a coffee can to pee in, because an entire subplot could be missed through one trip to the bathroom. Waiting in the ticket line of vehicles, plunked between my sisters, with car engines rumbling around us, I would look up at the green-painted concrete wall, illuminated by floodlights, with the silhouettes of palm trees bathed in moonlight cast upon it. Behind those walls, I would get a close-up look at the giant glow of the movies' illuminations and feel a rush of anticipation and excitement at what was to come. The promise of being lost in another world—and what a world!

The first movie I remember seeing at the Edgewood was *Lady in a Cage,* featuring Olivia de Havilland as a disabled widow whose home is invaded by sadistic freaks who trap her in a cagelike wrought-iron elevator and spend the rest of the movie physically and psychologically torturing her, just for the hell of it. Fun, I thought. Weird? Yes. Freaks? They were both attractive and repulsive. I can't remember feeling any compassion for poor Olivia, the way I did for Bambi. But was the movie thrilling? Absolutely.

Next there was *The Wild Angels* with pretty Peter Fonda and nitro Nancy Sinatra as sharpened black-leather-clad Hells Angels out for kicks however they could get them. I knew I was coming along for the ride right at the opening credits, when the first hit of that creamy, savage fuzz-guitar riff that kick-starts Davie Allan and the Arrows' theme song sent shivers up my spine and made cycle-delic tire tracks all over my clay-tablet brain. Little did I know then that my future career as a musician was already cemented. I ate up the hippie biker culture in the movie. This ain't the Summer of Love, said their sneers. Was that what adulthood meant? It was free and mean, intoxicating and scary, at the same time. If being bad was cool, I wanted to be bad. Not bad-bad, just good-bad, but not evil, as the Shangri-Las put it.

When LSD exploitation film *The Trip* came out soon after (also starring Peter Fonda), we were packed into the Booger Bus once again and hauled down to the Edgewood to see what a "square" might discover in an acid-laced sugar cube. Even though he did drugs, I think his character was an academic; that's pretty square, I guess, compared to a Hells Angel. I have this distinct memory of becoming quite titillated while watching the scene when Peter Fonda was trolling through a laundromat off the Sunset Strip while tripping heavily. He lifts the lid of the washing machine and becomes engrossed with the agitator as it spins and shakes back and forth. That scene stayed with me for a long time, shaking eight-year-old me down to my brown suede Hush Puppies. It made me feel excited and funny in a way that, at the time, I had no idea was sexual. I also vowed, right then and there, that I must take a "trip" of my own someday.

I wouldn't say I was a problem child, but my exposure to all this morally degraded popular culture clearly had an effect on my juvenile development. One night, we were all watching TV as a family in the den. The Shangri-Las were the musical guest on some prime-time variety show, performing "I Can Never Go Home Anymore," a song, appropriately enough, about a problem child. It was one of those vivid mini-dramas written for the group by their Svengali, Shadow Morton, sketched with pathos and etched in pain, in a way I would come to love. But that night, to me, it was just another song, albeit one with a convoluted plot that was really hard to follow in which the teenage heroine falls in love with a boy against the wishes of her mother, runs away from home, and quickly comes to regret it.

As the song hit its fevered emotional crescendo, right at the point where the girl, desperate and alone on the street, is flooded with regret at having wronged her mama, the group all dropped to their knees onstage to sing a lullaby refrain. Lead singer Mary Weiss let out a harrowing wail—"Maamaa"—and I blurted out, "What is that *son* of a bitch *crying* about?"

It seemed like a perfectly reasonable observation to me, but my parents were horrified. Given how often I heard my parents curse at home, they shouldn't have been too surprised. They were shocked nonetheless, not so much at my lack of basic human compassion for the poor, distraught Shangri-La than at my all-too-mature display of profanity. The reaction from my parents was swift. "Brian, go to your room and think about what you've done!" Sitting there, alone, while everyone else continued watching TV at the other end of the house, I came to the conclusion I must have done something right.

Brian, by the way, was the name I was given at birth. I don't know why that name in particular was picked out for me. It didn't have any sentimental or familial connection I knew of. There were no uncles, grandparents, or cousins called Brian. I guess it just seemed "right," and that was fine for me. When schoolkids would tease me, the very worst nickname they could come up with was "Brian the Lion." I thought that was pretty great. Being a lion gave me pride.

I can't remember a time when music wasn't a presence in my life in one way or another. I have been told by my sister Barb that I was even rocking out in the crib, such was my affinity for primal rhythms. Before I could even walk, I would get into my sister's record pile and she would look on horrified as I picked out my favorites, with hands smeared in baby food, and waved them around in the air, as if conducting traffic in a hurricane. From an early age, I was able to identify each record solely by the color and design of the label, and would become hypnotized as I watched them go round and round on the turntable. As a result, colorful spinning things continue to attract my attention today.

Growing up, I was fortunate to have two older sisters and a number of cousins who were all into music in a big way; I had access to lots of records at home. My sister Barbara adored blue-eyed soul groups like the Righteous Brothers, dance numbers like "The Twist" by Chubby Checker, and surf tracks like "Pipeline" by the Chantays. "Short Shorts" by the Royal Teens was heard so much in our house that some of the first words I ever spoke were from that song: "Ooh, man, dig that crazy chick."

At home, my parents mostly played Mexican music: female ranchera singers like Lucha Villa or the ballads of men like Cuco Sánchez, so revered he was known as the "Voice of Mexico." I didn't know any Spanish at the time, but I didn't need to. I could hear in the voices and their phrasing that these singers were in heavy emotional turmoil. In later years, I found out the songs were mostly about men doing wrong and having affairs, about drunken verbal and physical abuse and being cuckolded by their wives and drowning their sorrows in drink. It was our version of country music. Suddenly, I understood why the voices I heard were awash in grief and feelings of revenge. "If blood or murder was justice, so be it," they sang. Mom and Dad liked a drink or two (or three or four) and would blast this music on the hi-fi console late into the night, long after my bedtime. I could hear them from my room, singing along loudly, commiserating with the protagonists of the songs and letting loose with the occasional Mexican coyote yell. That was how I learned to sleep through just about anything.

Music was also a big part of family get-togethers at my grandmother's wood-framed house on Anderson Street in an industrial section of Boyle Heights, East Los Angeles. My immediate family was humongous, with aunts, uncles, dozens of cousins, and another extended family of friends and acquaintances. My cousin Theresa and I were the same age. We grew up together. Her younger brother, Ricky, often hung out with us also. Theresa's mother, my aunt Jenny, was a single mom who lived in a small duplex at the back of my grandparents' house.

All throughout my childhood, for years and years, a visit to Grandma Carmelita, my mother's mother, was a weekly weekend ritual for me and all my many cousins. She was a small but strong Native American woman, who grew up on a reservation in Socorro, New Mexico, and had received all the Native wisdom, traditions, and superstitions. When my mother would get a scrape or cut as a child, Grandma would grab a handful of cobwebs, which were plentiful in her old wooden house, and put it on as a salve to stop the bleeding.

She had all these witchy herbal remedies that were a great mystery to me. She was born in 1906 so, when I was a young child, she seemed ancient to me, a benevolent elder filled with great learning and empathy. Carmelita was our family matriarch, a giant figure in all our lives.

A typical Saturday at my grandmother's involved a lot of cooking, eating, and drinking. Food was a big part of the family gatherings at Grandma's. The smell of braised meat with lard and chilies filled the kitchen and hallways while the living room was given over to heavy drinking, loud singing, heated card games, casual dominos, and sometimes even jubilant family brawls. Watching over all this activity was a giant framed painting of Jesus that used to scare the bejeezus out of me. He wore a crown of thorns on his head, tears rolled down his cheeks, and this terrible, anguished expression was etched into his face.

At these parties, my father and uncles would play guitar and sing ranchera songs in Spanish. The ladies sang as well. As a matter of fact, my aunties Margaret and Sarah played guitar too. Everyone joined in. The singing went on for hours. They always seemed to be having a lot of fun.

All the kids, and there were a lot of us, were usually crammed into a guest bedroom with a tiny black-and-white TV that had terrible reception. The adults and their partying really held no interest for us, and we forgot about them altogether. We were in our own zone. Most of us have since done pretty well, so being glued to that gray fuzzy static can't have caused us too much harm.

Theresa and I loved to hang out for hours in our secret hiding place under Grandma's sink, spying on the adults and giggling our heads off with our hands over our gobs, trying to stop from being discovered. Sometimes we commandeered the record player with rock 'n' roll 45s and danced our own version of the Twist, spinning round and round until we were dizzy and nauseous. Rejuvenated after some Mother's Pride grape soda, we ran wild in the pickle-factory parking lot next to Grandma's rickety wood house, the lot carpeted with cucumbers we smashed under our Sunday-best shoes.

My parents were Catholic and churchgoing . . . to a point. They observed all the holidays but didn't really practice. However, they did want us kids to be raised in the church. I was baptized but never confirmed because my mom missed the deadline to sign me up for catechism classes. She went to the church school and said, "Oh, sorry, I missed the deadline by a day, I want to sign up my son."

They said, "Well, you *can't*, you've missed the deadline."

"*That's* not very *Christian* of you," my mom replied. "In that case, he's not going to be confirmed in this church." And I never was. So my official affiliation with religion was never completed, which might help explain the wandering soul I became.

Besides being scared of that gruesome painting of the crucified Jesus in my grandmother's house, I was never that god-fearing. But I was petrified of Santa Claus. You know when you see those pictures of kids screaming in Santa's lap? I was one of those kids. When my parents took me to the Movieland Wax Museum in Buena Park, I couldn't wait to jump into Frankenstein's lap, though. He was my role model. Frankenstein felt out of place, knowing he didn't fit in, in a society that did not accept him for what he was. He represented the otherness I felt as a Chicano kid growing up in a white world.

I would see the Shangri-Las or *Leave It to Beaver* on TV and, as much as I identified with white culture, and even aspired to be white on some level, I knew I wasn't and could never be a part of it. I wasn't at all ashamed of my heritage. On the contrary, we were told to be proud of our culture. But it became a source of struggle within me anyway. It seemed like the Mexican part of my family life existed in a bubble and was very contained: at the get-togethers in my grandmother's house, the food we would eat, and the music the adults would listen to.

My parents spoke Spanglish—Boyle Heights Spanish—but only when they were trying to hide stuff from us. Born in America to immigrant parents, both my mom and my dad had their own struggles with assimilation. They did not want us to be afflicted by what they went through.

La Puente was mixed but mostly Chicano. I didn't ever think about it in racial terms—not then. I was conscious of economic differences, as my father had a blue-collar job and my sister worked in a factory. We didn't know any rich Mexican people.

I used to see cholas in my neighborhood, though, and was very in awe of their whole vibe. There was this one girl named Vicky Frijo who lived around the corner from my house and had this very extreme look: immaculately applied jet-black eyeliner, like Elizabeth Taylor in *Cleopatra*, a giant beehive, and white pancake makeup. As a little kid, I would see her in the street and become entranced, unable to take my eyes off her. She was always very sullen. I never saw her smile. She looked as dangerous as she was glamorous, although, thinking back, the danger was all wrapped up in the glamour, at least for me. I was drawn to her otherness.

In those preteen years, my older cousins, Mike and David Noriega, were a formative influence on my future musical taste. They were already in their mid-teens and played guitar in a high school rock 'n' roll garage band. It was through them that I first heard Jimi Hendrix. They would play *Axis: Bold as Love* over and over and over again. I really dug all the spaceship-leaving-the-launching-pad sounds Jimi wrenched out of his guitar. The helium-voiced spoken intro to "EXP," talking up the possible existence of UFOs, always made me laugh and, at the same time, inspired dreams I might one day encounter a UFO myself. I would also sing along to "Castles Made of Sand," with its devastating lyric about a disabled young girl who "decided to die." Other than hearing creepy nursery rhymes as a child, that might have been the first time I was really wowed by poetry. I would hold the album cover up and stare at the fish-eye photo of the band, looking so awesome and exotic in psychedelic garb that conjured up an aura of Eastern mysticism. I was in thrall to their costumes and sense of style.

Not only did my cousins have great taste in music, they also had outlandish taste in cars. David drove a blue metal-flake woodie, which had the words *So Fine* inscribed in white script on the rear windows, a nod to cholo culture. It was 1967. I was eight years old. Hot rods and psychedelic music were already imprinted on my consciousness. I was ready to roll.

Around the same period, I remember sitting on the couch at home watching my teen sisters, Ruth and Barbara, and our cousins Irene and Lucy all getting ready to go out to a dance one night where an East LA Chicano band called Thee Midniters were playing. As they primped themselves in front of the mirror, chattering and dancing, their excitement about the night's event was palpable. I didn't know who or what Thee Midniters were, but I wanted to feel that kind of thrill and instinctively knew that music was the conduit. But, still way too young to go-go dance in a cage with the groovy set, I sat there steaming, feeling left out. Fortunately, another cousin, Steve, who was the same age as me and also barred from the dance-night fun, saved the day by suggesting we take our toy trucks out to the backyard and bury them. A Destructo Derby game was just the distraction I needed. Ahh, the sweet joys of youth!

It was my mom who encouraged me to channel my creative impulses into, shall we say, more productive pursuits. She had a passion for making art, not for public consumption, just for her own entertainment. She was extremely creative. I remember watching her make these prints of flowers she'd etched into Styrofoam sheets saved from packages of hamburger meat. She told me they were influenced by Andy Warhol. That meant nothing to me at the time, but, through her, I was exposed to art and artists from an early age.

We painted a mural together on a wall in the hallway of our house. It was trippy and psychedelic, full of astrological signs. She drew these eerily realistic spiraling tunnels on the way to the bathroom that looked like portals to another world. It felt like such an achievement, we dated it: 1971. Later that same year, Mom gave me a palette of watercolor paints for my twelfth birthday. Inspired, I immediately set to work that night on an impressionistic portrait of Jimi Hendrix, copied from the cover of his just-released *Cry of Love* album, which I'd also gotten for my birthday. My Hendrix obsession was still in full bloom. I gifted the painting to my mother. She was so proud, it hung in the family home until the day she died.

I always felt a little adrift from the norm. But now I come to think of it, maybe there never was a norm and my family was always off-kilter. Aren't all families a little bit strange anyway? Being a weird kid meant I fit right in! There was a story I would often hear, about the rather unorthodox courtship of my parents, Manuel and Beatrice, that seems to speak to that.

When they met, my father was working as a bar-back at a neighborhood joint in Boyle Heights called the Blue Sky. My maternal grandfather lived nearby and that was his local hangout. When my mother was of age, she began to frequent the bar also.

Two things my mother always liked to do was to drink and to party. She was kind of wild, a free spirit in the buttoned-up '50s. One night, she closed the bar. The owner called out for somebody to accompany Beatrice home, because the bar was in a dangerous neighborhood and it was risky for her to walk alone at night. My father offered to take her. He had been flirting with her for some time at the bar, but she wouldn't give him the time of day. He saw this as an opportunity to spend some quality time alone with her. So they got into the car and, the way my mother told it, "Suddenly, we were in the back seat furiously making out, and I had torn your father's shirt off." She remembered that a friend of my father's walked by, peered into the car window, and said, "Hey, what are you doing in there?," then briskly walked away, embarrassed, when he realized what was going on. For her part, Mom seemed secretly thrilled the journey home from the Blue Sky had turned torrid.

They stayed together from that night on, got married shortly after, and remained very much in love, partners for life, even though they seemed like polar opposites personality-wise. My mom was quite the hell-raiser, and my father was so affable that his brothers nicknamed him "Smiles," after his Spanish birth name, Ismael, because he was always smiling. The name stuck and that's what everybody called him: Smiles.

After my parents married, Dad got a job as a welder. He worked for Stainless Steel Productions and, being a lifelong Democrat and staunch union supporter, joined the United Steelworkers. They bought a house in La Puente, which was a brand-new suburb where lots of young couples were moving because it was both affordable and low on crime, a safe place to raise a family.

Beatrice was a stay-at-home mom after the birth of my eldest sister, Barbara. By day, she was the perfect housewife and mother.

By night, she'd drink and let loose. She loved my father and took care of him, but she was also frustrated at being confined to the home and would lash out. She had a mouth like a truck driver when she was drunk, and could become quite verbally abusive. I think she always felt out of place in the suburbs. My mom longed for the city life she had before they married. She was a voracious reader and devoured the newspaper back to front every day, especially the travel section, as if she was keeping alive a dream to one day leave La Puente and planning her escape. I guess I gave her a reason to stay. I was very attached to my mom, but I was growing up fast. No longer her little boy.

The touch paper of my own sexuality was lit in the locker room at Torch Junior High, the school down the block from where I lived, whose ultramodern circular buildings made me think of flying saucers. I don't recall a whole lot about my time at junior high other than that it was the first time I had to get changed in a locker room with other boys for physical education class.

I felt so self-conscious, and nervous as hell, taking off my pants and underwear to change into a jockstrap and gym shorts in front of all the other boys. Of course, it was probably their first time having to undress in public also, so it must have felt pretty strange to them too. If so, they sure didn't show it. I acted as nonplussed as I could, but, inside, I was overwhelmed with strange sensations I couldn't explain. Whenever Coach Doyle, our muscular gym teacher, made his entry into the locker room, I had to stop myself from staring at the short-shorts clinging to his deliciously fit bubble butt.

I wasn't particularly athletic, but I decided to try out for the track team, fancying myself as a long-distance runner, not realizing how useful a skill it would become, in later years, as a juvenile delinquent. More importantly, I picked a sport with no physical contact, but one under the tutelage of Coach Short-Shorts.

His wife taught the girls PE and modern dance. She also wore form-fitting tennis outfits and leotards that hugged her tiny waist and accented jutting torpedo breasts that stood to attention. Even to a young, sexually confused boy like me, her figure was deeply impressive. I'd never encountered body enthusiasts before.

Nothing much came of my running career, though. I just wasn't that competitive in the field, and because I was no track star, Coach Short-Shorts didn't pay me a whole lot of attention. My attraction quickly waned. Other than being a prime physical specimen, he was a bit boring.

Still unsure of what to make about my budding attraction to boys, I welcomed the advances of girls who seemed interested in me. Most of the other guys at school didn't have much interest in fashion. With my hip shoulder-length shag and groovy print shirts with long collars, I guess I must have been quite a catch. I made my mom buy me yellow-and-brown plaid extra-wide and cuffed bell-bottom trousers that fit over my brown-and-mustard two-tone platform shoes, and a chambray work shirt. The more adventurous girls, who always seemed so much more mature for their age than the boys, were attracted by my "otherness" and sense of style.

Elaine Diaz would make a point of sitting next to me at every lunch hour and engaging me in conversation as her friends made encouraging facial expressions while we talked. She was gorgeous: an exceptionally beautiful Mexican girl with dark brown eyes and long straight hair, like a Chicana Buffy Sainte-Marie. We connected over our shared love of music and started to hang out at my house after school. Elaine would bring her records over and we'd listen to music together in my living room. Being a quiet, sensitive type, she also had excellent taste. She introduced me to Laura Nyro; I played her Jimi Hendrix. We confided our teenage dreams in each other. It was sweet and she was great. But looking back, she was trying to be romantic, and I just didn't get it.

She asked me to be her date for the Torch Junior High School dance. This was another first for me. I had never been on a date with a girl. I got dressed in my hippest clothes. Perhaps it was the sense of occasion but, at the school dance, Elaine and I took it one step further, sharing more than just our dreams. We slow-danced to "The Town I Live In" by McKinley Mitchell, holding each other cheek to cheek. At one point she led me out, behind one of the saucer buildings near the cafeteria, for a smooch. During our fumbling lip smash, I knew what this was all about and desperately wanted to lose myself in the moment, but realized, without really understanding why, that I just wasn't into it. I wriggled away. We returned to the dance. Elaine was visually disappointed at this rejection, and I was embarrassed at my make-out failure. But I soon perked up when the record changed to Archie Bell & the Drells' "Tighten Up," and launched myself onto the dance floor. I was the only boy dancing, fearlessly, among a gaggle of girls but completely oblivious that I was just compounding the insult to Elaine. I was such a goofball, I didn't get how much Elaine was into me. Not even a "maybe." I felt bad for disappointing her, that I couldn't fulfill her teenage dream and be the boyfriend she wanted me to be.

After our disastrous make-out session, nothing more was ever said about that night. We both realized there was no future for us as sweethearts. Elaine began to distance herself from me, but we did remain cordial and friendly. She wrote a really sweet message in my yearbook: "Plant these seeds." Adolescent girls are so much more perceptive than adolescent boys. Maybe Elaine was the first person to realize I was gay, when she saw me furiously working it to "Tighten Up." Because I know that's the first time I figured it out for myself, even though my own sexuality was still a big mystery to me.

Some years later, I would see Elaine and her friends at punk shows at the Whisky a Go Go. I always knew she was cool. I'm so sorry I wasn't your dream boy, Elaine. But I owe you so much and am forever grateful you helped point me in the right direction.

The Enjoyment of Fear

They looked like '40s movie starlets gone to hell, then raised from the dead in skintight rayon dresses, with blue, black, and bleached-white hair. The ghostly Victorian pallor of their powdered faces, extreme kohl-rimmed eyes, and bloodred lip gloss reminded me of 1950s bohemian Vali Myers. All of which made these gothic apparitions of extreme femininity look that much more incongruous standing in the blazing California sun, in the parking lot of NBC Studios, Burbank. That's where I first saw them, while waiting in line to see the New York Dolls taping a performance of *The Midnight Special* TV show.

In the summer of 1973, I was a fourteen-year-old suburban curious cat, obsessed with glitter rock. The "glitter" look, a charmingly naive expression of futuristic fashion, was actually derived from vintage wear. Gaudy and colorful iridescent clothing was the height of fashion. Spangled, sequined teenage baby-whores in miniskirts and bikini tops roamed the Sunset Strip. Some of the better-known LA glitter girls of the time, like Sable Starr and Lori Maddox, even attained their own fame and notoriety after being featured in the pages of teen magazine *Star* as the "Sunset Strip Groupies." But glitter was also a throwback to the faded glamour of Hollywood's yesteryear. The phrase "silver screen" was bandied about a lot in the rock lyrics of the era.

In their low-cut blouses, tight pencil skirts, platform shoes, and vintage jewelry, the quiet, sullen-looking girls who sparked my curiosity in the NBC parking lot stood a mile apart from the crowd. They looked like elegant femmes fatales and evinced romance and danger. I immediately wanted to know who they were. I sensed a darkness about them that spoke to me, making me recognize something inside myself I had not previously acknowledged, a vignette around the edges of my luminous teenage daydream.

Maybe it was hormonal, or even adrenal, but as soon as I hit puberty, music started to play a much bigger role in my life. It became the medium through which I began to forge my own identity as a teenager. My own tastes and desires. My own sense of style.

I had fallen under the influence of some older high school guys in my neighborhood, who mentored me in all things popular culture. Foremost among them was Steve Escandon, an affable, jocular figure four years my senior, who took me under his wing. He was a painter, heavily into underground comics like R. Crumb and Furry Freak Brothers, and underground music culture.

Steve's favorite group was the Mothers of Invention. Frank Zappa was a god to him. I was so much under Steve's spell that I became obsessed with Zappa too and wanted to know everything about him. This was music unlike any I'd ever heard before—freaky, rebellious, full of snark and biting humor. It was all so strange to me but thrilling too. I immediately identified with the whole vibe.

Steve took his mentor role seriously enough that when he saw my burgeoning interest in all things freaky and weird, he encouraged it by taking me to my first concert in September 1972: Frank Zappa and the Mothers at the Hollywood Bowl. Frank was performing his new, yet-to-be-released album, *The Grand Wazoo*, with a small orchestra. The opening act was Tim Buckley, followed by the Doors, minus Jim Morrison, who had died the previous year, leaving the group he had fronted floundering for a career. They had just released a faux-Mexican novelty song called "The Mosquito" and went down like a lead balloon among all the rock aficionados there to see Zappa.

The next summer, Steve took me to concerts at the El Monte Legion Stadium, a legendary hall that was home to the LA Thunderbirds female roller derby team but also steeped in the history of Los Angeles rock 'n' roll. This was the venue at which Johnny Otis held his legendary weekly dances after the police forced him out of Central Avenue in Watts. Later, through local El Monte boy Frank Zappa, who embodied the melting pot of influences in Southern California and its contribution to the history of R&B and jazz, the Legion Stadium became the lodestone for the Mothers of Invention. And so, of course, Steve and I went to see everything Zappa-related there. There was this band, Ruben and the Jets, who were named after the Zappa album *Cruising with Ruben & the Jets*, and also Mothers drummer Jimmy Carl Black's band, Geronimo Black. They were all very theatrical, throwing jazz and R&B elements into a blender with offbeat weirdness. That lead me to Captain Beefheart, and from that point on, there was no turning back for me. Everything strange and discordant turned my head.

Steve had also turned me on to the delights of the Dr. Demento radio show, two hours of obscure off-the-wall novelty songs in any

genre you care to mention, and even more obscure outsider musicians. This was not the music I was used to hearing on the radio growing up, but it all made perfect sense to me now I was already in that
mindset. It was as if I was tuned in to my own private station at the
far end of the dial, on a frequency broadcast from the Outer Limits.

Around this time, I also became friendly with these older guys
who lived down the block from me: Mark Swenston, Jim Gaffney, and
Randy Crooks. They attended the same high school, Bassett High,
and played in a garage band called Hogwild. When I first met them,
they were heavily influenced by Black Sabbath. At some point, they
started getting into Bowie and Mott the Hoople. Through them, I
was introduced to glam rock.

When the New York Dolls announced their first West Coast
shows, a four-night stand at the Whisky a Go Go, the guys from Hogwild all bought tickets to see them. I was desperate to go too, but my
parents wouldn't let me out of the house because it was a late show
on a school night. That afternoon taping for *The Midnight Special* at
NBC was my consolation prize, and the Dolls did not disappoint.

I didn't get to see them play a full concert until almost a year
later, in July 1974, when they returned for a string of midnight shows
at the Roxy, playing after performances of *The Rocky Horror Show*.
Midnight was evidently too early for the Dolls, who kept everybody
waiting well into the early hours and riled up the crowd. Even so, it
was the first concert I'd been to that felt like a party. David Johansen
played the host to the hilt. He wore a white tuxedo over his bare
chest, and wielded a bottle of champagne in one hand, the mic in
the other. The other Dolls were dressed like Times Square street-
walkers—in tight spandex, stacked heels, big hair, and makeup—but
strutted like men.

The wings of the stage, already tiny, were packed with onlookers
done up in glam garb, as were the rest of the audience, all revved up

for the show. As the Dolls played, a wild, infectious energy rippled through the Roxy, from the stage to the floor and back again. It felt as if the audience and the band were one, a confab of cross-dressing kinks and kooks expressing their inner freakiness through song.

Ground zero for every switched-on '70s glam rock kid in LA was Rodney Bingenheimer's English Disco, an ultra-hip teen mecca that only played the latest British imports, located in a storefront at the lip of the Sunset Strip in Hollywood. I had read about it in music magazines and wanted to experience it for myself. The first few times I went to Rodney's, Jim Gaffney, one of the guitar players for Hogwild, came with me.

Rodney manned the turntables at the club, selecting from his collection of British glam 45s. At Rodney's, I was exposed for the very first time to records like "Tiger Feet" by Mud, "Blockbuster" by the Sweet, and "48 Crash" by Suzi Quatro. Rodney would obtain all these singles himself, often before anybody else in the country. This was music you couldn't hear on the radio, or anywhere else but this tiny club in LA, packed with hipster kids and music fans. It made Rodney, this glittery teen fantasia he had created around him, and everyone who gained entry to it feel all the more special, mysterious, and exclusive.

Inside the club, posters and album sleeves of Bowie, the Stones, Slade, and the Sweet were tacked up on the venue's brick walls, as if a teenager's bedroom had been transposed to a Hollywood dive bar. Next to the DJ booth was a small, walled-off area with a large window cut out of it, above which Rodney Bingenheimer's name was spelled out in silver, glittery lettering. Inside, there was a long table covered in a red tablecloth with red vinyl seats set around it. This was Rodney's famed makeshift VIP booth, where celebrities could sequester themselves away from the throng on the dance floor yet were still close enough to touch.

One of the main attractions of Rodney's was being able to see somebody super-famous in close proximity. Bowie himself was said to be a regular visitor, but I never got to see him there, or Jimmy Page, or Elvis Presley, who famously came to check out the action at Rodney's one night with his security detail in tow. I did see Iggy Pop, though, who was a regular, and Shaun Cassidy, who came to the club with his band, Longfellow, years before he became a teen idol, when he was still in the shadow of his half brother, David. Alex Harvey would come to Rodney's when he was in town, Sparks were often there, and Jobriath.

Then there were the people who were famous to me simply because I'd seen them in *Rock Scene* and *Circus*, like Sable Starr and Lori Maddox. To me, anybody who had their photo in a magazine was a rock star by proxy. It was all so exciting that I wanted to be near it, and I felt it was changing me just by osmosis.

Jim Gaffney wasn't as captivated by all this as I was. He didn't think of our trips to Rodney's as much more than a lark and stopped going altogether after our first few outings there. Hungry for experience, drawn to this after-dark interzone of Hollywood and the strange characters that populated it, I started venturing out on my own.

On my maiden solo night out of suburbia, I staggered into Rodney's wearing some girls' platform clogs, which seemed like an accessory appropriate for the occasion. That night, I was astounded to see the parking-lot girls I'd spotted outside the New York Dolls taping a few months earlier, along with a male friend of theirs. Maybe I looked kind of lost, or it was just obvious I was a kid hanging out on his own, but one of the girls approached me. She told me her name was

Pearl, after Pearl White—the silent-movie actress who starred in *The Perils of Pauline* films—but she was also obsessed with Jean Harlow. Pearl had her own distinctive take on the "vamp" look of the 1930s: face powdered white, eyes smoky dark, squeezed into dresses that accentuated her figure. Because we were both too young to drink at the bar and the only thing on offer for the teen patrons was a revolting cherry cola, I ended up drinking in the back alley of the club at Pearl's invitation. There, she introduced me to all her friends: Meredith, Sue, her sister Joan, and their male friend, Jamie. We would pass around a tall green bottle with a silver label—Rainier beer—and each take a swig. I wasn't used to the bitter taste of rank, cheap ale, but I quickly decided that I liked being drunk. If nothing else, it made me feel part of the group.

From that moment on, this would become our ritual, meeting early on Friday night with Pearl and her friends to drink in the alley, before heading into Rodney's to dance, hang out, and be seen while spying on whichever pop star or celebrity was positioned in the VIP booth.

The music I heard at Rodney's opened up new possibilities in record collecting for me. I was always excited that the B-sides of the singles were non-album tracks I'd never heard before, like "Barbecutie" by Sparks. Rare and unusual records were all I was interested in now. But more than that, glam spoke to my budding sexuality.

There could hardly have been a more perfect fantasy figure and foil for a gay teenager at the time than David Bowie. He was a rock star, of course, but androgynous to the extreme—both asexual and openly hedonistic. He was like an alien from outer space, which was exactly the experience of a gay teenager at the time—dispossessed on a hostile planet far from home. I even felt like an alien, growing into my body and experimenting with alcohol and drugs. I related completely and absolutely with the otherness of Bowie's image. Gay guys who rejected the cliché clone image of the day—flannel shirts and Levi's—found a home at Rodney's. Sexual ambiguity was the name of the game, whether gay, straight, or bi.

There was nothing ambiguous about my sexuality, though. Already sure I was interested exclusively in men, I remained closeted at home and school. But at Rodney's I could rock and roll and be as gay as a day in May, making out with older shaggy-haired types in a drunken stupor. One time, I even made out with Pearl's friend Jamie. We were drunk and got amorous sitting next to each other in the back of the car, but it never got further than that. I was having fun and that's all I cared about, chomping at the bit to explore music, counterculture, and my own sexuality. I followed my curiosity wherever it led me. It was all about the journey not the destination, testing my limits, consequences be damned. Jimi Hendrix asked, "Are you experienced?" I wanted to be able to answer, "Yes, I am!"

At the same time, Rodney's was kind of a "play" sexual cabaret. There was a lot of dressing up and a lot of fronting, mostly by heterosexual men in makeup and flamboyant clothes who were playing gay to get young girls. Runaways manager Kim Fowley, a well-known lech, was always lurking at Rodney's. His album, *International Heroes*, had just come out, which featured a portrait of him slathered with rouge and eyeliner on the cover. There were more than plenty underage teenagers in that place for Kim to hit on, stealing out, like me, for an all-night drunk, looking for adventure, and available.

I planned my weekly excursions to Rodney's so that I could stay there till closing. Then everybody would move over to the parking lot hang-out scene outside the Rainbow Bar & Grill, a few blocks up the Strip. After that, it was on to either the Rock 'n' Roll Denny's diner, which was open all night and catered to the music crowd, or Danielle's, a coffee shop on Hollywood Boulevard and Highland Avenue, which was frequented by drag queens, transvestites, and hustlers who worked the stroll nearby, on Selma Avenue. This part of the boulevard felt dangerous and alluring. A couple of blocks along, on the corner of Hollywood and Las Palmas, was another notorious pick-up spot and street hangout I would sometimes frequent, the Gold Cup. There was also Arthur J's on Santa Monica and Highland.

After-hours gay culture in Hollywood centered around these coffee shops. I didn't have money for a hotel room so I would go there, hang out, and hope nobody killed me. I was a little bit frightened by it all, but at the same time instinctively felt I was in the safest place I could be. I had no business with any of their business anyway, and always felt quite invisible, sitting there, drinking coffee, and people watching. It was as if I was conducting an anthropological study, observing these bizarre characters circulating in this little corner of the city whom I was fascinated by and wanted to know more about but didn't quite feel a part of. I'd usually stay till around 6 a.m., then catch the bus back home to La Puente.

My parents were none the wiser about my new life in Hollywood. As far as they were concerned, I was staying out late and sleeping over with a pal. That seemed like a pretty reasonable and harmless thing for a teenager to do, so they never inquired further.

Hanging out at Rodney's with all the freaky young glitter kids started to change me, giving me the confidence to become more flamboyant. I started to express myself through clothing. This was around the time my idol worship of David Bowie began. He had famously worn a dress on the cover of *The Man Who Sold the World*. I was starting to dress up in a glam style myself. However, I couldn't really afford any cool designer clothes at my age. No Kansai Yamamoto space suits or Fred Slatten platforms for me. So I was compelled to start making my own.

First, I got a pattern for flared trousers, designed to fit over my six-inch wedgie platform shoes, which I had festooned with rhinestones in the shape of a lightning bolt in a circle—a tribute to David Bowie's Aladdin Sane character. I also made a snap-up, Chairman Mao–style jacket/shirt to complete the look. I was actually quite adept at following the sewing instructions. I made two outfits using cheap satin; one in red, and one in white. I also gave myself a rather crude Ziggy Stardust spiky-top haircut, which ended up as more of a shag than a mullet, I'm relieved to say. I had no idea what my extended family or friends thought of the alien in their midst, but I didn't care either. I was emulating the styles and fashions I'd seen worn by others and in magazines, and felt that, by making them myself, they would be more unique—and so would I.

Even my mom seemed to sense there was something different about me. I remember vividly one night, apropos of nothing in particular, my mother confided in me that she once had a transvestite friend named Greta. She didn't go into detail, simply explaining to me that Greta was a man who dressed as a woman and had sex with men, as a woman. I tried to wrap my teenage brain around this information that, quite literally, turned my understanding of men and women, and the relationship between them, inside out. To this day, I have no idea why she told me. She never mentioned Greta again. I figured she was drunk and just forgot. She was also known, by my sisters and I, to sometimes play this game where she would reveal something unexpected about herself that she shouldn't have, just to let us know she was more worldly than she let on. Maybe Mom saw my interest in gender-bending and suspected she had a homosexual son, and that was just her way of letting me know that not only did she understand but she accepted me.

Through my weekend romps at Rodney's and my pre-meets with Pearl and her friends in the alleyway behind it, I was starting to feel part of the in-crowd and certain I belonged there. I was on a journey of discovery. And, of course, that also involved discovering everybody else's bad habits and adopting them as my own.

Quaaludes were the drug of choice for most. Seconal downers seemed to be everywhere too. As soon as the other kids told me they got pills from their parents' medicine cabinets, I went home and looked to see what my parents kept in their bathroom. Not quaaludes, but codeine. "Take two per hour" it said on the bottle. I followed that advice to the letter and got plenty high.

When you're young, too much is never enough. Moderation and tolerance were not in my vocabulary. Sometimes "too much" got the better of me. One night, after throwing up all over myself, Pearl took pity on me and brought me home with her, sneaking me in the back door of her family home, even though she was terrified of her asshole biker brother, whom she was afraid might wake up and kill us both. While she washed my clothes in the pantry, I hid in the closet. At dawn, she snuck me out again. I walked along the avenue to catch the bus back to the Valley, watching my sour breath freeze as it left my hungover mouth.

On another evening, around the same time, we stopped by a Spanish-style bungalow on Argyle in Hollywood, which reminded me of Joe Gillis's apartment in *Sunset Boulevard,* for a pre-Rodney's drink with a friend of Pearl's named Mickey. A delicate and feminine fair-skinned lady opened the door and let us in. She had soft, curled, golden-brown hair, a heart-shaped face framed by finely plucked, arched eyebrows, and full, soft-red-lipsticked lips. Perhaps used to Pearl showing up at her door in the company of stray pets, Mickey acknowledged me, but somewhat dismissively, before proudly showing off a black leather jockstrap she'd just purchased, holding it up

in front of herself like a new skirt or blouse. Mickey was a transsexual
street prostitute. The jockstrap, she told us, was to help her "tuck"
and please her clients. "Cool," we both said, in all seriousness.

My response to all this was very matter-of-fact. Meeting Mickey
just felt like my mom's story, about her friend Greta, made flesh.
At the same time, all this was still so exotic to me. It was like I was
meeting somebody from a completely different country or culture,
maybe even a different planet.

One day, I took the bus into Hollywood and was buzzing around in
my platform wedgies. I wanted to lose myself in the glamorous big
city and soak up the atmosphere, away from the constraints of small,
suburban blandness. On my stroll this warm fall afternoon, Lori
Maddox walked by me with some girlfriends. She looked me over in
all my casual finery and exclaimed to her friends, "How cute!" They
all smiled in agreement. I was flattered to be recognized by a famous "in-chick" of the Hollywood groupie scene, but then thought,
Cute? I wanted to be hip and cool, not cute, as only a fifteen-year-old
brat would think to themself. I had no idea that, to them, I looked
like exactly what I was: a fresh-faced little suburban Mexican boy in
platforms, skintight patchwork jeans, and chest-hugging T-shirt—far
from the newly world-wise teen I thought myself to be.

I walked on to Hollywood Boulevard, by the Gold Cup, and
headed down to Highland Avenue, to a secondhand record store
called Railroad Records. Just as I got to the Arby's drive-thru nearby,
a guy sidled up to me as if he wanted to talk to me. I was a bit taken
aback, but he looked friendly enough. Up to that point, I had felt
quite anonymous, despite walking around in glitter platforms. Now
this hip-looking cat wanted my attention. I was flattered, anxious,
and excited, all at the same time. I was not used to somebody paying

me attention in an overtly sexual manner. Even dressed in a style designed to attract attention, I felt invisible.

He was tall, buff, and squeezed into tight, worn jeans, probably all of seventeen years old, with blond, floppy hair. He asked me my name and what I was up to. I guess I looked somewhat aimless. I was on my way to visit some friends, I said. I had some notion to give myself an "out," sensing that he expected something of me.

He said his name was Tommy and did I want to follow him? He might have asked me if I wanted to "fool around"; I can't remember. I already knew, instinctively, that was the reason he wanted me to follow him. And I did, as if in an autohypnotic state, possibly out of a reflexive fear or survival mechanism. But if so, it wasn't working, because there we were, walking below Sunset to a residential side street, then down some back alley. I was more excited than nervous. I had never gone further than making out and wasn't sure what might happen. But I was too intrigued, and too scared, to say "Forget it" and run.

We came across an empty garage. At that point, the mood changed, everything became transactional. Tommy unzipped his pants, whipped out his big fat dick, and ordered me to get on my knees. Again, I complied. Finding myself eye to eye with his cock, I stared at it—and it appeared to stare back. Inside me, elation commingled with fear. But the apprehension at what was expected of me now was not enough to deter me from throwing caution to the wind and furthering my dalliance with "Mr. Big in the Pants."

In what seemed like an hour but was probably a minute, Tommy groaned, pulled out, shot a load, and wiped off. My first ever blow job was done. He zipped up and laughed. Giddy with excitement at my accomplishment, I wanted to laugh too. I had participated in this clandestine sexual act—and survived. What had I ever been scared of? But there was no time for reflection.

At that moment, we heard car tires rolling up to the garage and quickly ducked out a side door, making a mad dash back up to Sunset. Panting after our two-block sprint, Tommy asked if I wanted to hang out more. But I wasn't sure I needed to get to know him any better than I already had. Later, I would realize he was probably a hustler, trying to recruit me into the game. Being somewhat naive, I didn't take the bait. "Gotta go," I said and hopped on the bus back to La Puente.

I scanned the passengers around me. It seemed as if I was viewing them through a fish-eye lens, goofy and animated. I imagined I looked the same way to them, like a cartoon character rushing on endorphins. Laughing to myself, I realized the blow job was fun, but the enjoyment of fear was really out of this world.

Theresa

Tumbling into our teenage years, my cousin Theresa and I left the kid games behind. We started to talk earnestly about the latest music and trends. We devoured movies and music and magazines, developing a shared understanding you only get in a personalized teenage world. We discovered our own sense of ourselves. I spun crazier and crazier yarns for her about my adventures in Hollywood and on the club scene. Theresa told me about her boy crushes and close encounters with the opposite sex at parties. We spoke about sex, shyly, awkwardly, with imaginary bravado. Sensing she would be cool, I confided in her that I liked boys too. That she seemed completely unfazed by this revelation I took as a tacit acceptance and acknowledgment that nothing could come between us. The confidences we shared, the hunger we felt for new experiences, propelled us together through this strange new journey: adolescence.

Like any good teenage malcontent, I was utterly disinterested in any social aspect of high school. At lunchtime, I'd often sneak off the school premises to smoke a cigarette. That was what the cool kids did. You had to time it right, though, because if you missed the beginning of the period, they'd lock the gates so you couldn't get back in. One day, I saw this girl trying to scale the school fence in platform shoes and a satin skirt. Wow, I thought, that's some kind of style. Whoever that is, she *has* to be my friend. Her name was Debi Smith, but she would go by the name "Pester." She was a year above me. It turned out she knew the guys from Hogwild. We became fast friends.

The only nonacademic activity I engaged in at school was writing for my high school newspaper, the *Bassett*. Randy Crooks, the bass player for Hogwild, used to write the music reviews. When he graduated, he passed that mantle on to me, having faith I would continue the good work of subverting the student body through music.

I couldn't yet drive, but I was lucky to have my sweet sister Ruthie take an interest in going to see live music with me and Pester. She had a Volkswagen Bug that sputtered along the highways and byways as she drove us into Hollywood from La Puente to see the likes of the New York Dolls, the Sensational Alex Harvey Band, Sparks, Dr. Feelgood, and many others. Ruthie, who had already been my mentor in all things musical, felt she could justify taking us to shows knowing that, as the music editor of my high school newspaper, I always wrote reviews of the bands we went to see and was therefore engaged in a worthwhile activity that kept me off the streets.

Roxy Music hit LA in March 1975 for the last date of their US tour, at the Santa Monica Civic. I was already a huge fan of their music and just had to experience "the thrill of it all" for myself. The Civic was a three-thousand-seat auditorium, the next step up in LA for bands that had outgrown the club circuit. I decided to camp out at the venue the night before the tickets went on sale, so I could be first in line when the box office opened in the morning and get seats as close to the stage as possible. Proximity to the bands was incredibly important to me. I didn't want to just see and hear them from afar, I wanted to feel like I was almost onstage with them. I wanted to see the cut of their clothes and the sweat fly off their bodies as they played.

I packed my sleeping bag, headed out to Santa Monica, and arrived outside the auditorium to find that a bunch of other kids had exactly the same idea as me. Everyone was lined up against the building, with their sleeping bags laid out on the sidewalk. There was an instant camaraderie between everybody there, a recognition that we were all of the same tribe. I got talking to this redheaded girl named Marcy who lived in Orange County, near Laguna Beach. We bonded over our favorite bands and talked all night.

From that night on, Marcy Blaustein became another of my new best friends. Even better, she had a car and a license! She took over from Ruth as designated driver and would detour to La Puente to pick me up on her way to the city from Orange County.

By 1975, so much of my interest in new music was sparked via the new breed of rock 'n' roll magazines: *Creem, Circus,* and, especially, *Rock Scene.* These were my bibles. I devoured them from cover to cover every month with the religious fervor of a juvenile delinquent version of Aimee Semple McPherson. I could while away endless hours in my bedroom trying to imagine living the not-so-saintly lives of the rock stars who had become my devotional icons through the pages of these magazines. I pored over the photos in *Rock Scene,* wondering what it would actually feel like to sit between Lou Reed, David Bowie, and Andy Warhol at Max's Kansas City.

On the first Sunday of every month the parking lot under the Capitol Records tower in Hollywood was a big draw for music obsessives like me. That was where the Capitol Records Swap Meet took place, awash with collectors, tastemakers, or anyone interested in something other than records you could get in a store, all looking for rare used records, obscure out-of-print oddities, and the latest bootlegs. It was music nerd heaven. The swap meet became so popular that vendors started to set up their stalls in the early hours of Saturday. We'd go out all night and then, still buzzing from whatever we'd imbibed, head straight to the parking lot to sift through the vinyl. More than that, it was a big hangout and meeting place for a lot of people. Everyone who would become anyone in the first wave of LA punk bands was there.

That's where I first met Phast Phreddie and Don Waller. They were putting out a zine called *Back Door Man* that championed a raw rock 'n' roll style—mostly Detroit pre-punk—as well as local bands like the Motels, who started out with a much more primitive sound, and the Imperial Dogs, Don Waller's band, who had a hard-edged Stooges/MC5 sound.

Patti Smith I discovered through an issue of *Back Door Man* and ordered her single "Piss Factory" from the address listed in the back of the zine. The B-side was a cover of "Hey Joe," which I already knew from the Leaves and Jimi Hendrix versions. I completely fell in love with that record, in awe at the simplicity of its arrangement, using just piano, guitar, and voice. From that point on, I was a voracious consumer of everything Patti Smith. I discovered she wrote articles and reviews for *Creem* magazine and was often featured in *Rock Scene* as "New York underground star, Patti Smith." *Creem* even ran a poster of her holding a copy of Iggy and the Stooges' *Raw Power* album in front of her naked torso, with a caption that began: "This is Patti

Smith. She is a filthy slut with absolutely no respect for anything."
What wasn't there to love about Patti?

Horses came out at the end of 1975 and only furthered my obsession. Through Patti, I learned about Lou Reed's *Berlin*, was first
exposed to and started reading poetry. Whoever she name-checked
and praised, I would look up and listen to or read so I could be
on exactly the same wavelength as her. When Patti Smith Group
announced shows at the Roxy at the end of January 1976, Marcy
and I were first in line for tickets. John Cale and Buddy Miles were
at the show. Marcy's friend, photographer Donna Santisi, who was
very cool and unobtrusive, almost to the point of being shy, went to
shoot Patti at the Tropicana, and I tagged along. We also went to see
Patti at this intimate hippie venue in Huntington Beach called the
Golden Bear. Then, Marcy, Donna, and I drove up to San Francisco
to see her there also.

Patti was very much into mythologizing her life. As an uber-fan, I
followed her every utterance onstage and off. She would talk about
her family and the songs they had inspired, to the point it made you
feel like you were familiar with them. I knew her mother answered
her fan mail. So of course I had to write a letter to Patti's mother,
rather than bother Patti herself, and tell her everything I was thinking about at the time. This is the logic of a teenager. It was a very
candid, almost intimate letter, possibly too intimate, because I never
sent it. But the intention was there, to place myself one step closer
to my idol. Maybe she would read it, maybe she wouldn't. I felt compelled to communicate.

Every kid like me who ever discovered themselves through music eventually stumbles onto the one group that changes absolutely everything.

For me, the Ramones were that band. I was obsessed with them. I identified with them. I even started to dress like them, ditching my bell-bottoms and all the patterned shirts with the wide lapels, which suddenly felt so passé and outmoded, for a denim jacket and jeans, tight-fitting striped T-shirt, and sneakers.

I came across their photo in the pages of *Rock Scene* before I'd even heard them. They didn't look like any other band. They didn't wear makeup or have hippie-length hair. There was nothing glam or androgynous about them. They wore leather jackets, denim jeans, and T-shirts, and looked exactly like what they purported to be: working-class guys from Queens reared on '50s rock 'n' roll. They looked dangerous, mysterious, and the epitome of cool, all at the same time, with their matching pudding-bowl haircuts and cold, menacing, switchblade stares.

I wondered what these cute street toughs could possibly sound like to get *Rock Scene* journalist Lisa Robinson and her panties in such a twist. But, of course, I couldn't know unless I heard them for myself. I *had* to have their record!

When the Ramones' first album was slated to come out, I managed to find out precisely when it was going to ship to my local Music Plus record store and, on the appointed day, waited outside for the store to open. I'd imagined, as with concert tickets, there would be a big line of like-minded fanatics foaming at the mouth, and I did not want to miss getting my copy. It turned out I was the only freak who turned up, the sole customer waiting in the spring rain! I could have bought all five copies that the store had ordered for myself.

The second I got home with the LP, I raced up to my bedroom, dropped the needle onto the vinyl, and started laughing hysterically, jumping up and down on the bed, because the music was something else, a pure adrenaline rush of exhilaration. I'd heard the Stooges and seen the New York Dolls play live a few times, but the Ramones were faster and funnier than anything I could have ever imagined. They really were a dream fulfilled. I wrote them up in a breathless review for my column in the high school newspaper, trying my best to explain the sound to suburban teens.

Fortunately, the group of friends I had met following Patti Smith around California the previous year all got the memo about the release also. We shared a collective loner-with-a-boner rush for the Ramones LP and waxed enthusiastic in frantic, giddy phone calls about our experiences purchasing the album at various record shops around LA County. One phone call screamed they were coming soon to play the Roxy in West Hollywood, supporting the Flamin' Groovies.

Marcy and I bought advance tickets for both sets and, on the day of the show, rushed down for the hours-long wait in line for the best front-row seats. This time we were not alone but met by throngs of fruitcake fanatics with striped shirts, bowl-head haircuts, and leather jackets, waiting to be a part of history. For those few hundred of us there that night, this was going to be a legendary show. When the time came, none of us were disappointed.

Sitting in the front row during the first set, I became mesmerized by how tall the singer, Joey Ramone, was. At one point he lost his balance, swaying back and forth, teetering on the brink of falling over, like a giant katydid with vertigo. Whoa to the left, whoa to the right, whoooa backward for what seemed much longer than a New York minute. Until he did finally crash backward, into Tommy Ramone's drum kit, scattering the cymbal stands to the stage. That very act sealed the deal for me, convincing me of the sheer brilliance of their art. They didn't have to try to be themselves; they could *only* be themselves. From that moment on, I was a true believer in the church of Ramones. It was love, love, love, like I had not felt for any other band before. The Ramones were my first addiction, my first rush. It felt like we were inside one of those crazed *Mad* magazine crowd scenes, populated by people with their tongues lolling out or hammering nails into their heads.

A large part of what endeared the Ramones to me and all my fellow pinheads was how real they were. They put on a show, for sure. The Ramones were like a machine. Johnny, in particular, was quite the taskmaster. But then they would fuck up, messing up the beginning of a song, stop playing, and start blaming each other, right onstage. And that became part of the show also, for us, at least. It was refreshing, entertaining, and very unprofessional, which is precisely why it was so great. They were still comic-book heroic, but it was the human element, the imperfection and the faults, that made them so special. We would see them onstage, then they'd walk out into the club afterward and start talking to the audience. We were so used to groups being untouchable—stars, gods—but the Ramones were just like us. There was nothing standoffish about them. At that time it was a revelation to be able to engage with a band on a personal level. We had really not experienced that—ever!

The Ramones worked a lot. They played every hole in Southern California, Northern California, and, I imagine, the rest of America. That's probably how they ended up at the Fest Awe Fair in Huntington Beach. I can't think of any other reason why they would choose to play a circus in Orange County.

It was an outdoor concert at the end of summer. The weather was fine, but Dee Dee kept getting shocked onstage. There must have been a mic or an amp that wasn't grounded properly. One minute he'd be playing bass and singing, the next he'd suddenly leap back, high in the air, and scream "FUCK!" That happened a few times. The rest of the band were all screaming back at him, "Just do it! It's *good* for you." We figured it was all part of the show. I guess they eventually realized he was getting shocked really badly and cut the show short.

Afterward, I overheard Dee Dee ribbing Arturo Vega for the way he was dressed. Arturo was not only their live sound engineer but did all their graphics. He was a sweetheart, and no match for Dee Dee's tongue. "Oh, you changed the side you put your keys on because you're in LA," Dee Dee sneered. Even with my limited sexual experience, I knew the code. It signified whether you were a "top" or "bottom." Arturo had switched from one to the other.

Dee Dee, I already knew, was no stranger to that life either. He was a firm favorite among Ramones fans because he wrote so much of their material, but mostly for his song "53rd & 3rd," which was about being a male hustler. The Ramones dropped little crumbs of information about their real lives throughout their songs. We followed the trail and put the story together ourselves. They had a gritty, down-to-earth quality that only endeared them to us further.

I was getting more and more caught up in fandom, and the Ramones, when everything came to a sudden halt. One night, in October 1976, my life changed in an instant.

I came home after school and immediately felt something wasn't right. The mood in the house was stark and somber. My parents seemed distressed and upset. Eventually, my sister Barbara took me aside and told me the reason why. Theresa was dead. I learned she had gone out to a party in the neighborhood with a girlfriend the night before and never returned home. The next morning, their bodies were found in a nearby alley, lying side by side. They had both been shot in the head. There was no evidence of sexual abuse, and robbery had already been ruled out as motive. The pain and confusion of not knowing the circumstances of how and why she had been taken from us, or who had done it, made the tragedy that much harder to bear.

At the wake in my grandmother's house, I'd overhear my sister talking to a cousin about rumors it was gang-related, possibly an initiation, a drive-by shooting. I even heard it might have been a hit in retaliation for a drug debt owed by an older, junkie family member. All this I gathered from bits and pieces of conversation overheard between the adults. That rickety wooden house, which seemed to have played host to one long endless party, jollity and music, throughout my entire childhood and adolescence, was suddenly filled with a grim silence, solemnity, and grief. Grandma tended to her daughter who had just lost her own child. My parents were in shock also. And nobody could explain anything to me. Cast out to make sense of it all on my own, I was sure of only one thing—it was fucking awful. When Theresa was murdered, a part of me was murdered with her. The secrets I had brought back and shared with her from my nights cavorting in the shiny city lights all went back in the closet, the door slamming shut behind them.

There was an open casket in a room that smelled of flowers and ammonia, sickly sweet and clinical. I looked at the body, but it didn't feel like I was looking at Theresa—just an empty shell without the person I knew. I didn't sense her ghost but, rather, felt like a ghost myself. Drained. Hollow. Invisible. Floating above the scene of mourners. I had no words to express what I felt, only thoughts, rambling and incoherent. *Fuck off, murder. Fuck you. You make me want to kill myself.* It could have been Theresa's voice I was hearing, I realized, which made my ghost tumble back down into my body on this dingy, ruined earth.

That was the end of my innocence and naivete. My understanding of the world, of what it means to be alive, had turned on a dime. I didn't want to, and couldn't bring myself to, accept reality. Immersing myself in fantasy was the only way to go, I reckoned. If no adult was going to counsel me, I had to write my own manual on how to deal with death. But where to start? After all, Theresa's murder had shown me life was not worth much. In denial, and with any mind-altering substance I could get my hands on, I began a new search: for sense in the senseless.

Following Theresa's death, I felt nothing. I didn't want to feel anything. I became a typical sullen and introverted teenager. That was my way of soldiering on, retreating deep into myself. I needed something powerful to shake me from my doldrums. Music was the key. Punk rock was like a dynamite blast, propelling me out of my torpor and grief. From wanting to feel nothing, I wanted to feel everything. Theresa always leading the way, saying, *LIVE.*

The Prez

The Ramones were the smartest, dumbest rock 'n' roll band there ever was. The New York influence that came through the Ramones was quite different from anything I'd heard before: a new attitude and feeling, almost avant-garde in its simplicity, with rocket-fueled emotions wrapped up in lyrics so stupid they were insightful. Whatever it was, it was RIGHT for me. I loved them with a passion unmatched and all the fanaticism they deserved. I was so enamored with the group that, toward the end of 1976, I started their West Coast fan club. I wanted them to be huge, like something out of *Tiger Beat* magazine.

Although I didn't realize it at the time, throwing myself into this new venture provided me with something to focus on and pour my energies into after Theresa's death. It was my way of reaching out and connecting with others, especially this burgeoning community of freaks I was now a part of in the nascent punk rock scene. This was during that all-too-brief moment before punk became too cool or trendy. We were a group of really strange, disparate misfits, looking for something new.

I had a mailing list of twenty-four Ramones friends and fans I'd met at the band's first LA shows. With me as de facto "president," that made twenty-five of us. That seemed like a pretty good start. I sent a letter out to everybody announcing the formation of the club.

"Hello and welcome to the Unofficial Ramones Fan Club," I wrote. "I know that some of you guys have been waiting for a long time and we thank you for being so patient." The band's debut album had only been released in April, but eight months in teenage years felt like an eon. "The reason for this club being called 'unofficial,'" I continued, "is because we can't collect money without going through a lot of hassle. The main one being we'd have to pay taxes." Smart.

Among the core fan-club crew was a girl gang from Palos Verdes: Mary, Helen, Trixie, and Trudie, aka "the Plungers." Mary became known as Mary Rat. Helen chose one of the best punk names of all time: Hellin Killer. Trixie Treat was a tigress punk with black spiky hair, black absolutely everything, who seemed to always be in perpetual motion, moving, whirling, dancing, with rosaries flying around her neck. And Trudie Arguelles was, well, Trudie. She was truly exotic and dangerous-looking, with a dark shag and smoky black eyes. Her makeup was inspired by James Williamson, and her hair by Jeff Beck. She took her style from the male rock stars we all loved and made it her own.

There were also kids in our group who were even younger than me: sixteen-year-old Paula Pierce and her fifteen-year-old friend Robin Cullen were the bass player and drummer, respectively, of a precocious glam pop-punk band called the Rage, heavily influenced by both the Ramones and the Quick, at whose concerts I first encountered them. Paula later fronted all-girl garage band the Pandoras.

Jenny Stern from Mission Hills, known as Jenny Lens by all and sundry on account of the camera forever slung around her neck, was a few years older than us and already an accomplished artist, with two degrees from CSUN and CalArts, when I first met her at a Ramones show. Just as I had been inspired by the Ramones to start a fan club, Jenny picked up a camera and dedicated herself to documenting the LA music scene, bringing a unique vision drawn from her fine arts training. Patti Smith used to call her "the girl with the camera eye."

I had been a member of the official Sparks fan club. With that you got a newsletter and a photo with a badge. Although it was a one-man, DIY affair, I wanted my Ramones club to be as professional as possible. As I was already writing reviews for my high school newspaper, I decided to write, edit, and lay out the newsletter myself, taking a cue from *Back Door Man* and early punk fanzines I'd heard about in England like *Sniffin' Glue*, which were just photocopied sheets of paper stapled together. Jenny agreed to let me print the amazing photographs she'd taken of the group when they first came to LA, the year before, and use her test strips. It was so very punk to use the scraps!

The oldest member of the club was a schoolteacher, Herb Hammer. We met at a show too. He had curly hair and round glasses and looked like a professorial hippie. He was an adult among a sea of kids, just very young at heart. He didn't see any difference between his enthusiasm and our enthusiasm—and we didn't see any difference either. So he lent a helping hand to organize the fan club and, as I didn't have an ID, he applied for the PO box in his name so I could receive fan club correspondence. My Bassett High School friend Pester also made every Ramones show without fail and was a great cheerleader and supporter of my activities.

I grew the fan club by word of mouth, meeting others at shows, taking their addresses or having them send me a self-addressed stamped envelope. The band's record company, Sire, saw my grassroots efforts as a good thing for the band. Sue Sawyer, who oversaw the Ramones' publicity in LA, let me come to her office to print out my newsletters and used to give me all the latest dish on what was coming up in Ramones world. I also had access to all the Ramones promotional swag—like the special switchblade comb, posters, and publicity photos. Right before the Ramones' second album, *Leave Home*, was about to come out, Sue invited me to hear a test pressing in her office with Phast Phreddie of *Back Door Man* fanzine and Don Snowden, who wrote for the *LA Times*.

Plans were already underway for the first newsletter when the Ramones arrived in LA again for a week of shows at the Whisky with Blondie. The newly formed Ramones "unofficial" West Coast fan club decided to personally welcome our heroes to town. We even found out what flight they were coming in on and met them at the airport.

That week felt so significant, I memorialized the most noteworthy events on a scrap of paper for posterity:

1) Greeted Ramones at airport—Tues, Feb 15th. Brian, Marcy, Debbie, Robin, Helen, Mary, Herb, Roxy and Jenny.

2) Wednesday, Feb 16th—Called Sunset Marquis and talked to Danny Fields. Went and met him at the hotel. Saw Dee Dee by pool. Left and saw Dee Dee by elevator. Saw Johnny & Roxy in street and Tommy too.

3) Went to sound check at Whiskey and watched them tape "Metro News, Metro News." Robyn & Debbie talked

to Dee Dee & Joey after over. I observed and acted cool (my favorite pastime).

   4) Went to the show. Was a lot of fun. Sue Sawyer took me.

Jenny Lens and I actually went to the Sunset Marquis together. She had arranged to show the band's manager, Danny Fields, the photos she'd taken of them. I tagged along to tell him about my fanzine. By now, my identification with the group was complete. I had grown and cut my hair into a near-perfect replica of the Ramones bowl-cut shag that kissed my shoulders and dropped below my eyes. I looked like a mini-Ramone clone. Danny took a photo of me sitting cross-legged by the pool, examining the contact sheets of the photos Jenny brought with her. In front of me, Dee Dee flexed and posed like a scrawny Charles Atlas in his mini-briefs. I cornered Joey and got him to write a little note to the fan club. He hailed me as "the Prez." From then on, anytime my friends and I showed up at a Ramones show, he would announce, "The Prez is here!" It was a real thrill, and made me feel important and accepted, to be seen by the band as part of the movement helping to promote their music.

   Even better, they wanted to hang out with us, find all the good record stores, and go junk shopping. Everyone was driving them around; different people had different Ramones. My high school friend Pester had a car. Johnny wanted to go to comic book stores, so we took him and his girlfriend at the time, Roxy, who had a tough Chrissie Hynde kind of look with mascara and bangs. Roxy was a little scary but super-cool. All the girlfriends were as friendly to the fans as the band. We took Joey around a bit also, but Joey was in great demand; he was a fan favorite and the most approachable.

   That week, it really felt like we were connecting with the group on a personal level. This was something totally new in rock, though.

There had always been a strict demarcation between fan and band. With the advent of the punk scene, fans could not only talk and interact with their idols but be involved with promoting their music. At the same time, I understood I was still a fan, not a friend, and had no intention of stepping over that boundary. I didn't want to infringe on their privacy. I wanted to be respectful, not come in and take a seat at their table.

The highlight of Ramones week was a party held in their (and Blondie's) honor at a Craftsman house on Wilton Avenue in Hollywood, known as the Wilton Hilton, that was home to Tomata du Plenty and Tommy Gear, the front man and bandleader, respectively, of a group who were recent transplants from New York, the Screamers. I was in awe at the idea of being at a house party with the Ramones and Blondie. That night, the house was packed to bursting, and I met two girls there who would become my closest friends and allies: Pleasant Gehman and Theresa Kereakes.

Pleasant had the loudest laugh in the room. She was a ubiquitous whirlwind of energy and I was immediately caught up in it. I overheard this buxom broad waxing lyrical to her gayboy friends about author Eve Babitz—whose book *Eve's Hollywood* had also seduced me—and knew I needed to be one of her fag-hag coterie. Sensing I was eavesdropping, Pleasant turned to me and insisted, point-blank, to know who I was. She had recognized me as a fellow scene maker who was at all the parties and always backstage at the shows.

"You're the Ramones fan club guy, aren't you?" she rasped in a voice filled with excitable laughter.

"Yeah, what of it?" I said, trying to sound cool.

"You should write for my fanzine," she said.

"Of course I should," I said.

Just like that, I got my wish to join Pleasant's gang. She had just put out her first issue of *Lobotomy*, "the Brainless Magazine," for which the concept was *Sniffin' Glue* meets *Mad* and *Rona Barrett's Gossip*.

I would start writing for *Lobotomy* also. Through that, I inherited a whole slew of new friends, including the fanzine's cofounder, Randy Kaye—who remembered seeing me a few years earlier at Rodney's English Disco and being impressed as I strutted around in my stacked platform shoes customized with rhinestone lightning bolts. I also became friendly with Randy's Beverly Hills High School pal Dennis Crosby and Brad Dunning, a Mumps fanatic with whom I would start another fanzine, *Contempo Trends*.

On staff and in our lives was photographer Anna Statman, who was a bass player in a band called the Red Lights with someone I was yet to meet, Jeffrey Lee Pierce. I bonded with the other staff photographer, Theresa Kereakes, whose apartment on La Brea Avenue was paste-up central, and often party central. Theresa was artful, educated, and calm in the frantic storm we dished up for our amusement. She sometimes worked in the box office of the Whisky a Go Go. Holding down a real job was anathema to most of us.

Pleasant would become the loud to my quiet. We found common cause. Neither of us was a musician. We were just fans and wannabe groupies, eager to be as close to the music and the musicians as we could, wanting to be facilitators of making something happen, whatever that would be. Our extreme enthusiasm pushed us, and everyone else, forward during those heady days of the early punk explosion. For Pleasant and me, it was a riotous meeting of minds that were drawn to anything naughty, humorous, and askew. We wanted things to be crazy, wild, and out of control at all times. Fun, fun, fun 24/7 was the aim of the game.

At one point during the Wilton Hilton party, Pleasant and I and a few others were smoking a joint in the yard with Debbie Harry, who got so high she fell into a bush. One second Debbie was there, then she was not. "Are you OK?" we all chorused when she emerged. "Oh no," she said, "I was just smelling that bush."

A few weeks after that, we were back at the Screamers' house again for another wild party. This time it was for the Damned, the first band from the UK punk scene to make it to the West Coast. They arrived in Los Angeles in April 1977 for a show at the Starwood and stayed with the Screamers. That spring, it felt like I was always at shows, hanging out and meeting new people. At the end of May, another New York band made their LA debut.

When the Mumps came to town, I had to meet them. The band themselves were virtually unknown, but their lead singer, Lance Loud, was already a superstar—at least in our eyes—as the break-out character of the reality TV show *An American Family*, which had me glued to the TV every Thursday evening for weeks when it first ran in 1973. The Mumps and especially Lance's best friend, Kristian Hoffman—a brainy, shy, and instantly likable sardonic, musical polymath—were often featured on the show. Lance, Loud by name and loud by nature, was outrageously flamboyant and exceedingly and quite obviously gay—although not openly so. But we recognized him and we knew, and that was all that mattered. So it was no surprise when, during one episode of the show, he came out to his family. In fact, it was a cause of jubilation and inspiration for all us queer kids who were still halfway in the closet. Lance was square-jawed, tall, and athletic, like a queer Clark Kent, but also nervy, sensitive, and articulate. The cherry on top was that he loved the Kinks, who were my favorite of the British Invasion bands too.

So when the Mumps were announced as a support to Van Halen at the Whisky, Marcy and I knew we absolutely had to go to see

Lance, and the group, in the flesh. They may have been stars to us, but there was not a lot of starriness around them, and little in the way of fanfare or machinery. They had a manager in Joseph Fleury—who also managed another of my favorite bands, Sparks—but no handlers to speak of, so it wasn't that hard to get to meet them. We hit it off right away.

Lance and Kristian were a little older than us, but not so old that we didn't share the same unabashed enthusiasm and fannish devotion to our musical interests. That was a huge eye-opener for me: that these characters, who were just like us in a way—almost our peers, loved glam and rock 'n' roll, and were cute and funny and smart—could be up onstage but still so down-to-earth.

The same could not be said for the Screamers, who made their live debut a few days after the Mumps' Whisky show, at a party held in a studio on Pico Boulevard to celebrate the first issue of a new magazine called *Slash*, published by Steve Samiof and Melanie Nissen.

Up to this time, it should be noted, the Screamers were more a concept than an actual band. You couldn't see them and you couldn't hear them. They had no records and they had never played live. But they had already made themselves visible, building their own buzz in LA by posting flyers up all around town for nonexistent shows. When we did finally get to see them play, they blew our minds. It was like they had crash-landed on Earth from an advanced and as-yet-undiscovered civilization on the far reaches of the cosmos.

That night, the Screamers instantly became the most original band in Los Angeles. Already fully formed in concept and presentation, they were a future shock in sound and image. Their music was a discordant onslaught of distorted synths, keys, drums, and the pained yowl of Tomata du Plenty, who was undeniably charismatic and lovable and possibly/maybe also certifiably insane. The

Ramones sang "Gimme Gimme Shock Treatment"; the Screamers delivered it. They were conceived to be worshipped.

As the Ramones were already well on their way to stardom, I decided I'd take up a new project and make a fanzine for the Screamers. Tomata had already seen my Ramones newsletter and asked if I could do one for them also, with photographers Herb Wrede and Diane Grove.

My life, increasingly, was taken up by music and fandom. High school bored me. I was learning more about literature from Patti Smith than I ever did taking English. Through her, I'd been introduced to Burroughs and Baudelaire, French symbolist poets, and the Beats. A seed of romantic desolation was planted in a fertile teenage mind ripe for turning. Out on the scene, I had taken drugs, had anonymous sex, hung out with rock 'n' roll bands, and earned my stripes in street smarts and the joys of petty crime from my gang of teenage delinquents—all before my eighteenth birthday.

With an education like that, what could school really teach me? Nothing, of course. So I decided to quit school altogether. The tricky part was how to tell my parents. Being an Aries, I've always been quite single-minded. It's my way or the highway, and I will "ram" through my desires, consequences be damned. So one night, I boldly marched into my parents' bedroom, where they were quietly reading in bed, and announced that school was over for me. For some reason, they didn't freak out. Maybe they already saw the writing on the wall and had guessed there was more to my late, late nights and early, early mornings than sleepovers with friends.

I was a diligent student. I'd always managed to achieve a consistently high grade point average. My mother stressed education as the key to all things. I did not disagree, and I do thank her for that, no matter how reckless I became in my search of learning through raw experience. But in my haste to ditch my scholastic obligations, I'd forgotten one thing. I'd been trying to convince my folks to let me go on a school trip to Europe, a whistle-stop tour through Rome, Switzerland, Paris, and London in early August, during summer break. My parents asked for some time to think it over, and I retired to my poster-strewn room and blasted Lou Reed's *Berlin* while fantasizing about my new post-school life. Ma and Pa came back with a counteroffer. If I could pass the GED and high school equivalency tests, *and* graduate at the end of the year, they would pay for my trip to Europe. It sounded like a good deal to me.

Even though I still had another three or four months to wait out the end of school before my European vacation, I was already so excited that I started making plans, researching all the things I wanted to do and places I wanted to see. I scoured all the British music papers—*Melody Maker, Sounds,* and *NME*—jotting down the addresses of record stores and the dates of upcoming punk rock shows, and wrote to European pen pals in the Ramones fan club to ask for their suggestions as well. My friends ML Compton and Marcy Blaustein were planning a trip to New York around the same time as my return trip to the USA, so I penciled in a stopover there so we could meet up and make a pilgrimage to punk rock shrine CBGB's, a place I'd only ever read about in magazines.

In those last few months of school, I made friends with a senior named Sissy. She was an Anglophile, drove a Triumph sports car, and worshipped everything David Bowie. I was a pretty big Bowie fan, but nothing like Sissy. Her obsession was so all-consuming it seemed unhealthy. But who was I to judge? She insisted on being called Ziggy and somehow even managed to get her name listed as "Ziggy Stardust" under her senior portrait in our high school annual. There was something very sweet and endearing about her enthusiasm. The weirdo quotient at high school was so low that freaks of a feather would flock together. We naturally glommed on to each other. Ziggy was coming on the summer trip as well. She wanted to stalk Bowie in London.

Studying always came very easy to me. I passed my GED without too much effort and graduated early in the top tier of all my classes, an honor student. Having fulfilled my end of the grand bargain I'd made with my parents, I was ready to claim my reward.

August arrived. My parents dropped me off at LAX, seemingly unconcerned at sending their youngest off on a solo trip halfway around the world. I jumped on my first-ever jet plane with what might have been trepidation but felt like excitement, eyeing the barf bag in the seat pocket in front of me and praying I didn't need to use it. There were ten of us in the group from Bassett High, strapped into our seats on a red-eye to New York City, where we were going to spend a whole day before catching another evening flight to Rome from JFK.

In NYC, one of the teachers decided to take us to the iconic Empire Diner on Tenth Avenue and Twenty-Second Street, in Chelsea. I couldn't believe I was finally walking the streets of New York City, in the footsteps of my heroes. Tramping all the same streets namechecked in the lyrics of the songs and the music I loved. To me, these were the streets of Lou Reed, Andy Warhol, the Ramones, and Patti Smith. I sucked it all up. The sounds. The smells. The traffic. The honking yellow cabs. And the stench of garbage. I felt like I was in a waking dream, intoxicated by the grime, the noise, and the hustle and bustle of the city, walking through the soundtrack of my life. It was all so loud and intense, more exhilarating and overwhelming than anything I could have imagined and all the pictures I'd already conjured in my mind while listening to "53rd & 3rd" or "Walk on the Wild Side."

After lunch at the Empire Diner and a trip up the Empire State Building, we got back on the subway to JFK and boarded the red-eye to Rome. There, we met up with a much larger group of American students from other high schools. They housed us all in a dorm-type building in a remote part of the city and shuttled us around on buses: to the Vatican, Trevi Fountain, the Colosseum, and restaurant after restaurant. I didn't see one punk rocker in all the days we were there. Maybe punk hadn't hit Italy yet, I thought. To make up for it, there were lots of beautiful and exotic-looking boys and girls to ogle. I took away a love of great culture and real Italian food, and memories of nice, shapely Roman butts.

From there, we took a train to Switzerland, to a city surrounded by spectacularly beautiful mountains. On that part of the trip, I gravitated toward two earthy sisters from Pittsburgh, Pennsylvania, who were exceedingly proud they lived in the same town as wrestler Bruno Sammartino and were great fun to hang out with. They bought Tyrolean hats to wear, laughed a lot, and walked side by side as if in a somnambulist trance.

One night, we attended a teen disco in a little cottage and drank beer. This was a novelty for most of my classmates, who were still a few years off the legal drinking age, as was I. So they were even more astounded by my precocious ability to down beers at a prodigious rate and yet still be able to hold more liquor. Unbeknownst to them, I was an old hand where alcohol was concerned, with years of practice already under my belt. Perhaps it was a little too apparent I was a pro drinker. I drank so much that, to this day, I can't even recall the name of the town we were staying in. Maybe I got slaughtered out of boredom, because I do remember the teen disco was a damp squib. All they played were cheesy pop hits, none of the art rock I loved.

Next stop, Paris—a place that piqued my interest just from my daydreams of what it would be like. We took in all the sights: the Eiffel Tower, the Louvre, the art nouveau metro signs, the fashion ads in the subway, and the clutter of sidewalk cafés. I convinced Ziggy to sneak away from the group with me so we could go find Jim Morrison's grave at Père Lachaise. It wasn't too hard to locate. We followed directions scrawled in graffiti that read THIS WAY TO THE END, MY FRIEND. We knew we'd reached "The End" by all the hippie drunks hanging out beside the Lizard King's final resting place.

After that, we headed to Fnac, a department store where I'd read you could find French punk records. Just the idea of that seemed so decadent, civilized, and rebellious. Back home, where nothing was more antithetical to Main Street America than punk rock, it was easier to imagine the coming of Armageddon than a Ramones record racked up in Macy's. At Fnac, we located what turned out to be a tiny stash of punk 45s, but a selection nonetheless. One picture sleeve jumped out at me. It had black-and-white photos of five cute-looking scruffs, brimming with sullen French attitude. They wore leather jackets, plastic trench coats, and ties that hung loosely around their necks like nooses. These figures were pasted against a proof sheet of the group lurking around an industrial wasteland. At the top, in bloodred paint splatters, was the word PANIK. I loved the dystopian imagery and flipped the sleeve over. The B-side was titled "Lady Coca Cola"; that was enough for me, I had to hear it. I whisked the vinyl over to the listening booth. As soon as the needle dropped on the record, a crash of buzz-saw guitars and a robotic drum-machine beat blared out. They sounded as good as they looked. I was thrilled. They were like kissing cousins of my fave raves in LA, the Screamers, except they sang in French with clipped Gallic accents. Even though the only word I could make out was the title of the song, "Panik," their intention was clear and beyond language. I couldn't believe my luck, chancing upon this group. The band was called Métal Urbain. An instant fan, I eagerly bought the single and couldn't wait to play it for all my friends back home.

We had one last stop on our trip before flying back: London. The best was saved till last. It was the year of Queen Elizabeth II's Silver Jubilee celebrations. Overwhelmed to be in the land of our pop idols, Ziggy and I dropped off our bags, skipped the group dinner, and headed straight to Mayfair to locate the iconic red telephone booth Bowie had posed inside a few years earlier for the photo on the back of *The Rise and Fall of Ziggy Stardust and the Spiders from Mars*. When we found it, we were as elated as one could possibly be. To us, it was like the monolith from *2001*—a mysterious object that was the source of all creation.

The next morning, we were shuttled en masse again to all the tourist sights: Westminster Abbey, London Bridge, the Houses of Parliament, followed by watercress-and-butter sandwiches at a traditional tearoom. That last place was such a drag. I stopped by a newsstand to scan that week's music papers for what was happening in town. My eye caught an ad for a club called the Vortex. The name was spelled in cut-out ransom-note letters, the international calling card of punk if ever there was one. There were three bands on the bill I'd never heard of, the Slits, the Prefects, and Tanya Hyde and the Tormentors. I already knew they were three new bands I was ready to fall in love with.

Back at the hotel, I got changed into the punk gear I'd packed for special occasions. Decked out in ripped jeans, striped T-shirt, and a black leather biker jacket, I was ready for the show and made my way to Wardour Street, where I handed over £2 to the sullen cashier at the door and descended into the basement club. The stench of stale beer rose up to meet me the farther I went down. Stepping inside the Vortex was like entering the cabinet of Dr. Caligari, an expressionistic nightmare, awash with figures wearing severe, exaggerated makeup and squeezed into tight vinyl fashions and black leather. When the DJ dropped the needle on the Adverts' "Gary Gilmore's Eyes," the entire place erupted in screams. Bodies were flying, leaping, and crashing into each other. It was the loudest sing-along I'd ever heard in a nightclub. This was it, the feeling I had been searching for: total exhilaration. I looked over and, in wide-eyed wonder, saw Siouxsie Sioux, Steve Severin, Mick Jones, and Joe Strummer drinking at the bar. It was as if I'd walked into a dive in Hollywood to find Monroe, Bogart, Cary Grant, and Steve McQueen. I was totally starstruck, probably much in the same way my sisters had been when they encountered Elvis, the Beatles, and the Rolling Stones.

Just then, the Prefects took the stage and shook me out of my reverie, spitting out that oh-so-British punk noise with oodles of attitude, the audience pulsating as one in front of them as they played. Then the Slits came on. I was overwhelmed just by their visual appearance before they'd even played a note. They were a chaotic jumble of mismatched skirts and boots, coalesced in a look that was totally incongruous and, at the same time, somehow made perfect sense. I still can't explain how, why, or what it was about them that worked so well—they just were. Ari Up, the teenage vocalist, stared the audience down with feral menace, wearing commemorative Silver Jubilee knickers over her tights, a look both delightfully disrespectful and hilarious. For a split second, I was in that prissy tearoom again with the perfectly cut watercress sandwich squares on china plates. Then the Slits launched into their raucous, primitive din and snapped me back into the club with its crush of seething bodies, each freaking out in their own individual way. I was in heaven, so high and buzzing after the show that I walked back to my dorm in a trance.

Inspired, the next morning I went out, bought a pair of scissors, and started randomly chopping my '60s Ramones bowl cut into a spiky mane, leaving my previous look as a mess of silky hair all over the sink. After that, I ran down to the huge HMV store on Oxford Street and bought the Adverts' "Gary Gilmore's Eyes" single and every punk magazine I could find, before jumping back on the tour bus for our last day of sightseeing. On the way to the airport, I saw some punks out of the window of the bus. They looked back at me and waved. Recognition. Acceptance. I was a true punk now.

As we boarded the flight back to New York City, word on the plane spread that somebody important had died, but nobody knew who it was. I was too caught up in the Sex Pistols fan poster mag I'd acquired to care. Just after we landed at JFK, the flight attendant's voice came crackling over the intercom to announce that Elvis Presley had died. The hustle, bustle, and chatter of departing passengers hauling their bags out from the overhead compartments dropped to a stunned silence, broken only by wheels of the debarkation ladder scraping up the outside of the plane to the exit door. When the door opened, a gust of humid New York summer air blasted our faces like a hair dryer on max power.

In New York, I met up with ML and Marcy. We set about roaming the city. They had gotten there a few days before me and already scoped out the scene to come up with an itinerary for my arrival. First stop was to see the Heartbreakers at the Village Gate. The opener was some guy I'd never heard of named Alex Chilton. Hey, I was young, and no one really knew who Big Star were back then. It never clicked that he'd been the singer in the Box Tops, whom I loved as a kid.

I'd arranged ahead of time to meet the Ramones' New York City fan club president, a girl named Michael—Michael Trese. We figured we could have a powwow and compare notes on the ins and outs of Ramones fan-club-dom. We'd been corresponding for a while but had never met. She wasn't hard to spot, though. She wore stiletto heels and a long men's dress shirt with a John Holmstrom–style cartoon of a Ramones "pinhead" on the back. Johnny Thunders didn't disappoint. I'd seen the New York Dolls a few times by now, so hearing Johnny Thunders's guitar and Jerry Nolan's drums again evoked cherished memories of their trashy glamour.

After the show, the entire audience congregated outside, then marched down Bleecker Street to catch the Dead Boys' late set at CBGB. Michael and I walked side by side, filled with feverish plans to merge our fan clubs and help usher the Ramones toward becoming the biggest band on the planet. We came to a stop outside CBGB, and my breath caught at seeing that famous awning for the very first time. Michael introduced me to another Michael, a boy named Michael Alago, who was handing around flyers outside for his Dead Boys fan club. It seemed like everybody ran a fan club back then, and every band had to have one. The Dead Boys were as worthy of fandom as any other group. They played the snotty '60s sex brats to the hilt. During their set a huge fight broke out. Elvis was dead, but the Dead Boys were more than alive! And that was all we really cared about.

I left NYC the next day, feeling I'd achieved absolutely everything I'd set out to do on that trip. I'd discovered myself while exploring the world. Now I knew that La Puente and Hollywood were a small part of a much bigger whole, and I could see how easy it was to move around, put yourself wherever you desired, in fact, right in the middle of the action. From that point on, I was struck by a wanderlust that kept me on the move for years.

From the Closet to the Needle

The mundane reality of life in the 'burbs seemed even more stultifying when I returned from Europe to my parents' house in La Puente. I crashed down to earth, culture-shocked by my own culture. The punk scene in London and the record stores of Paris had given me a path, and a hunger, for further exploration of the music world at large. I'd come of age through the glitter scene in LA, which had served as more of a fantasy for me to look up to. But punk, as the press were calling it, felt like it was made for me.

When the Who came out with "My Generation" in 1965, it sounded snotty, even then. When Generation X updated it as "Your Generation" a decade and some later, it sounded even snottier. "Your generation don't mean a thing to me," they sang, and that's exactly how we felt. All the '60s bands my parents' generation loved seemed irrelevant. John Lennon and Paul McCartney had become singer-songwriters. The Stones had gone disco. Psychedelia had devolved into self-indulgent prog. Punk was an adrenal rush with a rallying cry: everything "boring" in music had to go.

I identified as a punk rocker now, wholly and absolutely, and was determined to immerse myself even deeper into this new world, in order to help spread word of this music revolution. After leaving high school, I was desperate to move out of my parents' place and exercise my newfound freedom. I was spending less and less time at home, and was couch surfing with friends in Hollywood so I could stay out late and go to shows. There was a whole wave of people like me, either forming bands or documenting them. Everybody had the same idea at the same time—perhaps inspired by the title of the Ramones album *Leave Home*—to move into the city so we could all be part of the scene. Group living in crash pads was a way to live cheap, and sometimes free.

One of the most notorious punk lodgings was the Canterbury Apartment Hotel, a dilapidated Mediterranean Revival–style apartment complex on North Cherokee Avenue, with rooms that were fitted with Murphy beds. Built in the 1920s, and looking as if it hadn't been renovated since, it was like something out of an LA noir, like *The Day of the Locust.* Fittingly, a plague of miscreant teenage punk rockers had descended on the Canterbury once word spread it was run by landlords who didn't bother with credit ratings or background checks. As it was walking distance from Hollywood Boulevard— almost opposite the Masque, the most popular punk club in LA at the time—newly formed groups were using rooms in the basement of the building for rehearsals. I was planning on rooming there with my friend Rod Donahue, a punk scenester from Gardena, who later became bass player for the Mau Maus.

One day, I was having a meeting about the Screamers fan club newsletter with Tomata at the Wilton Hilton, and told him about my plans to move into the Canterbury. "I'd rather you slept under our sink than have you move into that building," he barked in a fatherly tone. "You're far too nice to be there."

Tomata was a collector of stray pets. I was still pretty naive, and his main objection to me moving into the Canterbury was that I didn't really know what I was letting myself in for. He probably also saw in me a dedication and potential that would go to waste if I was swallowed up by all the degradation on offer there. I loved the Screamers so much that I couldn't pass up the opportunity to be around them all the time. I moved in there and then. I don't think Tomata even bothered to run it by his roommates, Tommy Gear and Chloe Pappas, the Screamers' personal stylist and makeup artist (who went by the punk name Chloe Maquillage).

I'd been using their walk-in closet as an office to peck out the Screamers fan club newsletters because it had a built-in dresser I could perch my typewriter on. I suggested we just throw a single mattress in there. I was already working for them for free; now I could at least contribute a bit to the rent. Tomata and I used to joke it gave the term "in the closet" a whole new meaning.

The Wilton Hilton had already earned its place in rock history. Miss Mercy of the GTO's, the groupie-gang-turned-band produced and mentored by my idol, Frank Zappa, had lived in the house six years earlier. The house was owned by the mother of Mercy's artist friend, Donna Bates, who was a drummer in her boyfriend's band. They would often rehearse in the basement.

Mercy was still very much a presence on the early punk scene in LA and responsible for many bands' hairdos (and don'ts). She believed the house was a "mystical creative portal into another world." It was also, she said, extremely haunted, "like something out of a Stephen King novel."

Tomata concurred with this. He told me when the Screamers first moved in, they found a giant pentagram painted on the living room floorboards. It was rumored witchcraft and cat sacrifices had taken place in the upper part of the house. Tomata had himself experienced ghostly cat sightings and poltergeist happenings. The house felt like it was located in a supernatural realm. The Screamers added their own spooky touches to accentuate the vibe. All the walls were painted jet-black, and on the landing was a framed copy of a front page of the *New York Daily News*, with a headline that screamed, "MARILYN DEAD" above a full-page photo of Marilyn Monroe, looking lovely and smiling with her beautifully troubled eyes.

By far the best thing about living in the Wilton Hilton, though, was being exposed to the Screamers' record collection, through which I was introduced to so much new music, everything from Mae West's rock 'n' roll album to Broadway show scores, '40s singer Pat Suzuki, and Nico's *Desertshore* album. They hipped me to krautrock groups like Neu! and all the German-language pressings of Kraftwerk's albums.

Dario Argento's *Suspiria* had just come out. Tomata and Tommy had seen it multiple times already and were obsessed with it. They knew the film backward and insisted I had to see it too. We all went out to the Nuart Theatre on Santa Monica Boulevard to catch a screening. They made sure I took notice of the sets, the lighting, and the art direction, which was like something out of a German expressionist movie but in Technicolor. I understood why that would appeal to Tomata and the Screamers, who were a futurist, technological, German expressionist nightmare themselves. Afterward, I was just as excited about the film as they were. As soon we got back home, they put on their import copy of the film's soundtrack by Goblin, followed by the lounge classic "Black Coffee" by Pat Suzuki.

That was the Screamers idea of a mixtape and summed up their aesthetic in a nutshell: kitschy and creepy.

Seeing that I was a sponge for anything put in front of me, Tomata took it upon himself to act as my mentor and delighted in that role. He introduced me to a whole new world of avant-garde art and underground film I had no idea even existed. He took me to see a double bill of *Thundercrack!*, which was like a low-budget, porno Douglas Sirk melodrama, and *Tricia's Wedding*, which Tomata had a cameo in. I was also schooled on the Screamers prehistory and discovered that, contrary to their seeming to appear in LA out of nowhere, they actually had roots in both the underground theater and drag scene in Seattle and the pre-punk scene in New York.

Tomata (which, for the record, is pronounced "Toe-may-tah") had been given that name as a child, so he claimed, by his grandmother. Nobody I knew referred to him by, or even knew, his real name, David Xavier Harrigan. Born in New York but raised in Montebello—an LA suburb just west of my hometown, La Puente—he'd hitchhiked to San Francisco in 1968, at age twenty, to hang out with notorious cult transgendered performance art troupe the Cockettes. Soon after, he moved to Seattle and was inspired to start his own experimental theater group, Ze Whiz Kidz, who were heavily influenced by the Cockettes. Tomata added "du Plenty" to his name. His then-boyfriend, Michael Farris, became known as "Gorilla Rose." Tommy Gear of the Screamers went by the name "Melba Toast." They staged plays and musical performance pieces at a lesbian bar called the Submarine Room, located in the basement of the Smith Tower.

Tomata and Gorilla Rose moved to New York in '72, where they became part of the downtown music and arts scene. There they connected again with Fayette Hauser and John Flowers of the Cockettes and formed another avant-garde performance group, Savage Voodoo Nuns. In 1974, they performed their "Religious Horror Show" at CBGB, still a fairly new fixture on the Bowery, with two New York bands as support acts: Blondie and the Ramones. Little did I realize when I attended the party thrown at the Wilton Hilton for Blondie and the Ramones that all this had come full circle. And Tomata and the Screamers were at the center of it all.

After another brief period in Seattle, where Tomata teamed up again with Tommy Gear/Melba Toast and formed proto-punk band the Tupperwares, the whole group sauntered down the coast and set about making their mark in the early LA punk scene. Gorilla Rose and a friend named Suitcase were part of this group also. Gorilla was always around the Screamers. I feel he had a lot of influence on the group, especially on Tomata and his lyrics, which were hilarious. Gorilla was an artistic director par excellence and, while there from the start, never got the glory, fame, or recognition he deserved. Through Tomata and Gorilla, I was exposed to the roots of the underground queer culture that had inspired so many of the artists and the music I already loved.

In our insular, hedonistic world, sexuality—whether gay, bi, or straight—was rarely discussed, it just was. Everyone accepted that to be the case, even if there was a strange disconnect between the way we behaved and the way we had come to think of ourselves. Sex was great. Love was dumb. Sleaze was paramount. And Pollyanna morals were unthinkable. There was no shame involved. We didn't feel as if we had to hide our sexploits or our sexuality.

We were the Blank Generation. We wanted to scare the hell out of everyone and shake up the status quo. For us gay kids, that meant the homosexual status quo. We did not fit into the "clone" or "disco" mentality of late '70s gay culture, nor did we want to. As first-wave punk rock gays, we weren't interested in being "out" either. Labels were strictly taboo. We were part of our own subculture of a subculture that didn't seek or want acceptance or validation from the outside world. We had a pretty separatist and militant attitude. You were either with us or against us. Our feeling was . . . fuck the system, or stay the fuck away.

"There's just two kinds of people . . . my kind of people and assholes," said Connie Marble in *Pink Flamingos*; that was our rallying cry. We knew all the dialogue from John Waters's film by heart. Divine was the fairy godmother of the counterculture, the gay Statue of Liberty, a beacon for the outrageous, the uninhibited, and the transgressive. Around that time, John Rechy's book *The Sexual Outlaw* had also just been published and made the rounds of all the literary punks. With its real-life episodes of underground gay sex in Los Angeles, it provided an illicit sexual map of the city, of locales in Hollywood and beyond that were already well known to us, while also acting as a detailed guide and primer for the rituals of anonymous sex, its philosophy and manners.

In the transition from glam to punk, disco to punk, and hard rock to punk, all of which took place during the pansexual anything-goes '70s, we crossed as many sexual boundaries as we could. Punk was the hangover after the sexual revolution. We were seduced by the most dangerous antisocial aspects of the sexual subculture. We flaunted the mark of the rebel, wearing leather jackets decorated with studs and S&M accessories, adorned with leather wristbands. Whips, torn pantyhose, and a hint of Sally Bowles's divine decadence in *Cabaret* was a style adopted by both men and women as more than just Hollywood Boulevard drag, but a true expression of the exotic eroticism we were drawn to.

In that first wave of LA punk, sexual adventurers were as plentiful as musicians. Among our gang: Tony the Hustler, sometimes also known as Tony the Tiger, who was a gay-for-pay male hustler; Cherie the Penguin, the gregarious dominatrix singer of the band Butch, from Utica, New York, whose graveled laugh one could hear several counties away; her boyfriend, a swarthy, hairy-chested greaser in tight jeans and torn T-shirts who was tough on the outside, tender inside. And then there was Jane Gatskill, a statuesque, Teutonic blond trans woman, whom Tomata and Tommy Gear dubbed "Jane, the giant model," our very own Nico.

In mid-January 1978, Rod Donahue's mom made a trip out of town. So, naturally, Rod threw a party at her house. A bunch of punk rockers showed up and did what punk rockers generally do at parties in other people's houses: We got stupidly drunk, took way too many drugs, played music at ear-splitting volumes, and trashed the place. The usual fringy hoi polloi from the LA scene were all there—Plungers and Lobotomites, Germs and Go-Go's. But one stranger stood out: a tall, lanky fellow dressed in black denim trousers, motorcycle boots, and a black leather jacket on top of a ripped T-shirt, spray-painted punk style with some kind of slogan of dissent that was extravagant in its offensiveness. He wore a look of perpetual surprise on his face, and his eyes were so heavily rimmed with black kohl you could barely see them. Hmm, I thought, dreamy, very *Scorpio Rising*. He must have seen the love-light in my eyes because he made a beeline for me and introduced himself as Don Vinil. He was the singer of a San Francisco band called Grand Mal, and a friend of both Penelope Houston of the Avengers and Tomata du Plenty. Grand Mal were already notorious, chiefly for their song "Fag-O-Rama," a crudely articulated defiance of the sexual norms in punk. We don't-give-us-any-damn-label gay punks down south had heard about this incredible song on the grapevine, despite the fact it had not yet even been recorded.

A few drinks later, Don and I threw caution to the wind and locked ourselves in Rod's mom's master bedroom for a fuck that went from zero to a hundred so quickly the entire bed frame collapsed beneath us. We crashed to the floor with a thud so loud that even over the din of Buzzcocks playing on the turntable below, a bunch of revelers came to bang on the bedroom door to find out what happened. "Oooh, YOU broke Rod's mom's bed!" one bratty punk cooed, sounding like somebody's annoying tattletale little brother. Fortunately, Rod took it all in good humor and laughed the loudest of everyone. The event became such a staple of LA fanzine gossip that when Don returned next year with his new band, the Offs, he became known as Don "Bedbreaker" Vinil in *Flipside* magazine, which was so full of snark they would jump on any excuse to humiliate. If only we could be humiliated.

At that time, the talk of the entire Los Angeles punk underground was the Sex Pistols' upcoming show at the Winterland Ballroom in San Francisco. Every self-respecting (or self-loathing) spike-haired, torn-T-shirt-and-studded-bracelet-wearing music lover decided they had to be there or life just wouldn't be worth living. Everyone was looking for a ride share or a pal to hitchhike with or was even, as a measure of last resort, calculating how long it would take to crawl up the coast on their hands and knees. As it was just over a week into the no-future till the concert, Don's parting shot to me at Rod's party was an invitation to come up and stay with him in San Francisco so we could have fun and break more beds. How could I say no?

Don lived in a Victorian group house on Page Street, not too far from the hippie haven of Haight-Ashbury. It was there that I met his best friend and roommate, Rico, a lovely, lively queer boy, brown like me in complexion and highly knowledgeable about all the latest British music. We quickly bonded. Rico had big orange polka dots dyed into his blue buzz cut, and an "eyes to half, lips to lemon" demeanor. It felt so great, and empowering, to be with these out gay punks.

As soon as I arrived, there was a swirl of activity in the house, a sense of organizational urgency. Don announced that we were all going out to a restaurant in Chinatown to meet a friend. On our way there, he confessed he was actually going to score some heroin from his "friend," and I could have some if I wanted. No stranger to drug taking, I was all for it. How romantic and seedy, I thought, my punk rock boyfriend is turning me on to smack. Just like in the movies, or that William Burroughs book *Junky*.

The Chinese takeout place only had a few tables and chairs. We sat and ordered and ate and waited, and waited, and waited some more until an unsmiling, trench-coat-wearing punk sauntered in, to the dismay of the guy behind the counter, who had evidently seen him plying his trade here before, day in and day out. By the time the dealer left a few minutes later, having completed his transaction with Don, the proprietor wore the same unsmiling look on his face. After everyone else had made the obligatory trip to the bathroom, for about fifteen minutes each, Don offered to take me to shoot up also. He told me I could do the "cottons"—the piece of cotton ball used to siphon up the liquid heroin cooked in the spoon—and that there would be more than enough in there to get me off as a first-timer. Wow, I thought when we were done, this drug is great. Even though I felt queasy, I was comforted that shooting heroin was almost exactly like the Velvet Underground song had made it sound. Don told me there was an urban legend about someone who had done Johnny Thunders's cottons and OD'd. I think he was just relieved I hadn't OD'd and was trying to break the ice. I was already plenty high and couldn't care. Scruples were out the window. Life and death suddenly had no meaning.

On our way back to Page Street we passed a hippie head shop in the Haight with a sticker in the window that read IF IT FEELS GOOD DO IT. I took it as a sign. Shooting up felt so good, I vowed to do it again, and again, and again. The next day, there was no more heroin, no more money, and a whole lot less sex. I should have taken that as a sign also, about the fringe benefits of heroin, but as a first-timer, I was too caught up in the romance of it all.

Fortunately, the LA reinforcements started showing up for the concert and provided a welcome distraction. In a wave of great élan, Hellin Killer, Trudie Arguelles, Mary Rat, and Terry Bag arrived from Dallas, Texas, having seen the Pistols play there a few days earlier. At a house party the night before the Winterland show, Hellin even waxed enthusiastically to us about bloodying Sid Vicious's nose with an accidental headbutt when he leaned a little too far out from the stage. It made for a great bloody-nose photo and facilitated an easy introduction to Sid, who became instant best mates with Hellin after the show. Hearing that, we resolved to get there early, so we too could be up front. It was clear there was going to be a big mess of people packed into Winterland's massive auditorium.

The night of the show, I got into the mood by getting blasted on vodka while Don went out to score. Returning empty-handed, he applied his makeup and we headed out to the concert with Rico. Inside Winterland, the atmosphere seemed more tense than jubilant. Possibly the assembled throng was unsure if their joy at attending the event should triumph over their expectations for a night of nihilistic entertainment. The crowd was dressed, but were they impressed? I flashed back to seeing the Dolls at the Santa Monica Civic Auditorium in 1974, where glitter rock fans, dressed to the ninety-nine thousands, were so happy and wired and wide-eyed that you could picture a champagne glass perched in everyone's hand. The crowd at Winterland felt like they were spoiling for some kind of test; maybe a study in self-consciousness was my drunk analysis.

The Nuns opened with their upbeat and smartly cynical pop-punk songs about sex and transgression. One of them was an ode to the use of smack through harm reduction, "Smoking Heroin." Newly turned on to the joys of that particular narcotic, the refrain stuck in my head like a spike in the arm: "You don't got to shoot it, baby, you don't got to boot it." Thanks for the tip, you crazy Nuns! But they left so many questions unanswered, like can you smoke the cottons? The Nuns' showstopper, which may very well have been at the top of their set, was a song called "Lazy," which featured the band's front woman, Jennifer Miro, a gorgeous blond ice queen who stood behind her keyboards, singing the line, "I'm too lazy to fall in love" in a voice that was drier than the driest martini. Everyone compared her to Nico from the Velvet Underground, but having been schooled by Tomata in the art of '40s film noir, I knew better. Her performance was pitch-perfect Marlene Dietrich, and more thrilling for it.

Following the Nuns, it was another hometown band's turn, the Avengers, with their fireball singer, Penelope Houston, whose high-energy hardcore punk anthems raised the mood several elevator floors. There was a hopeful revolution of the spirit in their music that communed with my spirit also and left the audience exhilarated.

As the Sex Pistols took the stage, Don and I pushed our way to the front. It felt like everybody in Winterland had the same idea at the same time. There was a surge forward. We were locked in the crush. My feet were no longer touching the ground—not metaphorically, literally. I was pretty drunk and stoned by this stage. The Sex Pistols' set was a blur to me then and has remained so since. I do remember that they played the hits, "Anarchy in the U.K." and "God Save the Queen," for sure. But it was Johnny Rotten's riveting onstage, in-person live-wire charisma that made the show for me and cut like a knife through my intoxicated state. I've heard charisma described as "attraction without the use of logic," and that summed up his presence to a T. He was so much more animated than I'd expected and his voice, amplified through the venue's enormous sound system, was absolutely harrowing, standing my already spiked hair farther on end. It seemed as if he was becoming more misanthropic and despondent as the show wore on. I'm so glad I was able to bear witness to the last gasp of Rotten energy that was the Sex Pistols' final show. That night, I only had eyes for Johnny, and my memory of the show is pretty much limited to him. Sorry, Steve Jones, Sid Vicious, and Paul Cook—I hardly knew you were there.

After the show, there was a house party where, word had it, Sid Vicious was going to appear. So that's where we all went. It was packed with the punks from LA and the punks of SF, all mixing it up and either drinking like the world was about to end, locked in the bathroom doing drugs, or both. Nobody, but nobody, as I recall, said their mind had been blown by the concert. Soon enough, Hellin Killer traipsed in with Sid in tow, drunk, goofy, and more than aware that all eyes were on him, including those of Don, who was transfixed by the presence of this punk superstar. I got it—Sid was cute, an alluring mess, and a Sex Pistol. I'd experienced this kind of sycophantic fandom around Patti Smith and the Ramones. But I was very attracted to Don and wanted all his attention for myself, even though, dammit, deep inside I knew I was no match for star power and heroin combined. Soon enough, Don locked himself in the bathroom, and there were no cottons for me and piles of smack for Sid.

Instead of drowning my sorrows in heroin with Don, I went off to sulk in a corner, where I ran into Chip and Tony Kinman of the Dils, a band I loved and had followed from their earliest days. The brothers Kinman had always been exceedingly friendly to me. They gave me a nickname, "Brian Haircut," because I had a new hairdo every time I'd see them. Chip told me they were driving back to LA the following day and asked if I wanted to hitch a ride down south in their van. I jumped at the chance. As the sun was coming up and the party edging to a close, I told Don I was leaving the next day. He offered no resistance. It had been an action-packed week, to say the least. From true lust at first sight in LA to first-time junk hit in SF, witnessing the Sex Pistols' swan song, and a Sid Vicious going-nowhere party that led to a breakup with my first punk rock boyfriend. No future for me in San Francisco, at least not that week. Little did I know, my week of high drama was not to end there.

There was torrential rain the day Chip and Tony picked me up. Perhaps the heavens were crying over our exit from the city. Or maybe it was just that time of year. But anyway, the highway was closed due to flooding. To get back to Los Angeles, you could either take I-5, which was quick but boring, or the longer, more scenic, coastal Highway 101. Both were closed that day, so we took a back road through the hills that intersected with the highway. The higher we went, we figured, the less flooding there would be. So up we climbed, the rain so heavy we could barely see out the front windshield. We inched forward at the princely speed of twenty-five miles an hour. We were in the van for hours, moving at a snail's pace. Noticing that the rain had let up a touch, we decided to seize the opportunity to take a toilet break at the side of the road. We got out of the car, the van's headlights illuminating the dark road ahead. Tony noticed there were rocks scattered in the middle of the road a little bit up from where we stood. A split second later, we heard a distant rumble, getting louder and louder. Fortunately, we had enough of our wits about us to realize it was an avalanche, heading straight for us. "Get under the van!" Chip yelled. I must have frozen in shock, because the next thing I knew Tony grabbed me and threw me underneath the vehicle. All I could hear were the sounds of rocks smashing one on top of the other, echoing around the canyon. When the sound subsided, we crawled out from under the van gingerly, without saying a word to each other, and saw a wall of boulders about ten feet high no more than fifty feet in front of us. "Well, Brian Haircut, I believe it's time we turn around," Chip said sardonically.

As the local punk rock scene in Los Angeles started to take shape in the spring of 1978, those of us at its core were already starting to feel restless. Like the protagonists in that Paul Revere & the Raiders song, kicks were getting harder to find. Boys and girls alike were starting to find themselves locked into serious habits. Speed and LSD, the punk rock drugs of choice up until that point, had been supplanted by downers and hypodermics.

The Mumps made a return to LA around this time to record another single. We attended the sessions and Pleasant and Theresa sang backing vocals. Kristian was accompanied by his boyfriend, Bradley Field, who invited us to come stay with them if we were ever in New York.

A few of us decided we needed a change of pace, fresh territory to conquer. New kinds of kicks. Trixie Treat, Trudie Arguelles, and Pleasant had all decamped to New York and were sending letters back home with feverish accounts of their activities and all the bands they were getting to see. With the encouragement of the advance guard, and not wanting to be left out of all the fun, we made the spontaneous, and somewhat impetuous, decision to hop on board a Greyhound bus to join them; impetuous because we only thought to buy $69 one-way tickets. The idea of coming back before we'd even left was thinking too far ahead and would have spoiled the fun. The only planning we did was to gather the supplies we'd need for the three-day journey to New York. Just the staples, though: candy, cookies, and booze. But more importantly, as many pills as we could get our hands on. That called for further raids on our family medicine cabinets. We pooled our haul together: Darvocet, a synthetic morphine called Talwin, and even Thorazine, swiped from somebody's baby brother—a grab bag of opiates. We realized it was going to be pretty boring sitting on a bus for three days, so we planned to be as drugged up as we could on the journey, the idea being we could sleep all the way there.

There were four of us on this cross-country adventure: my friend Rod Donahue; Hellin Killer and Mary Rat, the other two Plungers of Palo Verdes, California; and me. Soon after we left LA, I popped a Thorazine and stared out the window at the desert for what seemed like an entire day and a half. The next morning, I woke up slumped all the way down in my seat. I peered out the window and saw a huge banner strung across a main street in God-knows-where America. It read HAPPY BIRTHDAY GRANDMA BUZZARD! My punker friends were all still passed out in the seats around me. With their crazy-colored hair, black clothing ripped and pinned together, and faces pockmarked from dozing on studded bracelets, they suddenly looked like otherworldly creatures deposited in the monochrome world of Middle America.

Rod brought a small cassette deck with him for entertainment, and we played a trebly-sounding live Screamers tape over and over and over again, much to the chagrin of the other passengers. If that wasn't enough to get us thrown off the bus, we were probably fortunate not to get caught crushing pills and shooting them up in the bus station bathrooms during a rest stop.

On our arrival in New York, I was excited to explore all the parts of the city I'd been unable to see the previous summer. I still had this big fantasy image in my mind of what New York and the Bowery were like from watching *Taxi Driver* and *Midnight Cowboy*. It was as smelly, horrible, desolate, and bombed-out as I'd hoped it would be. A dream come true! We made our way to Kristian Hoffman's loft in Chinatown, stepping over bums in the street on the Bowery, risking rape and murder at every step.

When Bradley Field had invited me to come stay with him and Kristian in New York, he probably didn't expect I'd turn up in a matter of weeks—and with company in tow. As it turned out, he wasn't inviting me to stay with them at all. Kristian lived in a loft at 240 Grand Street, off the Bowery. There was a Chinese laundry and a doctor's office downstairs. Their landlord was Doctor Moy. Kristian's living space was like a crazy funhouse, stuffed with all this great antique taxidermy. They had a loft bed in a crawl space so small you had to shimmy up this little ladder and slither into it. They called it the "Witch Hole." It even had a guest book, the "Witch Hole log." But there wasn't room for four in the Witch Hole, so Bradley walked us a few blocks through an even more desolate section of the Bowery to another loft above a Mexican cinema on Delancey Street. "I'm staying with Kristian, you can stay here," he told us.

"Here" was the home of Lydia Lunch. Bradley played drums in Lydia's band Teenage Jesus and the Jerks, whom Trudie had raved about seeing in one of her letters back home. Lydia seemed fairly nonplussed that her drummer had dumped four teenage LA punks on her doorstep. But she didn't seem all that thrilled either. In fact, she ignored us. After the first night, the others peeled off and found other places to crash. I stayed put.

Lydia was dating Sumner Crane, from the band Mars, at the time. He was around the loft a lot. We watched her conduct these very militaristic rehearsals of Beirut Slump, her new group with brother and sister Bobby and Liz Swope, and Jim Sclavunos. Then she would have another brief fifteen-minute rehearsal with Teenage Jesus right afterward, with Bradley on drums. Both bands probably had twenty minutes of music between them. Not that they needed any more. Hearing them, and watching Lydia marshal everybody into action, I was in awe at how they managed to sound both stripped-down and abrasive. It was an unnerving exercise in aggressive minimalism that stayed with me for a long time.

It took a while for me to connect with or even engage Lydia in conversation. "You've been here a while and you haven't said a word to me," she finally said one day. "You seem pretty crabby. I like that." With that, the ice was broken. "Let's play," she said, encouraging me to pick up a guitar. Without any forethought or intention, I was about to cross the invisible line between fan and musician for the very first time. "But I don't know how to play electric guitar," I told her. "What? You think I do?" she said. Lydia had this exceedingly raw but extremely effective and innovative guitar style in Teenage Jesus, churning out slabs of primitive noise. "Just pretend like you're playing 'Rock and Roll All Nite' by KISS," she said. So I did while she savaged the drum kit. It was a lot of fun. That cemented our friendship.

There was no end of music to see in New York, no end of musicians to meet. I got to see the Cramps for the first time at CBGB. Trudie had been raving about them to us also. They didn't have any records out yet. Other than Trudie's description, all I knew was what I'd read in *Rock Scene*. Just from seeing photos of them, I was smitten. They looked weird and creepy. They did not disappoint.

The Cramps whipped up a rock 'n' roll energy that was overtly and unapologetically sexual, visceral, and raw. They were magical, shamanic, entrancing, and unlike any group I'd ever seen. Front man Lux Interior, in particular, was absolutely magnetic, and completely perverted, in the best possible way. Their guitarist and Frankenstein monster, Bryan Gregory, would scream onstage while holding a pose as finely balanced as a ballet dancer. He had this special trick he would do while playing that involved rolling and flipping cigarettes around in his mouth so the lit part was inside.

One song in, I was hooked by the Cramps and knew, instinctively, these were definitely "my people." The Cramps embodied what I felt inside and had never been able to express: They were freaks like me. Because they were so unbridled onstage, they gave license for their audience to let loose and behave that way also. We were all taken over by a lunacy that was infectious, exhilarating, and orgiastic.

That night, April 14, 1978, the Cramps were sharing the bill with James Chance and the Contortions, another out-of-this-world musical experience. The Contortions had a sound that was an unlikely mash of James Brown and Albert Ayler, and a performance style that was relentlessly aggressive. James Chance was confrontational in the extreme. He would lurch toward the audience, grab people's hair, and pull it. Both groups had a kind of showmanship that was very different from anything else I'd experienced. They were crowd invaders. There was something malevolent and scary at work that was so exciting to me. It was the same kind of thrill I'd gotten in my encounter with the Hollywood street hustler—a leap into the unknown, giving myself over to the enjoyment of fear.

One night, shortly after that show, I was introduced to James Chance and his girlfriend, Anya Phillips, at Kristian and Bradley's Grand Street loft, which was a meeting point for a lot of people on the scene. As I got to know Bradley better, I discovered he was quite the character too. He was from Cleveland, Ohio, originally, so he was friends with all the Ohio bands: the Dead Boys, the Cramps, and

Pere Ubu. He was small, looked like Peter Lorre, and was absolutely fearless. I don't want to say Bradley was a sociopath because he was always very sweet and friendly to me, but he would get drunk and hit a point where the worm turned and he would become this absolute monster—again, I stress, never to me. His MO was to be as base as possible. He could be virulently anti-Semitic and racist, wielding noxious sentiments as a weapon to provoke a fight. I think he actually probably just liked getting beaten up. There was something innately masochistic and self-destructive about him that he couldn't keep under wraps. I'd never met anyone like him. His misanthropy was bone-deep. If you were around Bradley long enough, you were guaranteed to get in trouble. At the same time, he was a riot and a lot of fun to be around. It made perfect sense that Lydia would pick someone so abrasive to play with her in Teenage Jesus. She would marvel at his unsavory behavior. There were a lot of people who couldn't stand Bradley, I found out, and thought he was beyond the pale. He and Kristian were such an odd couple. Kristian was tall, thin, and blond, a poppy, polka-dot-shirt kind of guy, and extremely creative. Bradley was a little devil.

Kristian and Bradley also introduced us to a bunch of other teenagers in New York who were part of their social network—fans like us, scrounging around on the scene, who were all in bands that formed the next wave of musicians in New York. There was Howie Pyro and Nick Berlin, who were in a band called the Blessed. They were billed as the "teenage Dead Boys," as if they were the children of the Dead Boys. They were sixteen going on seventeen, young, loud, and snotty, and played dirty, Stones-y punk rock. We also became friendly with another group of teenagers who were in a band called Student Teachers, through their keyboardist Bill Arning, who ran the Mumps fan club. Student Teachers were notable for having an all-girl rhythm section, in bassist Lori Reese (a friend of NYC Dead Boys fan club organizer Michael Alago) and drummer Laura Davis.

The rest of the LA crew and I inevitably ran out of money. We started to improvise in order to survive. We lived like savages and vagabonds. Stealing drinks off the bar while someone was in heated conversation was a common scam. We also took to cleaning up after all the pogoing punks at CBGB and collecting change off the floor at the end of the night. That proved surprisingly lucrative. One time, I even found a $50 bill under a barstool.

When nights were slow and there was no money to scrounge or steal, we would stop off at the local food stand on the corner of Chrystie and Delancey. It didn't have a name, just a sign outside that read RESTAURANT FRIED CHICKEN. We'd go in there and split a chicken meal between four of us, to save money. By the time we got there, in the early hours, the place was usually packed with transexual prostitutes and their pimps, junkies waiting to score in the park across the street, and drunks who had staggered out of bars at closing time. The prostitutes approved of our punk fashion choices—ripped clothes, stockings, and stiletto heels for the girls, and crazy color-streaked hair; the pimps paid us the ultimate compliment by not knifing us. When the pickings were slow at CBGB, we'd dive into the garbage bin behind the restaurant, having realized that's where they tossed all the uneaten fried chicken. It sounds gross, and it probably was—we were competing for the same food as the neighborhood rats—but we were so famished, it seemed like a feast to us.

When I outstayed my welcome with Lydia, I crashed with everyone else I possibly could until I outstayed my welcome there too. I was having too good a time to go back to LA. But I was also realistic about my chances of making it in New York if I decided to stay. I could see how tough a city it was to live in for a suburban California boy like me.

Through Howie, Nick, and the Student Teachers, I met Janie Heath, an NYU film student. "Come stay at my dorm," she said. A bunch of us went over there. Her roommate took one look at us, a band of scraggly LA punkers with short, spiky hair, and said, "These people are *not* staying with us." She threw us right back out the door.

Laura Davis, the drummer for Student Teachers, had just moved into a studio in the basement of a town house on Perry Street in the West Village that was being used as a storage space by Joe Butler, the drummer of the Lovin' Spoonful, whom she was babysitting for. That quickly became a punk rock crash pad. The Plungers, the Blessed, and I all descended on Laura's basement bolt-hole. There were boxes stacked up that contained Joe Butler's record collection. Some people started rifling through them for rare sides that could be sold on the open market at Bleecker Bob's.

One night, a few of us got the bright idea to shoot up some blotter LSD. That was an instant hit, in more ways than one. There was a poster of Alice Cooper posed with a boa constrictor pinned up on one wall and we sat and stared at that, "charmed," for what seemed like hours but was probably an instant. Then Howie, Nick, and I decided we needed to get some air before the snake squeezed the life out of us.

We went outside to take a stroll around the West Village. We walked and walked and walked, wide-eyed and intensely focused, in a psychedelic haze, barely even communicating with each other. Until, hit by a sudden moment of clarity, we realized we'd walked more than a hundred blocks, all the way from Greenwich Village to Harlem. We promptly turned around and walked all the way back again. Not even considering, in our acid-fried minds, that we could catch the subway.

We got back to Perry Street, shut the basement door firmly behind us—and the outside world with it—only to be confronted by the sight of Hellin Killer sitting cross-legged on a pillow in a muu-muu listening to the Doors. Wow, I thought, this hard-core punkette is really a hippie in disguise.

Eventually, there was no more money to scrounge, no more places to crash. Reality hit. I knew it was time to go home. But I couldn't even afford a bus ticket to Los Angeles. I called Marcy in LA and told her I was stranded. She wired me $69 and I made the long journey back, all the way home.

Lysergic Acid Delinquents

My first summer living at 909 Palm was one long psychedelic blur. There were so many people around, so much acid being consumed, it was hard to keep track of who was actually living there and who was just passing through to another dimension.

My friend Ann McLean and Pleasant found the apartment. It was perfectly situated for twenty-four-hour oblivion, conveniently located within walking distance of all the hot spots on the Sunset Strip: the Whisky, Roxy, Rainbow Bar & Grill, Tower Records, Licorice Pizza Records, and Granny Takes a Trip, but most importantly, Gil Turner's Fine Wine & Spirits.

Ann signed the lease and she and Plez asked me to move in with them. Completing the 909 gang was our other roommate, Dennis Crosby, the lovable and dissolute grandson of Bing Crosby, whose cherubic face conjured visions of "White Christmas" and swooning bobby-soxers dancing before your eyes. Among Dennis's many admirable attributes was his considerable skill as a paper hanger and script forger, both of which came in useful, in different ways.

Dennis, whom we fondly called "Denis Denis Doobie Do," after the Blondie song, was a one-man riot. His favorite drink was pink lemonade and vodka in a Claussen's pickle jar, a concoction we dubbed a "Gay Boy." Dennis was gay with a capital G, the most carefree, outrageously flamboyant homo I had really known. Dennis would borrow Pleasant's Peter Max–print minidress and trot down the block in cowboy boots for an Orange Julius and chili cheese fries. He was obsessed with Brad Dunning, a handsome bespectacled geek who made all the girls—and Dennis—swoon. Dennis would graffiti ILJBD everywhere, which stood for "I love John Brad Dunning." So if you ever walk past a tree or wooden telephone pole in West Hollywood, look for ILJBD carved in it. You will know Dennis Crosby was there.

Our friends Joan Jett and Lisa Curland shared an apartment two blocks away, on San Vincente, directly across from the Whisky. Up one block, on the corner of Santa Monica Boulevard, was a car wash and an Orange Julius hot dog stand, whose mascot was a red devil. The crossroads, perhaps? On one side of us was the Blue Parrot, a tropical-themed bar that was a mainstay of the West Hollywood gay scene and played host to lustful bodies, rich and beautiful. A five-minute walk in the other direction was Duke's, the coffee shop at the Tropicana, the rock 'n' roll motel, where we nursed many a hangover the morning after the night before with whatever band happened to be staying there. And across from Duke's was a lesbian bar called the Palms.

I was working at the North Hollywood branch of Licorice Pizza, which was staffed almost entirely with musicians, future record label owners, writers, and band managers. There was Danny Benair, drummer from the Quick; Lisa Fancher, who founded Frontier

Records; ML Compton who managed bands like Thin White Rope and Poster Children; DD Faye, the coolest chick around, who wrote for proto-punk fanzine *Back Door Man*; and me. More often than not, people were hungover at work, which took the edge off one of our most excruciating tasks: having to constantly restock copies of *Frampton Comes Alive!*, which was still on the record charts two years after its release. Occasionally, I even came to work still tripping on acid from the night before. For that, I thank the influence of my mom and dad's tireless work ethic.

Every morning, I would make the journey over to North Hollywood either by taking a long, winding bus ride through Hollywood or, on sunny days when I felt more adventurous, standing on the side of the road and jutting my thumb out to hitch a ride through the hills of Laurel Canyon. Being young and cute, I never had a problem getting cars to stop for me. Often it was an easygoing lady of the canyon driving a sports car. I guess nowadays they'd be called "cougars of the canyon." If you were unlucky, it was some horny perv looking to cop a feel. Thankfully, that never got beyond some occasional groping and hands sliding onto a knee.

If a Volkswagen van or VW Bug came by, you definitely had it made, as more than likely it was driven by a hippie, still cruising the Strip long after the Summer of Love. One time, I was with a couple of girls and we caught a ride from this hippie in a van. He was trying to impress the girls by playing them tapes of his own music. It sounded like a psychedelic mishmash to us. We were like "Yeah, yeah, hippie, OK." Until a song we recognized came on, "Pushin' Too Hard" by the Seeds. We suddenly realized we'd hitched a ride with the lead singer of the Seeds, Sky Saxon. Later, I'd find out he was playing us his first tapes as Sky Sunlight. He told us he was a dishwasher at the Source health food restaurant on Sunset Strip. Still, we were more concerned with getting to where we wanted to go: a motel party thrown by Phast Phreddie. When we told Phreddie that Sky Saxon had just dropped us off, he freaked.

On weekends, for kicks, the 909 gang used to go see the Los Angeles Thunderbirds roller derby team skate and fight at the Olympic Auditorium in downtown LA. The Olympic was a huge nine-thousand-capacity boxing arena that also hosted professional wrestling. Our usual drill was to get nicely drunk beforehand on cheap beer—the old Rodney's routine—and neck some speed, ready to let loose and scream bloody murder for our beloved T-Birds. Joan Jett and Sandy West of the Runaways would meet us there, along with Sandy's girlfriend at the time, whom we used to call "Sandy's mom" because she was quite a bit older than us.

We all, boys and girls alike, had the biggest crush on "Psycho" Ronnie Rains, the baddest of the badasses on the T-Birds men's team because he would beat the crap out of everybody, loose cannon that he was, slamming into his opponents and sending them crashing over the rail, all while racing at full pelt around the track. Psycho Ronnie was such an icon for us that we stuck a photo Anna Statman had taken of him on the wall at 909. Someone scrawled GOD underneath it in red lipstick.

Our favorite jammer on the ladies' team was Gwen "Skinny Minnie" Miller, a rake-thin Black roller derby star who would often race between the legs of opposing team members to snag the winning point at the last second. Along with the rest of the Olympic Auditorium denizens, we would heckle, curse, and cuss out bad-guy managers like the fat and obviously unethical El Fabuloso and the grim-faced, hard-boiled dyke Georgia Hase.

Every week, I would see this one woman sitting in the front row, a small-framed Black lady in high heels and a gold-sequined cocktail dress, who waved a rubber chicken and yelled at the skaters she disapproved of. We found out her name was Bobo. Whether she was a plant or an honest-to-goodness, chicken-waving maniac cursing up a blue streak was of no consequence; it felt like an honest means of expression.

The crowd at the Olympic were a mix of Latino, Black, and white, low-income and disenfranchised, drunk and pumped up by fake violence. Everybody was just letting off steam. It was the same primal energy you'd experience at a punk show at the Masque or the Whisky. Bobo and her rubber chicken were like the guy who used to glue a piece of liver to his bald head at Germs shows. The Ramones and the Screamers, our musical superheroes, were the equivalent of the roller derby teams. Like the music we loved, we embraced the ridiculous and sublime of the roller derby. It was just a different subculture, another fantasy to lose oneself in, a cathartic escape route. That's what I saw, and what I was living for. We identified, and knew we fit in.

When not losing our minds at the roller derby, the residents of 909 would often drop acid on a whim to add color to our day. On one of those occasions toward the close of 1978, as soon as we started to come up on the drug, we all became as one with a shared mind and common purpose that guided us toward the most perfect and important mission for the day: a shopping expedition at the brand-new Fiorucci store in Beverly Hills. Fiorucci had acquired instant rock 'n' roll cachet when Debbie Harry, Andy Warhol, and KISS all attended its opening earlier that month. Being in no state to get there under our own steam, we had the sense to call a cab to whisk us to this new-wave wonderland.

Fiorucci was located on Beverly Drive in the old Beverly Theatre, which was a mock Arabian-themed building, topped by a large minaret that looked like a giant boob. Walking into the store was a bit like entering Aladdin's cave, wall-to-wall with the garish and the gaudy. Inside, everything was bright, neon, and plastic, and the staff so stiff and serious they seemed to be made of plastic too. It was kitsch to the point of being ridiculous. Whatever caught our eye inspired fits of giggles. Somehow, we managed to keep it together enough to all pick out outfits and accessories for ourselves—aqua-and-pink see-through plastic jackets, clunky plastic jewelry, and flu-orescent eye makeup—and left the store wearing our purchases, looking and feeling appropriately plastic also.

Back at 909, all suitably glamorous and dolled up, we reasoned that our new getups demanded an occasion to match. There was only one thing to do: throw a party. We called Joan Jett and her roommate, Lisa Curland, who, like us, could not resist the call to excess. Joan was away on tour; Lisa came over in a flash.

Lisa was very much the archetypal California girl next door, a perfect, perky blond with a foxy, compact body. But her Little Miss Innocent looks were deceiving. Lisa was a she-devil in disguise. One of her favorite pranks was to make Popsicles with her piss and give them to unwitting boys for a laugh. She was also a devil doll for real, who had met and made the acquaintance of Anton LaVey, the fearsome-looking head of the Church of Satan. Knowing Anton's fondness for Hollywood blonds—for which Jayne Mansfield had once paid a heavy price, losing her head and her life in a car accident after Anton had accidentally cut across a headshot of hers—Lisa had written him a fan letter, making sure to include her own headshot, in which she looked exactly like the kind of bubbly, fun-loving girl who could turn the devil's head. Before you could incant "B-L-Z-BUB," Lisa was invited to the Black House, the gothic Victorian row house headquarters of LaVey's church in San Francisco. Her friends worried she might lose her head like Jayne, but

Lisa returned intact with tales of Anton. She said he was funny and played "That Old Black Magic" for her on his pipe organ.

When Lisa arrived at 909, I opened the door and put a tab of blotter acid on her tongue. Now that we were all tripping our brains out, the fun could begin in earnest. Dennis, Ann, and I climbed up onto the roof of the building and sat and lost ourselves staring at the pink plastic rosary we'd brought back from Fiorucci. Pope John Paul I had just died, thirty-three days into his papacy, the second pope to die in just over a month. We pondered this as we all carefully examined the molded-plastic ribs of the tiny Day-Glo Christ suspended on his crucifix. There and then we made a pact that if a third pope were to unexpectedly kick the bucket, we would all jump off the roof together in sympathy, like good Christians. At that moment in time, it sounded like a plan we could agree on.

Back in the confines of the apartment, we all began to drift off into our own little trips. Ann and Lisa secluded themselves in one of the bedrooms. Dennis lay on the couch in the living room, staring at the ceiling. Siouxsie and the Banshees' *The Scream*, which had just come out and was an immediate favorite in our household, was playing at full blast on the record player and set on repeat, filling the entire apartment with Siouxsie's chilling wail. Pleasant and I retired to the bedroom we shared and draped one of her sheer negligees over the small black-and-white television so as not to attract attention—of whom or what I have no idea. We then got deep into conversation about how an atomic bomb could drop on us at any moment and how lucky we were to be here, in our bedroom, the perfect bomb shelter. To ensure our survival, though, we had to keep it a secret between ourselves. At that point, we came up with an ingenious plan to dig a tunnel through the floor of our closet all the way to Gil Turner's liquor store on Sunset Strip. That way, we'd never have to step into the atomic wasteland outside and could still maintain an endless supply of vodka and pink lemonade to see us through the apocalypse.

Just then, the sanctity of our bunker was violated by a discordant air-raid siren—or was it the Banshees' "Metal Postcard (Mittageisen)"?—as Lisa Curland came crashing through the door, all sparkles and sunshine, to gleefully exclaim that she'd just called the Runaways' ghoulish manager, Kim Fowley, and invited him to join our party. "He should be here soon!" The end of the world was coming far sooner than we'd anticipated.

"I can't think of anything worse than having to look at Kim Fowley's face right now," I sputtered. Even stone-cold sober, the combination of Kim Fowley's Frankenstein visage, his twisted smirk, and the whining voice that emerged from it was enough to induce a bad trip. On acid, it would be a hellish nightmare from which there was no escape. "That's a crime against humanity," I wailed. Pleasant was in full agreement. This was a scenario we had not planned on, and one to be avoided at all costs. A nuclear holocaust in the company of Kim Fowley was a grim forecast of what life would be like in a post-mutation society.

Now Lisa, who had stumbled upon our secret lair, would have to stay here also to ensure our survival, lest she tell the others and reveal our hideout. So, after informing Lisa of our plan to wait out the apocalypse, we got her to agree to sit in the corner until we'd decided on our next move.

A minute later, or it could have been three hours, we heard a knock at the front door. "Shit," I whispered, "Kim Fowley's here. What should we do?" All eyes were drawn to our collection of switchblades that sat on top of the dresser. That was it, of course, the only thing we could do to protect ourselves: Cut Kim Fowley up into little pieces and toss him down the tunnel we'd dug under the closet. We figured that when the stink of itty-bitty Kim Fowley's rotting flesh eventually rose up out of the tunnel, our heinous crime would be discovered and we'd probably be arrested and brought to trial. It seemed like a risk worth taking. In any case, we felt supremely confident that on the weight of the evidence, any court in the land would see we had performed a vital public service by saving the world from the unpleasant experience of having to look at Kim Fowley while tripping on acid. We'd be found not guilty by the unanimous decision of a jury of our peers and freed! We'd thought it all through from beginning to end. It was the perfect plan! What could go wrong?

Pleasant and I each grabbed a flick-knife and made our way to the door to the apartment, cracking it open with the chain lock on and flashing the tiny knives with their mother-of-pearl handles. Then, the one thing we hadn't counted on happened. The second we saw Kim Fowley's monstrous, rubbery mug staring back at us through the crack in the door, we became frozen in horror. Meanwhile, Lisa, who had been privy to all our scheming, took the opportunity to flee from the bunker, run up behind us, and scream, "They're spies! Run! Run!"

Apparently nonplussed by the imminent threat to his life, Kim just shook his head, turned around, and left. Babysitting a bunch of teenagers tripping on acid was clearly not his bag. In our acid-ripped minds, though, we felt as if we had just saved the world from imminent destruction and should be treated like heroes, receiving a handsome reward for our immense bravery at facing down the cataclysmic mien of Kim Fowley.

At that instant, behind us in the living room, Dennis dropped the needle on a new record: X-Ray Spex's *Germfree Adolescents*. "The Day the World Turned Dayglo" came bouncing out of the speakers. Our bunker fantasy melted away like a mirage. Dennis, Pleasant, Ann, Lisa, and I all crowded into the tiny bathroom, still wearing our

Day-Glo plastic fashions, turned off all the lights, and sketched trails with lit cigarettes in the mirror.

A month or so later, Pleasant and I decamped to New York for a couple of weeks. The Screamers were making their East Coast debut at Hurrah and there was no way on earth we would miss it. We planned on staying in town the next week also, so we could see Pere Ubu and Urban Verbs perform at CBGB. Bradley Field had gotten hold of some purple microdot acid. We bought some from him, thinking it would be the perfect "color" for the Pere Ubu show. Bradley had been told it was extra strong and suggested we all take half a tab to start. So, as prescribed, we somehow halved the tiniest little sliver of LSD.

We started getting ready to go out, listening to music. Half an hour goes by. Pleasant and I give each other that do-you-feel-it-yet look. NAH! We decided to take the rest. The tab was so tiny, we thought, how strong could it be? My high school friend Pester, who was also visiting New York, agreed and the deed was done. We all walked over to CBGB, laughing and feeling just fine. That is, until we walked inside and caught the end of Urban Verbs' set.

I looked up at the neon beer signs suspended above the length of the bar and imagined I was in a rocket ship, the room tipping up toward the sky, ready for takeoff. We must have looked like we'd just sailed in from the Island of Lost Souls because our friend Chase Holiday, whom we knew from Los Angeles, took one look at us and led us to the pinball machine with instructions to "just stand here and look." Chase was a professional nanny and knew how to handle children, which made her the perfect "trip" babysitter. The whir-ring, swirling new wave of Urban Verbs came to an end. The house lights went up, some punk song came over the PA, and the mood shifted in an instant. Bradley wasn't wrong; this acid was STRONG. But at least we'd gotten past the first shocking "KABONGG!" when the drug came on.

From there on in, the night flew past like a series of snapshots. The most vivid of which was seeing Klaus Nomi, a good friend of Chase's, standing in an alcove by the coat check, bowing like he was ushering us into a theater. He was ushering us into a broom closet. I found out later Chase had tipped him off that we were tripping and he was trying to freak us out. That, coupled with his black lipstick, powdered-corpse-paint visage, and mechanical mime movements certainly did the trick. Chase, dressed as the antidote to Klaus Nomi's new-wave Nosferatu—in a Day-Glo taffeta party dress, with bright green and orange makeup on her face—was lit up like a gaily decorated birthday cake.

Bands usually played two sets a night at the clubs. Pere Ubu had decided to ditch their second set that night because their drummer had taken too many drugs. That seemed perfectly reasonable to me, as I had clearly taken too many drugs myself that evening and if I was their drummer, I wouldn't have entertained the idea of even playing one set, let alone two. Instead, Bradley invited me to join him, Kristian, and Pere Ubu's front man, David Thomas—who went by the name Crocus Behemoth—down the block, at Phebe's, on the corner of Bowery and East Fourth Street. Pleasant, Chase, and Pester decided to go and party with Bryan Gregory and Nick Knox of the Cramps at their basement apartment on the Bowery, across from CBGB.

At Phebe's, I was still tripping my ass off. I knew Bradley was as well by the insane grin and wild, unhinged look in his eyes. Well, Bradley *always* looked like that, but in my addled state, he was a veritable garden of unearthly delights. Sitting across from me was Char, the Cramps' manager and an Ohioan, like Bradley, who knew Pere

Ubu also. Before my eyes, her deep-red-lipsticked lips morphed from red to purple to glittery sparkles, then back to wet fire-engine red, fading into sparkly metal-flake blue. Everything was coming up colors. A green voice told me to look under the table. There, I saw two luminescent white gloves covered with rhinestones attached to Char's arms, which beckoned me to crawl underneath. I peered up above the table at Char to see gloveless hands with red-painted nails clasped in front of her. I looked back down. There again were the beckoning white rhinestone gloves. Did she have two pairs of hands? Had I never noticed that before? Oh well, I thought. And then that thought disappeared from my mind entirely, as if it had never crossed it. Everyone started ordering drinks and food. Sitting next to Char was David Thomas, who, befitting his Crocus Behemoth moniker, was a man of rather large stature. The Rolling Stones' "Beast of Burden" was blaring on the jukebox. I looked at Crocus and wondered, "What am I doing in a country-and-western bar with Jackie Gleason?"

Back at Bryan Gregory's Bowery apartment, things got even weirder for Pleasant, Chase, and Pester. Bryan lived in one of those apartments that was actually underneath the sidewalk, with metal doors that shut with a padlock, like the storeroom of a deli. Everybody there was tripping on the same acid Bradley and I were. In one corner of his apartment, Bryan had a human-size cage. He handcuffed Pester and locked her inside it. Pester told me later she practiced mind over matter, telling herself over and over, "I am made of liquid . . . I am made of liquid." And somehow, she managed to slip out of the handcuffs, like Houdini!

When the festivities at Bryan's finally wound down, Chase found herself on a bus heading up Third Avenue at 9 a.m., with throngs of commuters on their way to work. Standing in the aisle, she noticed a little boy, who couldn't have been more than six years old, staring at her all the way. Being a nanny—and not thinking twice that she looked the worse for wear in her ripped Day-Glo party dress, with makeup smeared all over her face—she smiled at the boy. The bus came to a stop and a rare moment of silence descended on it. The curious little boy looked up at Chase and blurted out, in a voice loud enough for everyone to hear, "Hey, lady, you look like a clown." At that, the entire bus erupted into laughter. Poor Chase was so mortified, she got off at the next stop and walked back to her apartment on the Upper East Side.

One morning in December, back in LA, the household at 909 was having breakfast at Duke's Coffee Shop with Bryan Gregory and Nick Knox from the Cramps, who had played the Whisky the night before. We were gaily, and loudly, recounting the debauched behavior of the previous night's after-party. The tables at Duke's were arranged family style, which meant sharing a big long table with other patrons. On the other end of ours was an Australian gentleman who couldn't help but overhear our outrageous stories and let on that he approved by smiling a lot. "You guys sound like a barrel of monkeys," he said. And with that he was one of us and part of the conversation. At that point, I had to leave for work and skulked out the door into the bright midmorning sunlight. Behind me, I could hear the table still roaring with laughter.

That night when I got home around eleven thirty, Dennis, Pleasant, and Ann were in the living room, conferring about something in a hushed but excitable tone. I was in a foul mood after a long day at work and a tiring journey hitching back over the canyon, and not in any mood to talk, so I hurried past toward my room. But Pleasant couldn't contain herself. "Dennis has stolen a car," she blurted out. "We're thinking about taking it to San Francisco to see Levi and the Rockats!"

"Are you out of your mind?" I said matter-of-factly and slammed the bedroom door behind me. A few minutes later, I emerged holding my overnight bag, swiped Dennis's Gay Boy, and took a swig. "OK," I said, "when do we leave?" Everyone giggled, then the crew filled me in on the backstory of how Dennis had obtained this stolen chariot we were going to ride to San Francisco.

Soon after I'd left Duke's that morning, everyone else drifted away also. All except for Dennis, who stayed behind with the Australian and discovered he was an antique dealer, in town on business. They ended up spending the entire day together, drinking and carousing before, well, getting down to business. Around ten that evening, back at the Tropicana, Dennis asked if he could borrow the Australian's rental car. He said he needed to take his mother to the supermarket. In reality, it was a ruse to take the car on a joyride. The Aussie, who was slaughtered and in no state to drive himself, tossed Dennis the keys and then promptly passed out on the bed. Dennis slid out of the motel and drove the car the few blocks to 909. I walked in just as he was hatching a plan with Pleasant and Ann to make the road trip to see Levi Dexter, lead singer of British expat rockabilly band the Rockats, whom Pleasant was madly in love with. She wanted to surprise him by turning up unannounced to their San Francisco show.

We were all in now. We had a car. The one thing we didn't have was enough gas money to get all the way up the coast. We started rummaging through the pockets of every pair of jeans or coat we owned, crawled behind the couch, and emptied drawers looking for any loose cash. When that didn't add up to enough, we started calling friends who had actual jobs and told them our harebrained *I Love Lucy* scheme. A few calls in, we piled into the rental car, picked up some cash from our friend Hoity, and after buying some cookies (as cover to shoplift some champagne) for the journey, we headed up the scenic 101 highway north toward San Francisco.

Grooving all the way to Gene Vincent playing on the car stereo, we reached San Luis Obispo around daybreak and stopped off at the Madonna Inn, a hotel with themed rooms so gaudy, it gave kitsch a bad name. Not having enough money to rent a room, we stuffed ourselves with pie and coffee at the restaurant. Crowded into a pink pleather booth, dazed from driving all through the night, the new day brought a fresh realization of what we had done. Pleasant slowly spelled out our predicament. Grand. Theft. Auto. The words ricocheted through our fuzz brains. We all shrank into our seats.

Until that time, it had not occurred to us that we'd stolen some-body's car and they may have called the police. Dennis was the only one of us who appeared nonplussed by a potential jail sentence for larceny. Ever the smooth grifter, he dropped a few quarters into the phone box and called Mr. Antique at the Tropicana. "Hi there," he said cheerfully. "It's Dennis . . . sorry I didn't come back yet with the car. My mom suddenly fell sick. I'm going to take her to the doctor. Hope you don't mind. I'll be back in a few hours." The Aussie believed every word. Whew! At least we'd bought our-selves some time before the cops would be on our trail. Relieved, we all jumped back in the car to continue our journey.

A few hours later, we made it to Market Street in San Francisco, racking our brains to remember how to get to the Peoples Tem-ple, where Levi and the Rockats were playing that evening, the very same building that murderous cult leader Jim Jones had occupied before taking his parishioners down to Guyana and making them drink the Kool-Aid a year earlier. Looking at a crumpled-up street map through blurry road-tired eyes, we rear-ended a Latino family in a Chevy Impala. Oh shit. Think, think, our collective brains yelled out, how to get out of this one?

Pleasant was in the driver's seat. When the furious father from the Impala walked up to her window, she burst into floods of tears. "My dad's going to kill me," she wailed. "He's visiting from Australia and let me borrow his rental car." Her outlaw psyche kicked in and she rolled out this amazing story, between sobs, that was only half a lie. "Well, let me see your insurance papers," Mr. Impala said, suspiciously eyeing our poker faces for any tell. Dennis, who was sitting next to Pleasant in the passenger seat, rifled thru the glove compartment and presented the rental agreement—which, thankfully, included the insurance policy. Mr. Impala looked it over, then asked Pleasant for her driver's license. "I don't have my license with me," she said.

That was it; we all figured our goose was cooked. But then, miraculously, Mr. Impala cut us a break. "OK, then what's your driver's license number?" Pleasant scrawled a bunch of numbers on a piece of paper and handed it back to him. Mr. Impala looked at it. A confused look crossed his face. "There's too many numbers here for a driver's license," he said. "Not in Australia," Pleasant replied, quick as a flash. Wow, I thought, inspired! Exasperated, Mr. Impala decided the insurance policy would do and went on his way without even insisting on calling the police to report the crash.

After that, Dennis took the wheel to give Pleasant a chance to come down from her nerve-racking, Academy Award–winning performance. He whisked us to 1859 Geary and sailed into an open parking spot right in front of the venue. Levi was delighted to see Pleasant. We breathlessly told Rockats manager Leee Black Childers all about our escapades. He rolled his eyes and, like a true southern gentleman, cracked a devious smile and bought us a round of drinks.

Living for the moment like some wayward Buddhists, we hadn't given a second thought on how to get back to LA with a stolen vehicle. By now, Mr. Antique would have almost certainly alerted the cops. As word of our shenanigans spread through our punk and rockabilly brethren at the show, people started patting us on the back and even took up a collection so we could either fill up with gas for the journey home or ditch the car and buy bus tickets. It was then I truly understood the term "thick as thieves," and even shed a tear at this gesture of goodwill toward us. Or maybe I was just overtired.

After the show, Javier from the Zeros and a foxy African American punkette named Johnnie wanted to come back to LA, so they jumped in the rental car with us, sharing expenses and driving duties. I slept the entire ride home, only waking as we reached the outskirts of Los Angeles and began to devise another plan, this time to ditch the car in the Hollywood Hills after wiping off all our fingerprints. But first we headed back home to 909 Palm.

We arrived to find a note tucked into the screen door. It read: "I'm worried about you, Dennis. Please call me at the Tropicana. Yours, Charles." That was the first time I'd heard his name. To us, he was just Dennis's Aussie mark. More to the point, how did he know where we lived?

Only later did we find out that he'd approached Bryan Gregory, who was in the room next door to Mr. Antique. Assuming that since Dennis had been with the guy all day and the panicked man was a friend, Bryan gave him our address. After reading the note, we all had the same screamed thought in unison. We. Are. Fucked!

Our friend Anna Statman had a brother at law school. Pleasant called to ask how we could avoid getting the electric chair. This was the way our teenage minds worked; the gravity of our crime deserved the gravest punishment. Anna's brother simply suggested we tell Mr. Antique the truth. There was no point in suing us, he said, because we had no money. And anyway, the rental car was fully insured. Unless he wanted to teach us a lesson, it was unlikely he would press charges.

So off we traipsed to the Tropicana and threw ourselves at the mercy of Mr. Antique, telling him the whole sorry story. He responded with hysterical laughter. "You are really crazed!" he said. "That's what attracted me to you guys in the first place. I shouldn't have expected anything less."

On bidding us adieu, he mentioned that, as he was leaving the next day and the car had been rented on a weekly plan, we were welcome to keep it another four days, provided we promise him that we'd return it on time. "And no more car crashes!" We promise, we said. He left and we kept the car for another month, miraculously without consequence.

Preachin' Blues

One balmy evening at the beginning of August 1979, I was standing in line outside the Whisky a Go Go to get into a Pere Ubu show. I was on my own and had adopted the appropriate antisocial stance for a solitary, awkward, self-conscious teen—head down, face to the sidewalk—when I spotted somebody moving toward me out of the corner of my eye. I looked up slowly, not really wanting to engage with anyone at all, and saw this truly eccentric-looking individual standing directly in front of me.

The punk scene in LA had grown to the point where there was a touring band passing through most nights of the week. At every show, you'd see the same gang of punky types, dressed identically in torn clothes, plastic trash bags, black on black on black, and leather, leather everywhere. The person in front of me looked nothing like a typical punk. He couldn't have been more atypical if he tried. He wore an oversized Debbie Harry badge on a white vinyl trench coat belted tight at the waist. He had ribbons and bows tied into his hair, and black-and-white saddle oxfords on his feet. It wasn't meant to be drag—at least, I didn't think so—but it was certainly confounding. Wow, I thought, who is this completely strange creature? Soon he had a name. "Hi, I'm Jeff," he said.

Jeff may have looked like an alien, but he wasn't alien to me. I'd seen him before, browsing through the racks of reggae imports at Bomp!, the record store gig I'd landed after quitting my job at Licorice Pizza. Bomp! was a record emporium much more attuned to my taste. The store was owned by Greg Shaw, a baby-faced, die-hard music enthusiast with a blond bowl cut, who had curated the store into his own treasure trove of rare vinyl, mostly from the 1960s. These were stored in the back and sold by mail order at collectors' prices while all the latest British punk and reggae imports and rockabilly and R&B reissues were racked up at the front of the store, where I worked. That's where I first saw Jeffrey Lee Pierce.

We never really spoke at Bomp!, beyond the kind of small talk record buyers and record store employees usually engage in. But I did become aware he had run a Blondie fan club, much like the one I ran for the Ramones. He seemed a lonesome figure when I saw him there, almost lost as he browsed the racks in a kind of dream state. But when I saw the albums he brought up to the register, I knew he had taste. They were all reggae twelves, things like Burning Spear, which was an obscure choice in LA in those days.

Despite his outré appearance, when we got to talking that first time outside the Whisky, he was very polite and soft-spoken. This guy's a real weirdo, I thought, but I *like* him. He was neither a slick city guy nor a hard punk rocker. He was something else, something indefinable, a weird mix of things. But I couldn't make heads or tails of what he was from the way he dressed. He had four different looks going on at once. That was another plus for me. I liked confused identities.

He offered me some alcohol out of a brown paper bag. As we passed it back and forth, each taking a swig, we struck up a conversation about music and almost immediately discovered we had something in common. We had both been gripped by a desire to search out new music, sounds, scenes, and people. Like me, Jeffrey had been to New York, where he had even tried to start his own band. And while reviewing reggae releases for *Slash* magazine, he'd gone to Jamaica to experience the music at its source.

The line started moving, and we filtered into the venue. That seemed to be a cue for Jeffrey. Apropos of nothing and entirely out of the bluc, he said, "You should be in a band with me."

"But I don't play any instruments," I said sheepishly.

That wasn't about to dissuade him.

"Well, you could be the singer," he said.

My immediate thought was No, I absolutely do not want to be the singer, and told him so in the most definite terms.

"OK, well, I'll be the singer and you can be the guitar player."

"I don't have a guitar," I said. "Or play guitar," I added, just so there could be no misunderstanding on his part.

He was like, "I have an extra guitar."

I said, "Well, OK, why not."

Jeffrey said he could teach me an easy method to play, open E tuning. "That's how blues musicians play slide guitar," he explained. "You can play chords with one finger." It sounded easy enough.

Jeffrey had one other trick up his sleeve to convince me to fall in with him and start a band. "We'll get free drinks and get into shows easier," he said with the glee of a carny who's hit on a surefire scam. If I was feeling trepidation before, I was all in now. Free drinks? Sold!

We went into the club. Pere Ubu blew our minds to smithereens. My brain was whirling with all the possibilities open to me, having taken the decision to form a band with my new friend. The idea of

being in a band, rather than just seeing and listening to them, cross-
ing over from fan to musician, was not something I'd ever considered, even though I had a lot of musician friends. But the way it had
been proposed, so matter-of-factly, and Jeffrey's confidence in me,
even though we were total strangers, made it seem entirely possible.
I didn't exactly know how, but I was committed. Not so committed
that I gave up my lifestyle, though.

I was living in a 1920s fourplex at 1553 Cassil Place that Marcy had
found. We moved in together, then invited Pleasant to be our roommate. She was seeing Billy Persons, who was playing bass with the
Weirdos. He dubbed the place Disgraceland, in honor of a plaster
bust of Elvis that sat on the mantel, which Pleasant had customized
with Alice Cooper makeup. From then on, our home became legendary in the annals of the LA underground rock scene as a 24/7
party house. Debauchery and hijinks, fueled by a never-ending diet
of drugs and alcohol, were our daily bread.

The Runaways had broken up earlier that year, and since then,
Joan Jett had been on a tear. On any given night, there always seemed
to be a party at Joan's place. One night in the fall, Pleasant, Jane
Wiedlin and Margot Olavarria of the Go-Go's, Dennis Crosby, and I
were heading out to party at Joan's ourselves. But first we decided to
go to the Mayfair Market on Santa Monica Boulevard to load up on
booze. Once you arrived at someone's house, it was a given that all
the alcohol you brought would somehow immediately disappear the
second you set it down. Pre-drinking was mandatory.

En route to the supermarket, Dennis suddenly remembered
his boyfriend, Phillip, had some quaaludes and Eskatrol stored in
the freezer. Even better, Phillip was out of town, and Dennis knew
it would be a cinch to climb through his broken kitchen window,

which didn't lock, to obtain them. What was the harm in a little petty larceny between friends, we figured, Phillip being Dennis's lover. By this pretzel logic, breaking, entering, and stealing drugs all seemed wholly innocent to us, as a means to an end for a good time.

After scoring two prescription bottles of uppers and downers from Phillip's refrigerator, we decided we needed to wash them down in style with some champagne. Being young and impoverished, we already had a wealth of experience obtaining supermarket liquor using a five-fingered discount. Eager to get the party started, even before our shopping expedition, Dennis doled out pills to each of us. I took one quaalude and pocketed the extra, along with some speed.

Inside the Mayfair Market, Dennis and Margot trundled up and down the aisles, one of them pretending to browse and select groceries while the other purloined the goods. Dennis managed to slip a bottle of fine champagne into his deep-pocketed trench coat. Margot followed his lead, stuffing a huge leg of lamb into her oversized, oblong shoulder bag—not nearly oversize enough, though, as the meat was still clearly visible. I guess with the quaaludes starting to take effect, she figured this was a good idea. Well, it was a very *bad* idea.

Jane, Plez, and I were waiting outside in the parking lot, and beginning to feel a little light-headed ourselves, when Margot suddenly came running over and jumped into the car, bug-eyed and breathless. "They have my bag!" she wailed. "With all the rent money I made selling Tuinals! Dennis is still in there! Arrgggghhh . . ."

They'd been busted buying a single roll of toilet paper at the checkout. Margot had bright green hair and wore a large black-and-white-checked man's shirt, green tights to match her hair, and sneakers. She couldn't have picked a more conspicuous outfit to wear while swiping a big hunk of meat.

When the security guard came to nab them, Margot bolted for the door, leaving the bag, and Dennis, behind. Dennis's usual fall-back in situations like these were the stunning baby blues he'd inherited from Grandpa Bing and a thousand-mile stare that was utterly disarming and charming at the same time. Right now, for whatever reason, Dennis's peepers weren't working their crooner magic.

From my vantage point in the back seat of the car, Margot's tearful, mascara-stained face made me think of Alice Cooper. I didn't see what all the fuss was about. Shoplifting a hunk of meat wasn't that big of a deal. I have to assume that the quaaludes were starting to cloud my judgment also because, believing I could be the singular voice of reason here, I offered to go back into the store with Margot and pay for the leg of lamb, apologize profusely to the clerk, and promise never to darken the door of Mayfair Markets again. That very ploy had worked like a dream one time before, when my friend Pester was caught hiding a bottle of Kamchatka vodka in a canvas shopping bag shaped like a Converse high-top.

Into the supermarket we boldly marched, Margot and I. The looks on the faces of Dennis, the clerk, and the security guard weren't as genial and welcoming as I was expecting, but undeterred, I swayed up to the clerk and launched into my routine, a slurry spiel of sorry-paying-and-splitting-forever-and-ever. Unmoved and stone-faced, the clerk told me the police had already been called and we were all now locked inside the store until they arrived. Bastards! Dennis and I traded blank stares. Margot dropped to the floor wailing and screaming at the top of her lungs. After a few minutes of her shrill cries, the clerk couldn't stand it any longer. "Beat it!" she told us. "Now! The police are on the way . . ." Maybe there was a God after all. And he condoned shoplifting under exceptional circumstances, and the influence of quaaludes.

I may look innocent . . .
Kid Congo Powers archive

My proud and stylish
parents, Bea and Smiles,
standing with infant me
in front their brand-new
house on Ahern Drive
in La Puente.
Kid Congo Powers archive

An early birthday, at home with
my big sisters, Barbara and Ruth,
in our La Puente kitchen.
Kid Congo Powers archive

Honing my dance skills with big sister Ruth (far left) and (next to her) my cousin Theresa, her brother Ricky, and friend Conchita, during Theresa's birthday party at Grandma Carmelita's house in Boyle Heights.
Kid Congo Powers archive

A freak like me. Frankenstein was my first role model. He represented the otherness I felt inside but didn't know how to express.
Kid Congo Powers archive

FRANKENSTEIN'S PHOTO GALLERY
MOVIELAND WAX MUSEUM
HYWAY 39
BUENA PARK. CALIFORNIA
© UNIVERSAL PICTURES CO. INC.

Mom enthusiastically encouraged my natural inclination towards artistic expression. Here I am showing off an early masterpiece: a watercolor drawing of Jimi Hendrix, copied from the cover of the first record I owned, his album *Cry of Love*.
Kid Congo Powers archive

Dressed to impress for a Sparks concert at the Santa Monica Civic in December 1975.
Kid Congo Powers archive

Vamping with my friend Pearl in a Hollywood Boulevard photo booth in 1976. Also the year I lost my virginity to a male hustler in Hollywood.
Kid Congo Powers archive

Ramones changed my life, in every way imaginable. And the lives of all the people I met through them also. We followed them everywhere, including to a circus they played in Orange County, where this photo was taken by their manager, Danny Fields.
Photo © Danny Fields

With my best friend and sidekick, Pleasant Gehman, in 1979 at photographer Theresa Kereakes's Hollywood apartment, which doubled as the office for their fanzine, *Lobotomy*.
Photo © Theresa Kereakes

Teenage dreamer with
a Keef haircut and a
Sparks T-shirt.
Photo © Donna Santisi

Here I am in full Ramone-clone mode, perusing photos in my
role as "Prez" of Ramones' West Coast Fan Club, while Dee
Dee Ramone poses as a street hustler Charles Atlas in Speedos,
by the pool at the Sunset Marquis Hotel in Hollywood.
Photo © Danny Fields

Zonked on purple microdot
acid with Pleasant Gehman,
having our minds blown
by Pere Ubu at CBGB,
New York City, 1979.
*Photo © Paul Zone (from
the book* PLAYGROUND:
Growing Up in the New
York Underground)

The Cramps in the UK, 1981.
Photo © Anton Corbijn

Playing with the Cramps in Vancouver, Canada.
Photo © David Jacklin

Seduced by Lydia Lunch, every young queer boy's sexual fantasy.
Photo © Marcy Blaustein

With my friends Cindy aka Lotus Lame, Dennis Crosby, and
Ruth Seidman at the Wilton Hilton, Hollywood, August 1981.
Kid Congo Powers archive

Goths in Disneyland.
With Siouxsie Sioux
and the Big Bad Wolf in
the "happiest place on
Earth," 1982.
Photo © Donna Santisi

With Jessamy Calkin at
Hollywood Forever
Cemetery, 1982.
Photo © Marcy Blaustein

The first date on the Gun Club's
Australian tour in 1983 was a date
with Elvis at a shrine erected in his
honor in Melbourne Cemetery.
Kid Congo Powers archive

Sitting on the sacrificial altar at Chichen Itza, 1983.
Kid Congo Powers archive

Jeffrey wading in the crystal blue waters of Cozumel during our vacation in
Yucatan Peninsula, 1983.
Kid Congo Powers archive

Hotel hijinks with Jeffrey in Naples, Italy, during the Gun Club "Las Vegas Story" tour, 1983.
Kid Congo Powers archive

Thinking about washing the dishes in my apartment at Chateau Trianon, Hollywood.
Photo © Jessamy Calkin

Backstage at Long Beach Arena when the Gun Club supported Billy Idol, 1984.
Kid Congo Powers archive

Stripped-down onstage with the Legendary Stardust Cowboy and Jeffrey Lee Pierce at the Pandoras Music Festival in Rotterdam, 1985.
Photo © Herman Nijhof

Getting up close and
personal with Anita Lane
and Nick Cave, 1988.
Kid Congo Powers archive

Shocked by Crowley
but only a bit . . .
Photo © Jessamy Calkin

Stranger in a strange
land. A Bad Seed in
Hong Kong, 1985.
Kid Congo Powers archive

Backstage at Große Freiheit 36 in Hamburg with fellow Bad Seed guitarist, Blixa Bargeld, September 1986.
Photo © Lilian Lohberg

Fur Bible, the band I formed when the Gun Club broke up, with Murray Mitchell, Patricia Morrison, and Desi Desperate, outside our digs in White City, London, 1985.
Photo © David Arnoff

With Nick Sanderson and Jeffrey, on tour with the Gun Club in Portugal.
Photo © Romi Mori

The Gun Club on fire, live in Germany, 1987, for the Mother Juno tour.
Photo © Jens Jurgensen

The Gun Club at the Acropolis in Athens.
Photo © Romi Mori

A portrait taken for the cover of *In the Heat of the Night,* my first outing as a solo artist, in 1989.
Kid Congo Powers archive

Downtime on the beach, wearing matching bathers and sipping coconuts with Nick Cave during the recording of *The Good Son* in Sao Paolo, Brazil.
Kid Congo Powers archive

With Jeffrey Lee Pierce in 1990, around the time of the Gun Club album, *Pastoral Hide & Seek.*
Photo © Richard Dumas

Mirror Mirror, on the wall,
will I stand or will I fall?
Photo © Romi Mori

Ron Athey inspired me
to embrace my true
personality and fall in
love for the first time.
Photo © Liz Seidman

With Sally Norvell, my
partner and muse in
Congo Norvell.
Photo © Ed Colver

Dennis and I grabbed the bag with Margot's Tuinal rent money, squeaked a grateful "Thanks," and ran to tell Margot to quit making a scene because we could now split. Margot was beyond method acting. She had worked herself into a panic attack and was genuinely distraught. When we tried to help her up, she started screaming and crying even louder. We each grabbed an arm and dragged her toward the exit instead. Eventually, she came to and managed to stand on her own two feet, still sobbing. We made it out the automatic doors right as the cops pulled up outside. They didn't need to do a whole lot of detecting to identify the punker leg-of-lamb looters attempting to flee the scene of the crime.

Facing imminent arrest, a brief spark of sense somehow prevailed in my drug-addled mind. "Get rid of your drugs!" I yelled, pulling all the pills out of my front pocket, throwing them to the ground, and crushing them underfoot. Margot reached into her pocket and swallowed hers, a cocktail of ups and downs. But poor Dennis, loaded up with both prescription bottles he'd purloined from Phillip's refrigerator, one in each front pocket of his trousers, with no way to dispose of them at speed, was at a complete loss as to what to do.

The cops promptly cuffed us, threw us in the back of the fuzzmobile, and hauled us off to the West Hollywood police station. Pleasant and Jane bore witness to all this from the safety of the car. Or they would have done if not otherwise engaged. The quaaludes had worked on them like an aphrodisiac. They were so busy finger-fucking each other in the car that they looked up just long enough, through the steamy windshield, to see us being carted away.

At the station we were all separated, fingerprinted, and had our mug shots taken. Lucky for us, the supermarket manager, realizing what pathetic thieves we were, refused to press charges. Margot and I were thrown into separate men's and women's drunk tanks to sleep it off. I could hear Margot howling down at the other end of the cell block all night. I was, however, pleasantly surprised to see what a modern-day drunk tank looked like. Mine had recently been renovated with a shiny new chrome sink and matching bench, which was affixed to a matte gray wall and looked exactly like the industrial minimalism so in vogue in the late '70s. I knew people who would have died to have an apartment that looked like my cell. I imagined myself at a party for the editor of *WET* fashion and lifestyle magazine, waxing lyrical about the design aesthetic of Hollywood drunk tanks.

Scanning the cell of passed-out people, I spotted Pat Smear of the Germs smiling back at me on one of the chrome benches. We looked at each other and cracked up. He had been to a party that night and was hauled in for fighting. Still both high as kites, we stayed up and gossiped between catnaps until we were released the next morning. I had no idea where Dennis and Margot were and didn't want to hang around the station to find out. Fortunately, our apartment was two blocks away, so I went home on foot.

Margot later told me she'd been thrown into a holding cell filled with prostitutes. The cops insisted on calling her "the green thing." She was so whacked out on the quaalude-and-speed cocktail she'd ingested earlier she couldn't stop crying and yelling. At first, the prostitutes comforted her: "Oh, honey, don't cry. You're gonna be all right, nothing bad is going to happen." But after an hour or so of her shenanigans, the ladies lost their sense of compassion and started screaming back at her: "Shut up already! We have to get back to work when we get out of here!"

Since he had all the drugs on him—and not in him—Dennis got the worst of it. He was booked on possession and taken downtown to LA County jail. Fortunately for him, when the cops located Phillip, whose name was on the prescription, he vouched for his boyfriend and spun a story that he'd asked Dennis to pick up the medications and bring them to him.

The next night, I got a phone call announcing that Joan was throwing another party. We didn't have to think twice. We were there.

While I set about learning how to wrestle with my instrument in order to become proficient enough to call myself a guitarist, Jeffrey and I decided to try our hand at being Svengali managers, largely to exploit the multifarious talents of our mutual friend, Pleasant, who was beautiful, charismatic, and seemed born to be onstage. It really didn't occur to us that her lack of experience as a performer was any kind of impediment. That was the way we thought back then. You didn't have to be good, you just needed imagination . . . and dedication.

We put together a rockabilly band for Pleasant and named it the Cyclones. The other members were Johnny Nation, a wily, handsome rascal who played guitar under the heavy influence of rockabilly rebel Ray Campi; Jon Oliphant, who was recruited to play upright bass because he owned one; and our friend Brad Dunning, who offered to play drums. I learned that Jeffrey had a natural talent for putting all the right people together to make music. I assumed the role of artistic director for the band. The only real direction I gave Plez was this: "Clench your fists and scream." I imagined I was molding her into Wanda Jackson or Janis Martin gone berserk. "If you freeze up or can't sing or dance," I told her, "just fling yourself onto the ground." This was the kind of sage advice I dispensed, so valuable and effective I would later employ it myself. All the songs were written quickly and rehearsed until they sounded gone, daddy, gone. Superstardom for the new group, we felt, was all but assured.

The Cyclones scored their debut gig at the world-famous Gazzarri's on the Sunset Strip, opening for all-girl punkers the Go-Go's,
who were already pretty well established on the local scene. Also on
the bill were the Last, who had released an album on Greg Shaw's
Bomp! Records, and another new band, the Urinals. The Cyclones
got done up in their best Western finery for the gig. Jeffrey debuted
the black-suited *Night of the Hunter* look he would later become
synonymous with. I wore a fedora and brandished a large cigar to
make sure everyone knew I was the manager. Maybe we were a little
too wrapped up in our roles as rock 'n' roll managers because we
proceeded to get drunk with the band before the show. All things
considering, the Cyclones' debut performance in front of a paying crowd started off pretty well. Plez and the band were rocking.
Suddenly, Johnny, who must have had one swig too many, began
to scream and holler, swinging wildly at the other band members,
turning into a one-man rockabilly riot. The well-heeled and -coiffed
Gazzarri's audience weren't at all prepared for this display and
seemed to take a collective ten steps back from the stage as the band
thrashed through their "hit," "Rockabilly Bondage," before implod-
ing into a human heap at the foot of the stage. There was no encore.
Backstage we toasted to a great future. But that was fated to be the
Cyclones' both first and last live performance.

When the Cyclones blew themselves out after one show, Jeffrey and
I decided we needed to get serious about forming our own band.
But first, I had to get my own guitar. My friend ML Compton gave
me one he hadn't been using, as a donation to the cause. It was a
prototype Rickenbacker solid body, of which only a few copies existed. Pat Smear had exactly the same guitar. Jeffrey handed me a
homemade cassette tape containing Bo Diddley's "Gunslinger" and

told me to play along and learn how to strum. It was an inspired choice because it was only one chord! Pretty soon, I was strumming that one chord like a blues master.

All we needed now were band members. That proved to be no obstacle at all. Besides playing in the Cyclones, our friend Brad Dunning had little experience as a drummer, but he did have his own drums, along with a similar taste in music and a shared aesthetic. That was good enough for us. More importantly, like Jeffrey and I, Brad had also run a fan club, for the Mumps. That alone made him a shoo-in. Jeffrey asked his friend Don Snowden to play bass, as they had already played together in Phast Phreddie's band Thee Precisions. Don was a music journalist for the *LA Times* and the only member of our new group who knew how to play. We looked up to him as a "real" musician.

We started rehearsing in the garage and living room of Jeffrey's mom Margie's house in Reseda, where he lived with his younger sister, Jacqui. Margie was amazingly supportive of Jeffrey playing music, and very welcoming to me also as I was learning to play guitar at his instigation. She was always extremely positive and encouraging of our efforts. Where my parents were products of their era, Margie was really hip, almost one of the crowd, albeit far more responsible because she held down a job as well as being mom to her two kids.

Marcy and I left Disgraceland because it had gotten way too crazy and messy. Even Pleasant would later admit it was a pigsty. When we moved out, Belinda Carlisle of the Go-Go's moved in and the notoriety of Disgraceland went from strength to strength. We moved back into the Wilton Hilton instead, which Chase Holiday had taken over after the Screamers had vacated it. She needed two roommates. Jeffrey started coming around to teach me how to play guitar. We'd sit on my bed, and he'd say, "Don't pay attention to what the chord is called. Just know that's number-one chord, and that's number-two chord." He taught me how to play open E tuning by memorizing the frets as numbers. He'd say, "Strum on one, strum on five, then strum on three," and I'd follow along. Instead of paint by numbers, it was play by numbers. I didn't figure out the language of chords until a good while later.

We booked some time at a studio on Selma Avenue and Mc-Cadden in Hollywood that a lot of the other punk bands were using as a rehearsal space. It was close by my current job, at Peaches Records on Hollywood Boulevard. That particular corner was where a lot of male hustlers worked their stroll, which added a nice atmosphere to our comings and goings.

Those first rehearsals brought a new meaning to the phrase "working it out." We started by tackling covers, like Bo Diddley's "Gunslinger" and Burning Spear's version of "People Get Ready." The latter was quite ambitious. We turned it into a dirge. We also worked up a very no-wave "Slipping into Darkness" by War. Dave Alvin of the Blasters heard us play it one time and commented to Jeffrey that it was slipping "a little *too* far into the darkness." Jeffrey played guitar also initially, so he and Don could take the lead and guide us. Brad kept up nicely on drums, and I felt around for a style. We were searching for a groove—or what we thought was a groove—using reggae bass lines.

I had not yet learned the fine art of tuning a guitar, or even timing, rendering my input rather diabolical. I knew the sound I wanted to go for—which was very influenced by the playing of Bryan Gregory in the Cramps, Pat Place of the Contortions, and especially Lydia Lunch in Teenage Jesus and the Jerks—but not how to achieve it. I was playing by instinct, going for sound and feeling in an expressionist style that allowed me to make the most of my limited technical abilities. Jeffrey was very encouraging about this approach, seeing that he could steer me in any direction he wanted to achieve the sound he was after for the band. He, too, innately understood the correlation between what we were reaching for and what the Cramps and the Contortions were already doing, with their deep reverence for rockabilly, psychedelia, and free jazz, Albert Ayler and James Brown, but wanting to blow it all apart to create a new energy, a new musical language. Not only a language people could understand, but also a language that people would want to learn and communicate with. We mutually agreed upon this much from the start. You would think this was an easy way of playing. Well, it wasn't. I had to sound horrible and bumble around until the sounds started to fall into place. But we knew the idea was king.

We played around with a folk song recorded by Mack Self called "Willie Brown," about the lynching of a Black man during the Omaha race riot of 1919. Right from the start, we were mining subject matter and material that was far darker than the average punk band. That song starts out with this little arpeggio. Once I'd mastered that, I thought, Wow, this really sounds like I'm playing. It was the first time I was making something other than just a skronking noise.

Jeffrey was much further ahead than all of us. He had some original songs already written. There was "Body and Soul," a sort of Mink DeVille slinky number; a song Jeffrey asked me to write lyrics to called "Going Down to the Red River" (which later became known as "Devil in the Woods"); and "Black Train," which was easy enough for me but had a train shuffle beat that drove Brad insane at first, even though he eventually mastered it. We also attempted a ramshackle version of "Tombstone Blues" by Bob Dylan, which should have been left buried six feet under. Better was another traditional folk song, "Railroad Bill," we tackled at punk speed. Jeffrey let me have a slide solo on that, which was a revelation. Then he showed us this '60s garage-punk-type song he'd written called "Sex Beat."

We would practice and drink, and practice and drink, guzzling Kamchatka vodka by the gallon out of a grapefruit juice bottle. We were drunk all the time and rarely complained of hangovers. It was the only way we knew to make our crazy brains and dreams work in sync, but it was our way of bonding as a unit as well. That sounds stupid, but it's true. We took drugs and drank and drank. A group mind was formed through intoxication, and somehow music, and a vision for it, was born out of that.

We came up with a name—Creeping Ritual—because we thought that's what the music sounded like. Dr. John's *Gris-Gris* album was a big influence. We had a lot of influences, a lot of ideas we wanted to draw from and did draw from. It's pretty amazing we were able to make something out of them, because I had never played music before. *Everything* was miraculous to us, every step, every advance we made. Slowly, it all started to take shape and make sense.

One day, Jeffrey came to rehearsal and told us we were going to play our first live show, at the Hong Kong Café in Chinatown. We were astonished and slightly horrified, possibly me more than anyone else. I'd only been playing guitar for a month, and now Jeffrey expected me to play onstage, in front of other people? And at the Hong Kong Café, no less, where a lot of our friends in bands also played and would almost certainly be in attendance. *¡Ay dios mío!* Shouldn't we rehearse for another two years before taking this step? What we didn't know at the time was that not only had he set up this date without our knowledge, Jeffrey had also conned his way onto the bill.

Dave Alvin of the Blasters had set up a string of weekly shows at the Hong Kong Café. Jeffrey got wind of it, called him up, and insisted that he'd already booked one of the dates for Creeping Ritual. Dave knew he was pulling a number but admired Jeffrey's chutzpah so agreed to let us play. Even that early on, Jeffrey was already going for these Colonel Tom Parker moves. "That's mine. That's my show." It was an omen of what was to come.

We played the show, made it through. Nobody booed or ran away. Our friends liked it. Keith Morris was there. Jeffrey had known him from when he was the singer in Black Flag. They'd become friends and roommates. Keith asked us to support his new band, Circle Jerks, the following month, also at the Hong Kong. We were becoming regulars!

We still sounded like a real mishmash of our influences. All the country music and murder and gunfighter ballads we loved, cut through with R&B and Jeffrey's obsession with reggae. Even so, it felt as if we were conveying something approaching a unique and coherent vision for the band, even if it wasn't yet fully formed. The few people who came to see us—mostly our friends, peers, and fellow musicians, like the Blasters and X—seemed to sense there was something interesting going on also.

Keith Morris had one pointed critique. "You need another name," he told us. "Creeping Ritual sounds too gothic." He came up with a list of alternatives for us that included the Ass Festival and the Sand Niggers. We picked another one: the Gun Club. I believe we chose wisely. Jeffrey traded Keith a song for the band name—a fair trade. It was called "Group Sex," which ended up becoming the title song of the first Circle Jerks album. No one could say we didn't have a sense of the absurd.

Right from the start, Jeffrey was extremely confident in his own presentation onstage. He was developing this preacher-man persona that was very Reverend Harry Powell. He relished playing this role, as the evil rock 'n' roll preacher. We both loved cinema and actors.

We would talk in feverish tones about our favorite actors: James Dean, Marilyn Monroe, Marlon Brando, Sal Mineo, and Montgomery Clift. Jeffrey even sat in on classes at the Lee Strasberg studio at one point. Naive and uninformed, but tenacious, we decided to incorporate "the method" into our music. *Rebel Without a Cause* became our cause. We were irreverent and snotty. We set out to destroy music as much as create it. Live, we wanted to be offensive and conjure up bad vibes. We were huge Dr. John fans. Bad juju was the only kind of juju for us.

At the end of May 1980, we played a show with X and the Blasters at Club 88, a former strip joint on Pico in wild West Los Angeles, where some of the concert sequences had been filmed for Penelope Spheeris's punk documentary *The Decline of Western Civilization*. That night, Jeffrey seemed possessed and went full backwoods preacher man, bringing a Bible onstage as a prop, which he proceeded to fling on the ground, stamp on, and flagellate with a chain. In retrospect, he probably had a plan to upstage all the other bands. In actuality, he succeeded in getting us banned from the club by the owner, Wayne Mayotte, who, as a retired engineer and Korean War veteran, was a pretty straitlaced guy and outraged by Jeffrey's antics. But they served their purpose. Now the Gun Club were notorious. Outlaws, just like the gunslingers we sang about.

Immediately after that show, the Gun Club almost broke up. There was no connection between the two, though. Not a drummer by choice, Brad used to get tired and would signal his frustration to the rest of us by throwing his sticks into the air mid-song. Eventually, he decided he didn't want to play drums at all. At the time, he was also working on a book about *I Love Lucy*. Don, too, decided to forgo his position on bass. He already had a day job, writing for the *Los Angeles Times*, and the Gun Club was never going to become his main gig.

I felt pretty much the same way. We didn't have a record deal, barely had an audience. It was little more than a hobby. I resolved to be a musician second and a journalist first. I was already writing for various fanzines—for Pleasant Gehman's *Lobotomy* and for *Contempo Trends*, the zine I'd started with Brad Dunning. I had also been taking classes at Los Angeles City College: a journalism class, a typing class (because I figured journalism and typing went hand in hand), and one in philosophical logic, for similar reasons. I soon realized there was more math than philosophy associated with logic, so I dropped that one.

Becoming a music journalist seemed to be the logical next step for me. That way, I figured, I could still be involved in music, have a vocation that could blossom into a career, and get free entry into shows. It was a decision I reached, under Jeffrey's influence, through equal parts pragmatism and opportunism. There was never any thought that the Gun Club would amount to anything.

Jeffrey and I decided to soldier on anyway. We recruited drummer Terry Graham and bassist Rob Ritter, the rhythm section from the Bags, who had just disbanded. Terry and Rob came as a package deal. Handsome and quiet with a devilish sense of humor, Rob was a record nerd, like us, who held down an office job at the same time he played with the Bags and now the Gun Club. A fan of the artier end of punk, he had a Throbbing Gristle badge permanently pinned to his crisp, clean blazer. Terry was a much pricklier character but played with a feeling and nuance that was far more accomplished than many of his peers on the punk scene. We started rehearsing with them and were shocked at how good they were. Uh-oh, these people *can* play, we thought, not *kind of* play. We had to step up our game. But that's when it really took form and became less ramshackle.

Jeffrey handed each of us a tape of songs. "My Brand of Blues" by Marvin Rainwater was on there, Marty Robbins's "Big Iron," "Somebody in My Home" by Howlin' Wolf, "The Ballad of Hollis Brown" by Dylan, and "Prodigal Son" by the Rolling Stones. He wanted the Gun Club to be a combination of every element of those songs. It helped solidify our direction. This was not the kind of material the average punk rocker in LA was listening to, and that was the whole point. We wanted to stand out from the crowd, not just in our performance and attitude, but in our aesthetics and taste.

Rob and Terry really liked the no-wave aspect of my guitar playing, mixed with the country, rockabilly, Bo Diddley, and blues influences. They also liked the idea that we were odd and amateurish. Playing with them, Jeffrey and I gained confidence every day and started to write more original songs, knowing we now had accomplished musicians to interpret them. I wrote a song called "For the Love of Ivy," in praise of Poison Ivy Rorschach from the Cramps, a band we both loved and were very inspired by. I took the words from this funny old book I found called *2000 Insults for All Occasions* and cut them up William Burroughs–style. Jeffrey reworked them with this violent blues imagery, making the song's stop/start, quiet/loud structure all that more dramatic.

Then we really started to stretch ourselves. We attempted to learn Robert Johnson's "Preachin' Blues" and make it our own. The song was half improvised, structured only by the vocal cues. Jeffrey was incredibly encouraging as a teacher. He taught me to feel the song, to trust in my ability and find the right notes later. That song was rooted in beat and rhythm. The changes don't follow a traditional song structure but track the vocals, and the vocal line comes in whenever it comes. We never knew how long Jeffrey was going to draw it out, when we were going to have to let loose, or if we were just going to have to stay the course and keep it rolling. We just followed Jeffrey's cues. That was my introduction to improvisation, and it felt like another huge leap, not only in establishing the mood and the groove of the group but also in showing us what we were capable of. Even we were shocked and surprised at how we sounded.

After a couple of months' practice, we felt we had enough cover songs down and enough originals in our repertoire for a set—including most of the songs that would later end up on the Gun Club's debut album (like "Jack on Fire" and "She's Like Heroin to Me") and "Railroad Bill," a cover I helped arrange. It was time to go out and perform them in public. We played a string of shows through July and August 1980 at the Whisky, Jett's Cafe, Madame Wong's West in Santa Monica, and other clubs.

Jeffrey started to come into his own as a performer. A lot of people wrote off his singing as this horrible howling, but he persisted and began to find the voice that really helped define what the Gun Club became. He was a very odd sort of boy—obnoxious most of the time but very sweet too. The people who loved him often wanted to murder him. He used these extremes of light and dark, perversion and charm, and the way he swung between them, to great effect onstage, giving our shows an edge. Every Gun Club show was volatile, unpredictable, and often crossed the line between entertainment and punishment.

We would be playing "Preachin' Blues," and, during the bridge, he would start berating the audience, telling everybody to "fuck off" and what "losers" they were. We'd be laughing and playing at the same time, waiting for him to give the signal to come back in. The middle eight would become a middle thirty-six because he was having too much fun telling the all of five or so people in the audience they were "butt fuckers" until he got the reaction he was looking for and they started walking out. Then he would break the spell by saying something witty and hysterical, and we would all fall back in. It never failed to surprise us how he would pull it all together. He had discovered how to create something completely magical out of chaos and disorder.

In the space of a year, I'd gone from being a fan of music to a musician myself. That was a magical transformation also, entirely self-actualized.

Acquiring Congo Powers

"What would you sacrifice to be in the Cramps?" said Poison Ivy.

She and Lux Interior had come to see me at the Wilton Hilton shortly after they'd moved to Los Angeles from New York, in the late fall of 1980. They were short a guitarist after Bryan Gregory had abruptly left the band. Kristian Hoffman and Bradley Field had recommended me as a replacement and told Lux and Ivy they should check me out, playing with the Gun Club.

I guess you could say I was a friend of theirs, but I was still more of a fan and willing slave. A fan-slave, if you will. I was also very in awe of them. When the Cramps would come to LA, Pleasant, Marcy, Trudie, and I were always the welcoming party who would escort them around town and suggest places to go, the same role we'd adopted for the Ramones. That's how we got to know the band off-stage and became friendly with them. Lux and Ivy always seemed so much older and more worldly.

This wasn't a friendly visit, though. Lux and Ivy came with a purpose.

"We want you to be our guitar player," they said. "Do you want to be in the band?"

I couldn't think of anything I wanted more, but I was so taken aback at being asked, completely out of the blue, I was almost too stunned to answer.

"Yeah, of course," I said. "Don't I need to audition or something?"

They just looked at each other, looked at me, and that's when Ivy asked me what I would sacrifice to be in the Cramps. It was a perfectly reasonable question, but not one I'd given a whole lot of thought to. That I would ever be asked to join my favorite band seemed so out of the realms of possibility, it had never crossed my mind. Even so, now that Ivy had put the idea into my head, she might as well have asked, "What wouldn't you sacrifice to be in the Cramps?" The answer was nothing. And everything. Other than the Ramones, there wasn't a band I loved more.

"Do you mean you want me to quit my band?" I wondered aloud. "Relocate? Quit school?"

"No, nothing like that," said Ivy. "I mean would you sacrifice something like . . . a finger. Would you cut off a finger to be in our band?"

I had to think for a second. It seemed quite drastic. Not least considering they wanted me to play guitar. But what the hell, it was only one finger. I had ten. The upside was . . . I'd be a Cramp.

"You know," I said, "I think I would."

"OK," said Ivy, "then you can be in our band."

It was that easy. They even let me keep the finger. The only thing I gave up was my freedom. Total allegiance, I would soon discover, was a cardinal rule for becoming a Cramp. That meant I would absolutely have to quit my other band. I was torn. It seemed almost worse than losing a finger. I had formed the Gun Club with Jeffrey. At the same time, we were always on the verge of breaking up.

Shortly after Lux and Ivy came to see me, the Gun Club played a show at the Arena bar in Culver City, supporting the Blasters. Rob Ritter did, in fact, quit the band that night. He was forever quitting the band, mostly in frustration at Jeffrey, who was an exacting and mercurial front man. Rob walked offstage in the middle of our set, handed his bass to Anna Statman, who was in the audience and had played with Jeffrey in the Red Lights, and told her to take over. It felt like an omen.

"I don't know what to do," I told Jeffrey. "The Cramps want me to join them, and I'll have to leave the Gun Club."

"Are you insane to even ask?" said Jeffrey. "Of *course* you should join the Cramps." Then, ever the opportunist, he added, "I won't be mad as long as you get us some gigs with you." He was already planning a new incarnation of the Gun Club the second he found out I was leaving. It never even entered his mind the band would cease to exist without me.

"You have to have a Cramps name," Lux and Ivy told me. This was one of the first orders of business. "Make a list of names," they said. I asked all my friends to make suggestions. "Thing" was an early one, after the hand in *The Addams Family*. Then Pleasant said, "Oh, your name should be Brian Gris-Gris." That was a good one. I liked that it incorporated my own name and made it voodoo-sounding. Lux and Ivy rejected that outright. They didn't want another Brian in the band, or anything that would remind them of Bryan Gregory.

Bryan had announced his resignation from the Cramps a few months earlier by disappearing mid-tour, after a show in Berkeley, taking off with not only the band's van but also all their equipment in the dead of night. There were rumors he had joined a satanic cult. Bryan was a sweet man with a caustic wit but also very strange. Anything was possible. Bradley Field once told me Bryan used to favor older women as lovers because their skin felt soft like crepe paper.

The Cramps finished the tour with a fill-in guitarist: a woman named Julien. She played with the Mad, a New York horror-punk band fronted by Screaming Mad George, who later became a huge horror movie special-effects artist. The Mad were extremely theatrical and I'm sure that's what probably drew Lux and Ivy to Julien. They gave her a more fitting, Cramps-sounding name: Julien Griensnatch. I saw her onstage with them during the *Urgh! A Music War* concert at the Santa Monica Civic and thought she was great. But Lux and Ivy wanted someone who was going to be a more permanent addition. That was me.

They came up with their own suggestion for a name. "You should be like Kid Thomas," they said. Kid Thomas was a crazy, screaming rhythm-and-blues piano stomper from New Orleans, who had this giant jelly-roll hairdo and a pencil mustache. He looked great and I was a fan. Being the youngest in my family, I was often called "Kid" by different family members, especially my auntie, so the name already felt familiar.

Then, one day, we were sitting around their apartment. Lux was looking at this Santeria votive candle, which had writing all over it. "When you light this candle," it read, "congo powers will be revealed to you."

"There's your name," Lux announced. "Congo Powers." It had a great ring to it, for sure. Magical, and sprinkled with old Hollywood glamour. As if Tyrone Power had been reincarnated as an orisha. We married that with Kid Thomas and I had my Cramps name: Kid Congo Powers.

This was a great talent of Lux's, coming up with characters and assigning roles to everyone. He even came up with a name and backstory for my mother. There was an old '50s pulp magazine in their apartment lying open at an ad for Elura wigs, these fake-fiber hairpieces made by Monsanto. "Your mother was a Mexican vampire actress," Lux said, "named Allura Monsanto." In Lux's imagination, the mundane became magical. After all, he, too, had received his name as a transmission through the ether, after hearing a car commercial talking up the vehicle's "deluxe interior."

Once I had my Cramps name, I had to get together my look. The Cramps already had a very particular and defined style, mostly centered around anything that was sleek and black. They were into tiki culture and voodoo. My earliest look was very much in that vein. I wore a necklace made of bones and a crazy-looking turban I'd grabbed at a vintage store. It was huge and unwieldy, like something Elizabeth Taylor would wear. Or a Sikh. I bejeweled it. Later, I downsized to a more manageable and form-fitting New Orleans–style satin one. I looked like a voodoo guru, the Maharishi Screamin' Jay Hawkins.

The Cramps had all their clothes custom-made by a tailor in LA. We went shopping, Lux, Ivy, and I, to pick out material for trousers and other things. We also bought clothes from Strait Jacket, a vintage clothing store on Crescent Heights owned by Genny Body, who had been a member of early LA all-girl punk band Backstage Pass.

My look developed over time, but I'd already decided I wanted something very specific, something that would both pay homage to and further the role of my predecessor in the band. Bryan Gregory had such an iconic image that he was almost the face of the Cramps. He had a very powerful presence—a scary sexual cocktail of androgyny and machismo, like a weird cross between Boris Karloff and a leather daddy. I knew I wanted to incorporate that idea of being half androgynous and half scary, something that would fit comfortably within the world of the Cramps.

I was a huge fan of '60s girl groups like the Ronettes and the Shangri-Las when I was a kid. I hit upon the idea of a look and a character that was a combination of those girl-group singers and the bad-boy biker boyfriends they sang about. Willy DeVille's wife, Toots, was another inspiration. She was such an extreme-looking character. Toots had her hair teased up into a great big beehive, wore tight black dresses, and looked as if she would sooner kill you than fuck you. I had seen her in New York and was fascinated by her. Likewise, Roxy and Vera, the girlfriends of Johnny and Dee Dee Ramone, whom I'd been around quite a bit. They were paragons of exaggerated '50s femininity but also street tough and not to be messed with. They were terrifying and captivatingly beautiful at the same time.

One more element, I decided, was needed to complete my role in the Cramps. I went to a tattoo parlor on Hollywood Boulevard and got my first tattoo. At the time, people didn't really have tattoos. At least, not ones they showed off. Bryan Gregory had tattoos on his forearm that were very much part of the fearsome aspect of him I was so intrigued by. It made him seem like some hardened sailor. I decided I needed a "scary" tattoo also. I thought of it as image building.

The tattoo shop was run by some Filipino guys. It was the kind of place that dealt strictly in street tattoos for marines on leave. I looked over the flash on the walls. My eyes were drawn to this drawing of a shrunken head. I imagined a Vietnam War vet who had gone insane in the jungle, chopped off somebody's head, and got that tattoo to memorialize it. It was very voodoo-looking. The kind of tattoo no one in their right mind would get. It was perfect! As soon as it was inked on my forearm, I began to feel much more Cramps-like.

The Cramps believed they were a magical entity. They believed in psychic phenomena, ghosts, and spirits. And that all misfits and freaks, like them, were people who came from some other planet, or some other plane, and had somehow landed here. That *we* were the aliens who walked the earth. To Lux and Ivy, any true nonconformist was viewed as a magical person. They were always on the lookout for individuals with an essence. I think that's why they picked me for the band. It certainly wasn't because I was a skilled guitarist.

They were such misfits—and *worldly* misfits, at that, which was one of the things that drew me to them also—that they could only trust other misfits. Once they saw anybody conforming, that trust was gone. They were a bit like a band of feral cats. That was part of the magic too. You were either in their sphere of influence, and accepted as one of them, or you weren't.

I ended up connecting with them on that magical misfit level. It was completely intuitive, just feeling each other out. I felt completely accepted, particularly as a gay rocker. Lux, in his role as a shaman, was almost pansexual, and not homophobic in the least. That sense of freedom—that you could be true to your nature, create your own persona to express it, and not be judged for it—was liberating and exhilarating. Setting yourself apart, whether gay, straight, sane, or insane, was to be celebrated. The Cramps embraced perversion, in all its facets and in the best possible way. I knew they were my people.

Lux used to say he hoped the Cramps would be "a whole thing entirely separate from this world." He wasn't just paying lip service to this idea; he meant it. The Cramps' entire raison d'être was to fulfill that goal. To me, it didn't seem out of reach. You just had to believe in it, as they did, and fervently, to bring it into existence.

They lived on the top floor of a two-story building on North Edgemont, in the shadow of the huge blue Scientology building on

Sunset Boulevard. Scientology was not their bag, as far as I knew, but I'm sure they were intrigued. Lux was even an early adherent of Transcendental Meditation.

Moving to Hollywood made no sense whatsoever for their music career. It made perfect sense for them as a band, and as people. For Lux and Ivy, especially, because they had immersed themselves in the culture of Hollywood, particularly '50s Hollywood—the look, the style, the mode of being, the glitz and the glamour, the scandal and the crime, the esoteric philosophies and the occult. It was a place that had been brought into being, and continued to exist and sustain itself, entirely through magical thinking. And magical thinking was central to the Cramps also.

Their apartment was a pure expression of their devotion to the aesthetics of this "thing" they'd created, a time capsule of '50s outsider culture and a living shrine to their obsessions. The walls were adorned with framed B-movie posters and pinup girls. The furnishings looked as if they had been lifted out of an episode of the Jetsons, all midcentury modern. There were nods to tiki and voodoo culture, with outré touches here and there, like the pulp paperback that sat on their coffee table, entitled *Concentration Camp Bestiality*. They also had the biggest record collection I had ever seen and a vintage '50s jukebox filled with rare singles. I was already an obsessive record collector myself, as were most of my friends, but nothing compared to Lux and Ivy's collection, which was huge and varied, and was meticulously arranged and cataloged by style and year and label.

I was already a fan of rockabilly music, but mostly the obvious things like Gene Vincent. Lux and Ivy furthered my education, hipping me to more obscure cuts I would never have discovered on my own. The *Pebbles* compilations had started coming out around this time, which collected all these super-rare, pre-punk garage cuts on one album. They gave me some of those to listen to and directed my attention to songs like "Green Fuz," "Goo Goo Muck," and "I'm Five Years Ahead of My Time" that they were thinking of incorporating into their set.

I had only been playing guitar a year and had very little technical ability or knowledge. Like Jeffrey, Ivy took it upon herself to further my education, showing me how to play rockabilly scales on guitar. She was very patient. She even showed me how to use a fuzz pedal. With the Gun Club, I had no effects; I just plugged straight into the amplifier and turned it all the way up. Lux and Ivy mentored and schooled me. I wanted to know everything they knew. I listened, and hung on every word. They molded me in their image, filled me with the requisite knowledge and training I needed to become a true Cramp. Fortunately for them, I was young and malleable, willing to do whatever they said, and took their direction well.

Ivy was very influenced by Bo Diddley, most obviously in the Cramps' visual presentation, which was like a ghoulish revamp of Bo Diddley and the Duchess, but also in the starkness and simplicity of their music. Lux would hypnotize the audience like a snake charmer. Ivy would lay down these sleek, rhythmic guitar lines. Together, they worked a voodoo magic, a merging of the masculine and the feminine, harnessing its raw power and conjuring up a primal energy to infect their audience like a zombie virus.

Ivy gave me very specific instructions about the function of my guitar and where it fit within the Cramps sound. "Think of it like a horn, squawking and honking," she said. "And the solo as some wild sax solo." So that's what I did, played my guitar like a horn, blowing out these great expressive slabs of sound. The horn intro to Andre Williams's "Bacon Fat" was a major reference. The Cramps were all about rhythm. Rhythm was magic, and mastering it, they believed, was the key to unlocking that wild, unbridled sexual power that underpinned all the greatest rock 'n' roll.

About a month after I joined the Cramps, I got a strange foretaste of fame as a member of a notorious rock band. We hadn't yet played a show or made any public appearances as a band, but word had already gotten around that the old Bryan had been replaced by a new one. When Siouxsie and the Banshees arrived in LA at the end of November to play four nights at the Whisky on their first US tour, I was hauled out of the audience by their publicist, whisked backstage for an audience with the queen herself, and introduced as the "new Cramp." I was already a huge fan of the Banshees' first album. Lydia Lunch had turned me on to them. She said Siouxsie was one of the only women in rock worth paying attention to. This was high praise, indeed. Lydia hated *everything*. And she was right, of course, Siouxsie absolutely was worth paying attention to; I was eager to meet her and the band, never expecting to find myself sitting next to Siouxsie in the dressing room. Deborah Schow snapped a photo of us chatting for *Trouser Press*. Then, almost as quickly as I arrived, I was unceremoniously thrown out. I felt like a toy being used in a game. It was weird and unsettling.

The Banshees were everything I had hoped for live, though. Sioux stalked the stage using the microphone cord as a whip, as if she was ready to stamp out a cigarette on the face of some poor unfortunate in the front row without warning. The Banshees had that kind of vibe: transgressive, dangerous, and unpredictable. Seeing them in such an intimate venue was intense. They were mesmerizing.

Post-show, we were all invited back to their hotel to party. The band were staying at the Tropicana on Santa Monica Boulevard in West Hollywood, a notorious rock 'n' roll motel once owned by baseball star Sandy Koufax, which was a second home for anybody who partied on the music scene. In a drunken haze that night, we made plans to meet for breakfast at the motel's diner, Duke's, then I would show Sioux and Budgie around town.

The next morning, we attempted to nurse our collective hang-over while shopping on Melrose Avenue and, when that got too much, decided to partake in the hair of the dog at the Palms, a les-bian bar across the street. It turned out to be the perfect place to drink, not just because of its close proximity, but because none of the punk crowd would be hanging around in there to bother the band. Our little crew was always looking for somewhere different to hang out when we were hungover. The standard "punk" places were getting too crowded. The scene was becoming so claustrophobic. You would see the same people over and over and over. I was glad to have an excuse to travel and explore virgin territory with the Cramps.

The night I made my live debut with the Cramps, in New York, John Lennon was assassinated. We were playing at the Ritz in Greenwich Village, sixty-one blocks south of the Dakota building. I can't re-member if we found out before or during the show, and I was so traumatized I couldn't think of anything other than how to play my three chords, but I have almost no recollection of the show itself—as if I've blocked it entirely from my memory. The show at the Ritz was a warm-up for the main event, a headline appearance at the Lyceum in London. We flew there immediately afterward.

The Cramps were a big deal in the UK. There was quite a lot of excitement and fanfare in the British music press leading up to the concert because this was going to be the first show they'd performed since Bryan Gregory had left. I was very conscious, perhaps *too* con-scious, that it was going to be a landmark show of some kind and, as the newest member of the band, unknown outside a small scene of people in LA, I had to make my mark. I also knew how brutal and unkind the press could be in the UK, usually at the whim of whatever journalist was reviewing the show. To make matters worse, a lot of the musicians I idolized and admired would be there in the audience, scrutinizing my performance. Siouxsie and the Banshees and the Damned, both big fans of the Cramps, were coming. All of this was playing on my mind when we arrived in the UK.

I'd never played in front of more than a handful of people in the Gun Club. Most of them were my friends. The Lyceum was a big two-thousand-capacity venue in the heart of London's West End theater district. To say I was nervous is an understatement. It felt as if I was about to embark on a trial by fire. I was petrified and convinced I was going to fuck everything up. Everyone would know I couldn't play guitar for shit, and I'd be kicked out of the band.

Miles Copeland, the Cramps' label boss, was out of town so we stayed at his place in Maida Vale. It was a nice house, quite large, and stuffed with all these Middle Eastern artifacts that looked as if they belonged in a museum. "Wow, what a great collection this guy has," I said, admiring some small but extremely ancient-looking statues on display. "His father was in the CIA," Lux replied.

Miles's father, Copeland Sr., was a jazz musician who started out playing with Glenn Miller's band and ended up a CIA operative, helping to foment revolutions and support numerous coup d'états across the Middle East. "This stuff must be clandestine," said Lux, who imagined these relics, prior to becoming family heirlooms, had been spirited out of whatever country Copeland Sr. had been stationed in using diplomatic bags.

That night, I woke up in the middle of the night and felt very strange. At first, I put it down to preshow nerves, or wondered whether I'd woken up drunk. But it was a much weirder feeling. The house was silent. Everybody else was asleep. I could see a light on in the hallway. I got up to get a glass of water. It felt like the room was moving sideways, as if I was walking through a fun house, struggling to keep my balance. The whole room felt distorted and misshapen. I felt disoriented and weirded out. Is this even happening? I thought. Am I losing my mind? Or is it just jet lag? When I walked out into the hallway and spied all those antiquities again, I figured, Oh, that's what this is. All these statues, plundered from some tomb in Egypt or Damascus, were making their presence felt. Having lived in the Wilton Hilton, I was no stranger to hauntings and psychic phenomena.

In the morning, Lux told me he'd gotten up in the middle of the night also and had exactly the same experience. We figured the artifacts and the spirits inhabiting them were not best pleased at being shut up in Copeland Manor. "How do they live with all this going on in the house?" I wondered aloud.

"Oh," Lux said, "Miles has no consciousness. This would never affect him anyway."

But it might have affected our performance at the Lyceum. The band thought it was a terrible show and that we were under-rehearsed. Thankfully, nobody laid the blame on me, even though Steve Severin of the Banshees later told me he could see my hands shaking while I played.

After the Lyceum show, we headed straight into the studio in Los Angeles to work on the new Cramps album. This too was virgin territory for me but slightly less nerve-racking. At least if I fucked up this time, I wasn't doing it in front of an audience. We were recording at A&M Studios on the A&M lot in Hollywood. Miles Copeland's IRS Records was distributed by A&M in the United States, and part of the deal was that their acts were able to use the studio. I was in awe, walking in there for the first time and seeing all the gold records on the walls. Joni Mitchell. John Lennon. David Soul. All the greats. The place was steeped in history. It had started out in the '20s as a movie studio built by Charlie Chaplin, who had designed it as a replica of an English country village, and was later owned by Red Skelton before Herb Alpert and Jerry Moss bought it in the mid-'60s as the headquarters for their label, A&M.

The Cramps had recorded their first album with Alex Chilton at Sam Phillips's studio in Memphis. This time Lux and Ivy were producing themselves. They had a very clear idea of what they were after and wanted to break away from the rockabilly sound on the first record. Ivy wanted to slow everything down and make it grinding, swampy, and sexual.

Everything about the sessions was appropriately magical and ritualistic. We decided we should stay awake as long as possible. Not by taking drugs, but through sleep deprivation, to get out of ourselves and let the muse take over so that when we were playing we'd connect on a purely instinctual level, not an intellectual one, and our animal minds would drive our creative impulses. It felt like we were engaged in a spiritual and philosophical fasting, in order to achieve an otherness. To achieve otherness, you have to become "other." We became a spectral presence, almost like ghosts.

We felt possessed by the muse and played our roles accordingly. Everything was recorded live. We would use these very small vintage amplifiers turned up to the max. There was a song called "Caveman." I played the guitar solo on it to make it sound like . . . a caveman, deliberately brutal and unsophisticated. It was very high-concept. On another song, "Beautiful Gardens," we played and played and played the same repetitive rhythm until we couldn't feel ourselves. It was intended to be a psychedelic-shamanistic-ecstatic conjuring.

We also worked on a cover of the Hasil Adkins song "She Said." We ran through it three or four times, but for some reason it just didn't click. Lux wasn't happy with the vocal. We decided to give it one last try. This time, Lux grabbed a Styrofoam cup and shoved it in his mouth. Suddenly, he sounded like a toothless hillbilly, and everything fell in place. That Styrofoam cup was the conduit to make the magic happen.

Toward the end of April, we played Friday and Saturday shows at the Roxy in West Hollywood to kick off a promotional tour for the album that would take us across Europe and back through the United States. These were the first shows I'd ever played with the Cramps in Los Angeles, so all my friends were going to be there. Keeping my promise to Jeffrey, I arranged for the Gun Club to take the support slot. On the first night, my parents came to see us play. Lux pointed out my mother, Beatrice, from the stage, introducing her to the audience by the Cramp name he had assigned her, "Allura Monsanto, the Mexican vampire actress." My mom proudly took a bow. What vampire actress doesn't love applause?

If I wanted to make an impression on the hometown crowd, then the show on the second night would not be forgotten in a hurry. Halfway through our set, we'd play Lux and Ivy's song "I Was a Teenage Werewolf," which would segue into a version of Dwight Pullen's "Sunglasses After Dark." While the audience was hypnotized by an assault of feedback, rhythm, and flashing strobes, Nick Knox would duck down behind his drums to retrieve a pair of dark sunglasses and put them on, and Lux would yank his out of his pants, giving him an opportunity to do one of his favorite things onstage—expose himself. Ivy and I would turn our backs to the audience and walk toward our amps, on top of which we had votive candles and our prop sunglasses. Then we would all turn around again and reveal ourselves, cast in shades.

That night, I leaned just a little too far over my amp to fetch my sunglasses. A spark leapt up from the candle onto my hair, and, *whooosh*, it all went up in flames, igniting the Aqua Net Extra Super

Hold hair spray I'd used to make my Ronnie Spector hairdo even more voluminous. The whole outer shell of my hair was now alight, like a flaming wig-hat. Except I didn't know I was on fire because, one, I couldn't see the top of my head, and two, I was wearing sunglasses.

Girls in the audience started screaming. Wow, this is so great, I thought. Who would know the Cramps would inspire something like Beatlemania in LA? Seconds later, Bradley Field, who was tour-managing for us, put a damper on things by running out from the wings and showering me with beer. Then Nick Knox jumped over his drums and beat me on the head with his sticks. Wait a minute, I thought. Was I playing that badly? What did I do to deserve this?

By the time I realized what was happening, the flames had been extinguished. The smell of burnt hair lingered, wafting through the entire venue like a funeral pyre of human flesh. The screaming turned to cheering. Without missing a beat, Lux, great shaman that he was, announced to the audience, "Ladies and gentlemen, the days of miracles have not passed. We present to you Kid Congo . . . the burning bush."

In Washington, DC, we played the 9:30 Club. This British journalist named Jessamy Calkin came to interview us for influential UK style magazine *The Face*. She walked in with big crimped hair, wearing something like a rubber French maid's outfit and sunglasses so dark they were almost opaque. She created quite a stir in the Cramps camp. We were all quite taken with Jessamy, even more so when she told us she was currently living in a vintage Cadillac that was up on blocks in her brother's garage in DC. After the interview, Ivy was breathless in her enthusiasm for our encounter with this exotic creature, who felt like one of us. Coming from Ivy, who did not do "breathless," such compliments were exceedingly rare. But we were all in complete agreement about Jessamy, who would remain in my life for years to come.

Soon after we finished the album, we went into the studio again to record two new songs as B-sides for an EP of "The Crusher," a wrestling-themed garage-punk novelty song by the Novas I'd first heard on the Dr. Demento show, which we'd recorded for the album. One of the new Lux-and-Ivy songs was called "New Kind of Kick," which had started out as a riff on the Electric Prunes song "Get Me to the World on Time"—not the chords, just the vibe of it. It had the same swampy psychedelic sound we'd been mining, taken to a whole other level. The Electric Prunes song ends with this crazy single-note guitar crescendo. I told them I wanted to try and re-create that with fuzz guitar. "Oh, that's a really good idea," they both said. That was a proud-making moment for me. A pat on the head from Lux and Ivy felt like having the acceptance and support of your parents.

I played the solo; Ivy turned the knobs on the tremolo. Together we produced this incredible insanity-inducing sound that seems to speed up, slow down, and turn in on itself all at the same time. It was just the kind of expressionist playing I'd been reaching for and felt like a great success. The way the track was mixed, the guitar leaps out of the speakers, grabs you by the throat, and doesn't let go. It remains one of my proudest achievements from my time with the Cramps, not solely because I had a hand in its creation, but because of my sheer astonishment that a sound like that could exist on *any* record I'd played on. It felt like we'd created something both assaultive and transcendent.

By the time our album *Psychedelic Jungle* was released, Lux and Ivy were at loggerheads with the record label over their failure to provide proper accounting or royalty payments. They even filed a million-dollar lawsuit to compel them to do so. Miles Copeland seemed to genuinely love the Cramps and took it personally. He played hardball with them. They wanted off the label and Miles had them under contract for a certain number of records. So they were in stalemate, circling around each other, knives drawn, waiting to resolve this through the courts. The litigation was a drain on Lux and Ivy's time, energy, money, and creativity. Until the dispute with IRS was settled, they decided they weren't going to give the label any more new material. We were playing live all the time just to support ourselves, which started to wear us down.

When there were disagreements between Lux and Ivy on tour, it was terrible. This deathly silence would descend upon the van. Nick and I wouldn't know what it was about, we would just know that an argument was either brewing or had broken out, and we'd better keep quiet and not get involved. A lot was left unspoken in the Cramps. There wasn't always a lot of discussion about things, whether it was business, our personal lives, or even playing music. We mostly followed cues and instincts.

The Cramps were one of the most heavily bootlegged bands around at the time. Every major show they played ended up on vinyl, often within weeks, no matter how poor the quality, and was widely distributed. With no new material being released officially, bootlegging of Cramps shows became even more widespread. We only played cover versions, no Rorschach/Interior originals, for which they would never receive any publishing if bootlegged, and definitely no new songs. It was a vicious cycle that, along with the war of attrition being fought with IRS, only served to further demoralize the band. During my second full year in the Cramps, we didn't play more than a couple dozen shows, most of them between April and July 1982. I was left to flounder with nothing to do.

Siouxsie Sioux provided a welcome distraction to my torpor when she returned to LA on vacation in the summer of 1982. The Cramps and the Banshees had crossed paths a few times while we were touring *Psychedelic Jungle* and they *Juju,* even sharing a bill on a gothic horror double-header the summer before at Ancienne Belgique in Brussels. I befriended members of the Banshees' crew and extended family, like Billy Chainsaw, their fan club president and roadie, and guitar tech Murray Mitchell, and grew fond of the other band members, Severin, Budgie, and guitarist John McGeoch. A very intense relationship developed between Siouxsie and me, built on a mutual admiration and identification—part personal and artistic, part fag hag meets fag.

We took her to the Palms, where we sampled a new melon-flavored cocktail they'd added to the menu, named Midori, which seemed like the height of '80s kitsch. This time, the girls at the bar all recognized Siouxsie as a star and treated her accordingly. Randy Kaye and I became honorary lesbians by association. We got totally blasted and danced all night to tunes on the jukebox. We hatched an ambitious plan to take Siouxsie to Disneyland the next day, which seemed less and less likely to be realized the longer the night went on and the messier it got. The evening ended in the early hours at a Lotus Lame and the Lame Flames party, my memory of which is so fuzzy that all I remember is Craig Lee of the Bags and myself hiding in a closet, playing peekaboo, while Siouxsie and Marcy Blaustein terrorized some poor goth boy with witchy mind games.

The next day, we got up bright and early, nursing hangovers the size of Los Angeles but still determined to fulfill our plan to make

Siouxsie's day at "the happiest place on earth" her happiest day on earth for real. As a Cramp in good standing, I only ever dressed in black, onstage or off, from head to toe, my hair teased up like candy floss with a can of Aqua Net. That day, Siouxsie dressed for the occasion too, in a black leather miniskirt, sheer black top, black stockings, and thigh-high leather boots with stiletto heels. We set off for Disneyland—myself, Siouxsie, Marcy, Randy Kaye, and photographer Donna Santisi—stood in line for tickets, and felt ourselves regressing into giddy children the second we walked through the gates into the Magic Kingdom.

We hadn't walked twenty steps down Main Street USA before a group of Disney cops bearing walkie-talkies stopped us in our tracks. It seemed Siouxsie's leather miniskirt was just a tad too *Night Porter* for them. I guess they figured some innocent corn-fed child would catch sight of this black-clad dominatrix witch from hell and be transformed, not into a pumpkin, but a deranged pervert, or worse . . . a female impersonator. We attempted, in vain, to convince the Disney cops that Sioux was not only "famous" but "foreign." Both those things seemed to be equally good reasons for them to overlook the antiquated moralism of the theme park's dress code, but they would not budge. Siouxsie would have to change her clothes or we would all be deported from the Magic Kingdom back to the dreariest place on earth—Los Angeles! Fortunately, Randy's standard-issue dress code at the time was a trench coat. That day, he'd had the good sense to pick out a black one. Siouxsie threw it on, and the cop let us continue our tour around the theme park. We rolled into Tomorrowland, this strange group of black-clad misfits in a Technicolor fairy-tale dreamland. The hours flew by. We boarded rocket jets, bobsledded down the Matterhorn, dodged headhunters on the Jungle Cruise, posed with the Big Bad Wolf, and had the ultimate goth experience . . . visiting the Haunted Mansion. Siouxsie left happy as a clam. Mission accomplished.

Their relationship with IRS at an impasse, with no hope of resolution, Lux and Ivy eventually decided to take matters into their own hands and record their own official bootleg. They set up shows on two consecutive nights in April 1983 at the Peppermint Lounge. It was a nod to everything they loved about rock 'n' roll, their way of paying respect to and celebrating an iconic New York venue, as well as an homage to the Joey Dee and the Starliters live album recorded there.

It seemed like we were finally doing something for ourselves. We took it very seriously, even going into the studio to rehearse the set beforehand. There was a sense of occasion to the shows. It was all very exciting and reminded me why it was I joined the Cramps. We played three more dates in March and April, at the Channel in Boston and the Country Club in Reseda, California. Then, nothing . . . *Smell of Female*, the live album we'd recorded at the Peppermint Lounge, was released almost as quickly as a real bootleg, but we didn't tour to support it.

I had a lot of time on my hands. I was a rock star without portfolio, but a rock star nonetheless. Bored, I indulged my taste for excess and the opportunity to party. Everyone I knew drank a lot, all the time, but was somehow still able to function. A lot of the people around me now were on heroin, others on coke. Often both. Speedballs were popular. Heroin had become the in-thing among the in-crowd. It was almost "normal." A lot of my downtime was spent on downers.

I was living at the Trianon, a grand apartment building behind Hollywood and Western, built in the style of a French château, that had quite a history. Mary Pickford and Douglas Fairbanks had commissioned its construction in the '20s and lived in the penthouse. Now it housed Cramps and Go-Go's. Belinda Carlisle had an apartment there at the same time I did. I was hanging out with a lot of fashion people. We were all very chic, very wonderful, and all very on heroin.

We didn't see heroin as a dead end. Not then, anyway. It was more of a release, of inhibitions and euphoria, an elegant method to strip away everything that came between the ego and the will, allowing us to move through the world unencumbered by emotion and anxiety. Like LSD, it made you feel as if you were reaching a part of yourself that wasn't immediately accessible. We thought we were far-reaching—intrepid travelers of inner space. We were looking to people like William Burroughs who had trodden that path before us. We were a very well-read bunch. Our decadence had literary roots.

Another figure who was very much on our radar was Harry Crosby, the dissolute bohemian playboy poet and mystic who founded Black Sun Press and published Hemingway, Joyce, D. H. Lawrence, and Edgar Allan Poe, among others. Geoffrey Wolff's biography of him, *Black Sun*, had recently come out, and if there was one book on every punk rocker's bookshelf, that was it. We always used to joke that everyone had a copy, but how many of them had actually read it?

Crosby died aged thirty-one, as part of an apparent suicide pact. Fitzgerald at forty-four, from the effects of chronic alcoholism. This seemed innately glamorous and quixotic to us. To be young, decadent, and reckless, to live fast, die young, leave a beautiful corpse and an undeniable body of work. We were driven by the idea of decadence as its own reward, of attaining nirvana through drugs. Or else falling into an abyss. And most of us, myself included, would have embraced either of those fates, salvation or destruction, wholeheartedly.

This was a decidedly un-Crampsian philosophy. I was starting to come into myself more, exploring my own interests, distancing me further from the group—that, and my drug use, which, because the group was barely working, became more of an occupation for me than making music. I'm sure Lux and Ivy knew about my dalliances, but they never said a word or gave any sense of disapproval.

Jeffrey, who had never quite left my life, was in a similar situation. Very fucked up on drugs but, unlike me, working all the time. For him, drugs were more of a crutch to deaden himself from his deepening frustration and disappointment with the Gun Club. He just couldn't keep members in the band. Rob Ritter rejoined, then quit again after the Gun Club's second album, *Miami*. Terry brought Patricia Morrison in to replace him, who had played with him in the Bags. Tav Falco's guitarist Jim Duckworth replaced Ward Dotson. Then Terry left and Dee Pop from the Bush Tetras took his place. He only lasted eight months before Terry rejoined the band again. The Gun Club had gone through five lineups in three years. Jeffrey and I started talking about maybe working together again while the Cramps were in flux.

I was conflicted. I had started to feel as if I wanted to break free, creatively, from the very proscriptive world of the Cramps. It was strictly forbidden to work on outside projects or with other musicians. I was made aware of that one time when I jumped onstage with the Gun Club and Lux and Ivy got very cross with me. "You can't do that," they told me. "You're in the Cramps. The Cramps don't do that." I wanted to have fun, play with my friends. I didn't want to be told "you can't do that." It reinforced my desire to rebel. At the same time, the Cramps provided for me, they were my sole source of income, the key to my musical identity.

Fortunately, I didn't have to make that difficult decision myself. One day in mid-September 1983, I got a phone call from Ivy. She told me they still didn't know if they could record and wanted to rethink everything they were doing. "Maybe you should go and do what you want to do also," she said. I was being fired, but nicely, and without any drama. They probably knew I was taking way too many drugs and everything was getting messy. Fortunately, I was taking enough drugs that being fired didn't affect me emotionally either, other than thinking, Ugh, I'm out of a job.

Then, two weeks later, another gig magically dropped from the sky. I got an urgent call from Jeffrey. "I need you to come to Australia." He sounded panicked. It turned out he had good reason to be. Half the Gun Club had quit on the eve of their first Australian tour. Jeffrey and Patricia got on their flights to Melbourne. Terry and Jim Duckworth never left the United States. Jeffrey arrived on the other side of the planet to find his drummer and guitarist had bailed on him. Rather than cancel the tour, he decided to soldier on and play the first date solo, acoustic and unplugged. An Australian audience baying to hear the Gun Club's screaming, metaphysical blues were confronted instead by Jeffrey Lee Pierce performing a "folk" set. It didn't go down well.

"The promoter's freaking out," he said. "We need somebody with a name." That somebody was me. Jeffrey wasn't shy about exploiting his friends if he felt it served his own ends. The Australian promoter had signed up to this idea too, that the tour might be salvaged if only the guitarist from the Cramps suddenly showed up to play.

"If I send you a ticket, will you come?" said Jeffrey. "Tomorrow?"

"Sure," I said, "why not." I certainly didn't have anything better to do. Just like that, I was back in the Gun Club again.

This would become a pattern in my life. Opportunities presenting themselves with little or no warning, often at just the right time, when I was either looking for, or needed, a change of scene. I didn't have to think too hard. There was no agonizing over my decisions. Saying yes was simple and obvious, offering the chance of a new adventure. As if all I had to do was snap my fingers or click my heels to be transported to another place.

After I got off the call with Jeffrey, the promoter arranged to send me a ticket overnight. I picked it up at the airport the next day and off I went, crawling out of the deep, on my way to the ends of the earth.

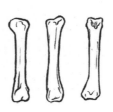

The Las Vegas Story

Elvis Presley never made it Down Under before he died, but I did. I guess it made some kind of sense that my first port of call when I got to Australia was to go pay my respects to the King.

Jeffrey met me at Melbourne Airport with two voluble musicians in tow, Spencer P. Jones and Billy Pommer, the guitarist and drummer, respectively, of a local country-punk rockabilly band called the Johnnys. They had been booked as the opener for the Gun Club on the tour. As Jeffrey had arrived with half his own band missing, Spencer and Billy were also commandeered as replacements for Jim and Terry. Being huge fans of the Gun Club, they gladly stepped in, the bonus being they already knew all the old songs. That didn't make Jeffrey any less anxious about getting his new impromptu version of the band up to speed for the tour. "We've got to start rehearsing right away," he blurted out almost the second we were reunited after I got through customs.

He had a point. We had a gig that night at the Seaview Ball-room in Melbourne. Spencer seemed nonplussed. "OK, but we're going to stop at this graveyard first." The two Johnnys drove us out to Melbourne Cemetery. It felt like the size of a small village, with long winding roads lined with thousands upon thousands of gravestones, and elaborate statuaries and crypts. We stopped near this crazy-looking stone grotto, covered in plants, that looked like something out of a fairy tale and had, at its center, a giant black tombstone with gold trim inset and a white column featuring two engraved headshots of the King: Elvis Presley.

An anonymous benefactor, so the story goes, paid the Elvis Pres-ley Fan Club of Australia to have this shrine built in his memory just a few weeks after Elvis died, making it the first monument to the King erected anywhere. And it was *truly* impressive. Jeffrey and I had our photos taken standing beside it. Then we went to rehearse. I was impressed, too, by Spencer and Billy's sense of priorities: fun first, work second. It gave me some indication of what to expect for the rest of the tour. I would come to find out the Johnnys were a band after our own hearts, reckless and impulsive, prodigious con-sumers of illicit substances, and the heaviest of drinkers.

As soon as I got to Australia, everywhere we went I heard this ob-noxious and awful new-wave novelty song called "Bop Girl." It was a huge hit and played on the radio constantly. Spencer and Billy told us the singer, Pat Wilson, was the wife of a big-time pop/rock musi-cian and producer named Ross Wilson, one of the most famous and influential figures in the Australian music industry. That didn't in-crease our appreciation for the song; it only made us loathe it more.

The real Bop Girl made the mistake of turning up at our first show. "The Bop Girl is here, the Bop Girl is here," somebody told us excitedly before the show. Jeffrey, never one to pass up an opportunity to cause mischief, made sure to let everybody else in the audience know she was there also, in his own inimitable style. But at least he waited until the end of the set. We often closed with a free-form version of John Coltrane's *A Love Supreme*. That night, as the music reached its apogee of discordant noise, Jeffrey started screaming, "*Kill* the Bop Girl! *Tear* her head off! Bop Girl! Bop Girl! I want to *fuck* the Bop Girl!"

After the show, we heard the Bop Girl was no longer there and had fled the venue in tears. Being completely obnoxious was part of Jeffrey's MO. It was mean but also hilarious. We considered it sweet revenge for the torture of having to hear that horrible song on the radio when we headed out on the road.

As an American from California, Australia felt strangely and instantly familiar to me, especially Melbourne with its beaches and palm trees. The tour took us up and down the east coast for three weeks, to all the major cities: Melbourne, Sydney, Canberra, Brisbane, and back to Melbourne again. We traveled everywhere by car. Passing through the smaller towns, we got to see the real Australia, which was redneck-y and conservative. We must have looked extremely freaky to them: Jeffrey with his bleached-blond hair, mine jet-black with a long, hanging fringe that masked my eyes, and Patricia resembling a cross between Elsa Lanchester and Morticia Addams. If there was any potential trouble from somebody eyeballing us at a truck stop or gas station, Spencer was always quick to defuse it and excused our oddness by telling the locals, "Oh, they're Americans."

Much of the trip was a blur. We would party a lot with people wherever we were, get drunk, go out, and get into all kinds of trouble. When we got to Canberra, one of the Johnnys made the mistake of offering Jeffrey the chance to take the wheel. That quickly turned into a hair-raising hell ride. The car was a right-hand drive, and he was drunk, or hungover. Jeffrey put his foot on the gas, careened around corners, and drove the wrong way down a one-way street at high speed as everyone else screamed for their life.

That night, the support band asked if they could use a smoke machine and if we wanted to use it for our set also. Sure, we said, that would be great. We decided to turn it on during "Cool Drink of Water," this long, slow, dirge-like blues song by Tommy Johnson (by way of Howlin' Wolf) we used to play toward the end of our set because we could stretch it out as long as we wanted. The machine was turned on. Smoke poured out, and poured and poured, until it was so thick, we could barely see each other, let alone the audience. Lost in a haze, we turned the song into a psychedelic drone, driving it up and up in volume and intensity. After about ten minutes, we stopped. The air around us began to clear. Almost the entire audience had split, driven away by the smoke, apart from two hippie chicks head-banging at the front.

Thrown together for the first time in chaotic circumstances, Patricia and I had to figure out on the fly how to coexist in the band, as well as navigate Jeffrey, who was still being Jeffrey: a crazy man, acting out in the same way that had convinced Terry and Jim to bail on the eve of the tour. It was the first time I really got to know Patricia. She and I shared an affinity for big hair, hair spray, and makeup. That's how we bonded, over the ritual of costuming to create an alternate identity from our real-life selves. Patricia's image was as strong and unwavering as Lux and Ivy's. She was the "Queen of Goth," after all, something that was entirely self-made and a natural extension of her personality.

She had her way with Jeffrey too, who responded to her very differently than he did to me. Being brought up in a matriarchal household with a single mom and a kid sister, he got along with and looked up to women. To him, they were the rulers and the goddesses. Patricia was not one to take any shit, from Jeffrey or anyone else. She was very earthy, liked Bacardi rum, and could drink with the best of us. At the same time, she was always extremely aware of what was going on around her and the band, and told it like it was. She was a quiet force and power in the Gun Club, a positive, stabilizing influence on all of us. She did not need to show her hand.

That is why, when Terry and Jim announced they weren't getting on the plane to Australia, she did not automatically join them in solidarity. She had enough of a sense of responsibility and loyalty to say, "I'm going to Australia. I'm doing this." When Patricia decided on something, it was for her own personal reasons, and she stuck to it.

When we got back to Melbourne, the promoter pulled Patricia aside. We still had two more shows left to play, but he told her he didn't think there was going to be anything left to pay us at the end of the tour because he'd lost so much money. There wasn't even enough, he confessed, to buy my return flight back to the United States. He probably figured the girl in the band would be a soft touch to break this terrible news. He didn't count on Patricia, who wasn't one to take any nonsense, storming off and immediately coming to tell us. We'd gotten a ton of press and had been playing to packed houses almost all the way, so we couldn't understand how the tour could still be in the red. To make matters worse, we'd been traveling with a full sound and lighting crew. The promoter didn't want to pay them either. They were a tough, hardened group and wanted to kill him.

Spencer, being extremely well connected and much loved in the local music scene, came to our rescue again. He set up a last-minute show at a popular pub in Melbourne, Strawberry Hill, and arranged for us to get all the door money. Contractually, this was strictly forbidden, but our attitude was "Fuck this guy." Spencer called up all his music friends to participate. Nobody turned him down. Members of the Hoodoo Gurus and the Scientists played at a moment's notice. The place was full to overflowing just through word of mouth.

With the venue at capacity, people even came to listen to the gig from across the street. It was quite a scene. Inside, the place was so packed, the stage quickly became overrun with people. We handed our instruments to the audience, stood back, and let them get on with it. The night was triumphant, crazy and wild. It felt as if we'd made the best of a bad situation and, despite the rip-off, ended our trip Down Under on a high note.

After the Strawberry Hill show, Jeffrey and Patricia flew straight back home. I stayed on at Spencer's place in Sydney for a few days waiting for my flight. He was just about to start recording an album with his new band, a supergroup of Johnnys, Scientists, and Hoodoo Gurus called Beasts of Bourbon, who had taken their name from the headline of an article about the Gun Club. Spencer introduced me to their singer, a charismatic and striking-looking nineteen-year-old kid named Tex Deadly, who led his own band, the Dum Dums. I was astounded by Tex, a teenager with a voice that sounded as if it emerged from a '50s jukebox, as deep and commanding as Sun Records–era Johnny Cash. They wanted me to record with them, but, unfortunately, my flight left before we could get into the studio.

Back in LA, Jeffrey asked Terry to rejoin the band. He agreed and they buried the hatchet on whatever petty dispute between them had made him quit. We played a Halloween show in Hollywood at the Cathay de Grande with the Mentors, a group of shock-rockers who wore executioners' hoods and would say and do anything to get a rise. Unsurprisingly, they were one of Jeffrey's favorite bands. It was the first time I'd played with Terry since before I'd joined the Cramps. Something clicked between us all.

There wasn't any discussion between Jeffrey and myself about whether I was going to continue playing with the Gun Club. I think we both just assumed I would. An Italian tour had been booked on the heels of the Australian one at the end of November and, after that, more UK dates. We arrived in Italy to discover we'd been booked into these large, prestigious venues. In Rome, we played at the twelve-hundred-capacity Teatro Palladium, a historic 1920s venue first built as a movie theater, and sold it out. There was a lot of excitement around the tour. Coming off the back of the Australian trip, it was weird to discover we'd become superstars in Italy without even knowing it. There was always a certain amount of chaos and unpredictability around the Gun Club. Still, it seemed like the only possible way we could screw this up would be to derail it ourselves. We discovered our Italian tour manager had a brother who was a heroin dealer. From then on, our fate was sealed. Jeffrey and I were lost in a fog of opiates for most of the tour but also somehow managed to keep it together.

The Italian shows were crazy. Gobbing was popular. In Naples, so much came our way, it felt like the audience had been saving up all their spit for us. We stood our ground. Afterward, Patricia looked as if she'd walked through a cobweb. The fans were so excited they followed us all the way back to the hotel and surrounded the van, banging on the windows. We also played a huge indoor gymnasium in a small southern Italian town called Bari. "What are we doing here and who's going to come see us?" we said. It turned out that the whole town came out to see us, people from neighboring towns also, and they all sang along to the songs, despite not knowing any of them. They just wanted to sing.

We returned from tour triumphant but dope sick. I was aching all over, couldn't walk, and was throwing up all the time. I didn't put together what it was. I thought I had a bad flu. From then on, drugs would no longer be fun, they became a chore.

By the spring of 1984, Jeffrey had worn out his welcome at his mother's place in the Valley and was living on the couch at the Trianon with my roommate Cindy Schwartz and me. Cindy was a bank executive by day, and a party animal by night. We'd met through Dennis Crosby, who brought us to legendary parties Cindy and her then-husband threw at their house on Griffith Park Boulevard. A fashion maven with wild frizzy hair and a thick Brooklyn accent, Cindy fronted a notorious faux-rap group of girls called Lotus Lame and the Lame Flames. My friends Ann McLean and Lisa Curland, the blond Satanist, were in the group also. The Lame Flames appeared for the most part at a West Hollywood leather bar, the One Way, performing choreographed dance routines, dressed in leather-man caps, jockstraps, and thigh-high boots, to original songs with titles like "Fist Funk" and "Bad Sex" over instrumental B-sides from the newly popular Sugar Hill label. It was a very LA take on rap—wild, irreverent, and of the moment.

Jeffrey and I found a very different way to entertain ourselves. We did heroin and read a lot of William Burroughs, two activities that seemed entirely complimentary, if not mandatory. *The Western Lands* had just been published and Jeffrey even went to meet his idol at a book signing in Los Angeles. We had both come to Burroughs through Patti Smith. Whoever she praised, we devoured. Through

Burroughs, we found out about Brion Gysin and his cut-up method of writing. It was all archaeology. One excavation led to another.

Sitting across a coffee table from each other in the living room of my apartment at the Trianon, we decided to put the cut-up method into practice one day. We had a typewriter and Jeffrey would type something, then I'd get up, go to the typewriter, and type a line. We went back and forth like this for a while, trying to out-Burroughs each other with absurd and grotesque imagery. Then we cut the page into strips, jumbled them all together, and took turns to pick them out, randomly rearranging the pieces into a new whole, like we were casting a reading from the *I Ching*. Out of that came this short story, bearing the obvious and very heavy influence of *Naked Lunch*, about the apocalypse of Las Vegas, burning down into a "pile of dog shit." We titled it *The Las Vegas Story*.

It seemed to fit with the songs Jeffrey had been writing for the album we were about to record—about the underbelly and decline of America as seen through the lens of iconic locations associated with a particular type of tawdry glamour, now sunk into disrepair, places like Las Vegas, Miami, or Hollywood, an emerging theme in his writing.

The record label had high hopes for the new album. The Gun Club had signed to Blondie guitarist Chris Stein's label, Animal Records, for their previous album, *Miami*. But by this time, Blondie had broken up, partly because Chris had gotten very sick with a rare autoimmune disease. The parent label, Chrysalis, which was also Blondie's label, had taken a larger role in Animal. They had released Iggy's *Zombie Birdhouse* album and then turned their attentions to the Gun Club, feeling we were poised to make it big. Chrysalis hooked us up with an LA character named Denny Bruce as a manager. He had started out as the second drummer in a pre-*Freak Out!* Mothers, with Frank Zappa, then later managed John Fahey, T-Bone Burnett, and the Blasters—just the kind of pedigree that appealed to us.

The label was surprisingly accommodating to our wishes, possibly because Jeffrey had such a close relationship with Chris Stein and Debbie Harry, first as a fan and fan club president, then as an artist they had supported and mentored. Chrysalis asked who we wanted to produce the album. Our first choice was John Cale, who wasn't available. Then R.E.M.'s producer, Mitch Easter, was suggested, but that seemed a little too tame. Denny Bruce came up with a guy named Jeff Eyrich, who had just produced a T-Bone Burnett album we really loved, called *Proof Through the Night*, which was both dreamy and tough in just the right combination. We wanted to try for something similar. Commercial-sounding with an edge.

Chrysalis booked us into Ocean Way Recording on Sunset Boulevard, a legendary studio that had hosted Michael Jackson and the Beach Boys, for two weeks with Jeff producing. We'd already been playing a lot of the new songs on the Australian and Italian tours, so we were very well rehearsed and laid down basic tracks live in no time at all.

We were young, cocksure, and determined to make the best record we could. By then, Jeffrey had two albums under his belt, I'd done one with the Cramps, but we both had a lifetime of listening to all kinds of music, from Chicano rock, blues, and reggae through R&B, free jazz, and world music, and had studied our favorite records religiously. We knew what sounded good and interesting, and how we wanted it to work on our own record. Jeff Eyrich was impressed by how many ideas we had and how fully formed our vision was. He never pooh-poohed our ideas, just suggested ways to make them better.

We were in our jazz phase still and often performed this noisy free-form interlude based on Pharoah Sanders's "The Creator Has a

Master Plan." Jeffrey got this idea to segue from that into a version of Gershwin's "My Man's Gone Now" from *Porgy and Bess*. We all got really excited about that but didn't exactly know how we were going to pull it off. Jeff, who was really into this idea too, said, "Oh, I know Julio Iglesias's piano player, Randy Kerber. We'll get him to play on it."

Julio Iglesias was huge at that time. Although it seemed improbable his pianist would agree to perform on our record, it was no crazier than the Gun Club tackling Gershwin. Jeff called him up; he came down and played a heartfelt rendition of "My Man's Gone Now" for us on the piano. Then Jeff said, "Oh, I know Andy Williams's nephews. They sing really great operatic tenor." They had sung on the T-Bone Burnett album Jeff produced. He got them to come in also and sing these beautiful, ghostly backing vocals on the track that somehow perfectly complemented Jeffrey's wail.

We were working the graveyard shift at the studio, so we went in at midnight and left at dawn, which suited us night owls perfectly. One night, at about 2 a.m., a white stretch limousine pulled up outside Ocean Way. The door opened and one white knee-high platform boot emerged, then another, followed by a plume of feathers and then, cloaked in a black velvet cape emblazoned with a rhinestone peacock, Stevie Nicks, the witch herself—"Lady Nix," as we took to calling her. A seemingly endless stream of assorted flunkies, both male and female, exited the carriage after her, similarly attired in glitter and turquoise. They entered the building and immediately headed, with almost military precision, to the bathrooms, the clanking of their bangle bracelets making it sound like a chain gang being marched to work. And there they stayed for the rest of the evening, anxiously awaiting the witch's frequent visits to powder her nose.

At one point, Jeffrey was sitting by himself in the studio lounge, which was dark and dank through being perpetually over-air-conditioned and reserved for artists being driven mad by listening to a single track over and over and over again. There, one could de-compress staring at a gigantic rectangular TV, surrounded by cocoa-colored wood-paneled walls, or merely sit twiddling your thumbs on the brushed corduroy sofas. I decided I needed a break myself and popped into the lounge for my own moment of Zen thumb twiddling. Upon entering, Jeffrey looked up at me with an incredulous but dev-ilish grin and started shouting, "Rats! Rats!"

"What rats?" I asked, startled, poised to spring onto the turd-colored couch. "Where are the rats?" He just kept shouting "Rats!" It took me another few seconds to realize he was just saying something crazy to amuse himself. Jeffrey was often the only one in on his own jokes. Although we shared a sense of the absurd, I just wasn't in the mood this time. I turned around and went to the liquor store next door at Gower Gulch.

Sometime well past midnight, Lady Nix flowed into the lounge, velvet robe billowing behind her. As soon as she stepped into the room, Jeffrey screamed "Rats!" at her as well, like one of the pos-sessed in *Invasion of the Body Snatchers*. She stared at him, stock-still, completely unruffled, like the feathered peacock embroidered on her cape. But for a split second, she was betrayed by her eyes, and in them, Jeffrey saw a torrent of rage, like a swarm of rattlesnakes lunging for a strike. Assuming her to be a magical and mystical be-ing, Jeffrey decided to convey in poetic prose, likely intended just to vex her further, that he meant rats had scurried behind the giant rectangular TV. "Yonder, over there in the bramble," he said theat-rically, pointing to a pile of magazines dumped in the corner of the lounge. Lady Nix clicked her platform boots and disappeared into the bathroom with her gaggle of goons.

Our friend Amy, who was in the studio that night also, happened to be in the bathroom. We used to call Amy the "Napalm Heiress," because her father was one of the people in the brain trust at Harvard who developed napalm. She told us that her father later switched to making orthopedic devices for handicapped people; we were like, "Oh, he's making amends." When Amy heard the bathroom door open, she hid in one of the stalls, crouching on the toilet. Lady Nix came in wailing about the state of the world and a lawsuit with her cleaning lady. We never heard the end of the story and, after that night, we didn't see her again. Rats!

On another night, Jeffrey and I started hearing this sound wafting through the building. It sounded so familiar and alluring. "What is that?" we said to each other. It sounded, strangely, like Jim Morrison. Or maybe the ghost of Jim Morrison making his presence felt. "Where is that coming from?" We decided we had to find out. We followed the sound around the building, like bloodhounds sniffing out a scent, until we came to the door of this room sequestered in a far corner of the complex. We knew what lay behind it.

On our first day of recording, we'd been given the grand tour of the studio by the studio manager and were shown the echo chamber—less a room than a long, dark corridor with these reverb machines placed inside. To us, this was the most hallowed and mysterious spot in the whole studio. We were fascinated by it. We snuck inside, Jeffrey and I, crawling back and forth, our ears to the wall, to find the best spot to listen to this weird, ghostly reverberation of the Doors. "Over here, it's a bit louder." I wonder if they heard us down there in the control room. Someone told us later that the Doors, minus Jim, were in the studio, remastering their records for compact disc. If they had the tapes running, they might have even captured us whispering and sniggering to each other in the echo chamber. Then Jeffrey and I could legitimately say we were members of the Doors. We must have lost track of time up there because we were gone so long, Jeff Eyrich, who was waiting back in the control room, sent out a search party to find us.

That wasn't even our last brush with a rock legend during those sessions. It happened that Ry Cooder was in the studio next to us working on the soundtrack for the Wim Wenders film *Paris, Texas*. He had left all these incredible vintage amps and weird percussion instruments lying around. It was like being let into Santa's toy factory. "I wish we could use this," I said, picking up one strange-looking object. "Oh, I'm sure that's quite all right," said Jeff Eyrich, unwittingly giving us the green light to mess with Ry's precious collection.

Phast Phreddie had come down to Ocean Way to hang out as we recorded. While waiting for some setup or other, he went poking around in the next studio, picked up this serrated plastic tube of Ry's, and started whirling it above his head. It made a sound like the wind whipping around a house in a gale. Terry Graham's wife, Lois, started doing the same thing. Then I walked in, saw how much fun they were having, and said, "This is great!" I picked one up and started whirling it around. Between us, we got a force 10 hurricane going. Little did we know, Jeff was in the control room. He heard what was going on, hit Record, and got it all on tape. We ended up using this very creepy, ethereal sound as the intro to the title song on the album.

After wrapping the album, we did some shows up and down the West Coast. We were going through a big obsession with free jazz, especially the ABC Impulse! catalog of the '60s and '70s, and albums by John Coltrane, Pharaoh Sanders, and Eric Dolphy. Jeffrey had acquired a trumpet. He couldn't play it, like *really* play it, and never showed any actual interest in learning how. He simply played it how he *thought* it should be played. We played jazz that way too, almost as if we were pretending to be jazz musicians. "Let's just *think* like jazz," Jeffrey would say. So that's what we did, adapting what we heard in jazz to what we were capable of playing, which was really just making a lot of noise and trying to insert some feeling into it, like when we'd started performing a version of *A Love Supreme*, ending the sets with this wild, free-form noise jam. Everyone hated when Jeffrey played the trumpet, with a passion. I didn't hate it so much. It was obvious he couldn't play. I embraced it and was amused by it.

This girl, Summer Bankin, would often duet with him on sax. She played in LA art-goth band Die Schlaflosen, which was meant to mean "sleepless" in German but was grammatically incorrect. Summer was not his girlfriend, but Jeffrey was infatuated with her, so she was around a lot at the time. Jeffrey always had these girls that wanted to mother him. He was that type, the typical rock guy—brilliant and fun, but utterly incapable of dealing with practical mundane everyday tasks in any responsible way. So Jeffrey was attractive to women, like Summer, who wanted to take care of him.

We played the Music Machine on Pico Boulevard. Die Schlaflosen were the support. Jeffrey was drunk off his ass, possibly stoned. I'm sure I was too. In fact, I know I was because Jeffrey and I joked that the only people on our guest list were our drug dealers, Juan and Leroy, who did not have last names.

We had gotten very into Chilean folk music through this old album we'd picked up on Nonesuch Records and decided to include one song we liked, "Los Cholitos," in our set. We got some serapes, cut a hole in the middle, and wore them onstage, dancing around and playing our version of Chilean folk music. We had something of a flair for the theatrical when we put our minds to it, as well as a love for embracing the happy accident. Which was fortunate because, at one point, my amp blew up and caught fire. There were flames rising out of it. I kept playing, Jimi Hendrix–style. After all, it was just an amp. I'd already had my hair on fire. The audience was impressed. Exene Cervenka was at the show and thought it was the best thing she'd ever seen. Nick Cave, Mick Harvey, and Blixa Bargeld also came to see us play, chaperoned to the show by Henry Rollins. I'd met them the previous night when the Bad Seeds played Perkins Palace in Pasadena, their first shows in LA. They were promoting their debut album, *From Her to Eternity*, which had come out that week.

Jessamy Calkin had introduced me to Blixa a couple of months prior to this, when she came through town road-managing Einstürzende Neubauten. Day in, day out, Blixa wore the same rubber gum boots and leather trousers. Jessamy said his feet stank. She begged me to gift him a fresh pair of socks. As it happened, my mother had given me a packet of white tube socks for Christmas that I never opened because, of course, I strictly wore black. I donated them to Blixa. He was happy, his feet were happy, Jessamy was overjoyed.

Jeffrey and Nick had already met earlier that year in New York and become fast friends. Jeffrey turned Nick on to this book we were both obsessed with at the time, Malcolm Lowry's *Under the Volcano*. It was about an alcoholic English diplomat living in the shadow of two volcanoes near Mexico City, drinking himself into an early grave as he sleepwalks toward oblivion on the Day of the Dead. I can't imagine why that would have appealed to us.

We were both fascinated by Mexican culture, Jeffrey and I, having grown up as Mexican American kids in LA. We often used to talk about how we were Mexicans, but also not. We wanted to belong but didn't speak Spanish. We were not one thing or the other—not really American because we're Mexican; not really Mexican because we're American. We were caught in limbo, racially, socially, culturally. We felt as if we were stateless. Nobody ever told us how to make ourselves feel whole. We both gravitated, separately and then together, toward exploring and embracing that feeling of otherness and displacement, seeking to establish our own identities through music. In the LA punk scene, at least at first, no one cared who or what you were. We were all misfits together.

Even so, that sense of estrangement from our mother culture remained with us both. It was also, ironically, one of the things that bonded us, creating this very strong, almost brotherly kinship. We felt a great yearning to connect with our roots. I'd only ever visited Mexico once, with my parents when I was very young, to visit an auntie who lived in Mexico City, but had no real memory of it. Jeffrey had never been.

This was when Jeffrey was in his "Indiana Jones" period. He was *very* into *Raiders of the Lost Ark*—obsessed, actually—and anything to do with adventurers. He even took to wearing a khaki-green fedora and utility jacket onstage. When *Indiana Jones and the Temple of Doom* opened, about a month after we'd finished recording *The Las Vegas Story*, Jeffrey went to see it over and over again. He'd also been reading this book *Incidents of Travel in Central America, Chiapas and Yucatan* by a real-life Indiana Jones character, the nineteenth-century American archaeologist and explorer John Lloyd Stephens, who rediscovered and documented Mayan culture.

Duly inspired by pulp movies, modernist literature, and swashbuckling archaeologists from another age, and aching for adventure ourselves, we decided a trip to Mexico was in order. Jeffrey and I had spent a lot of time together on the road and off, but we'd never taken a vacation, or any kind of trip, just for the sake of taking one. We had one other very good reason to go away. We were both thoroughly hooked on heroin. My body had become acclimated to the drug. I had been "chipping," bingeing and stopping to try to keep a tab on it. I had chipped one time too many and chipped over into addiction. Using was no longer a luxury but a necessity, another job. The romance had turned into a chore. Heroin had gotten its claws into me.

Knowing we had to go out on a long, possibly grueling tour in support of *The Las Vegas Story*, we made the remarkably sensible decision, at least for us, that we didn't want to pack our habits and take them on the road with us. We figured it would be easier to kick and clean up if we were away from home for a few days, far from all the distractions and invitations that came our way daily. Not least, our drug dealers who were on call at all hours and delivered heroin to our door like pizza.

We left LA with a plan of sorts, to make a pilgrimage to Chichen Itza, the largest existing Mayan city, and climb its huge pyramid. But we also wanted to let loose and have some fun, so we booked rooms at a place called the Hotel Mara on Cozumel, a small island off the coast of the Yucatan Peninsula. On our first night, we ended up at beach club bar Carlos 'n Charlie's, drank ourselves silly on cheap booze, and started talking to a couple of British tourists. At first, it was all friendly banter back and forth, then it quickly escalated, not quite into violence, but close. Jeffrey would recall me challenging them. I remember an antagonistic insult fest. Thankfully, that situation passed. Then I was sitting talking to this woman, who was very friendly and wanted to hear all about my story. Flattered, I obliged. At one point, Jeffrey came over and sought my attention with some urgency. "You know she's a prostitute?" Well, I did now. And apparently, just in the nick of time. Her pimp, who had a vantage point to the negotiations somewhere else in the bar, had told Jeffrey in no uncertain terms that there was going to be trouble if I didn't pay for the privilege of enjoying his charge's company.

By the time we got back to our rooms, we were so drunk the door kept swaying out of reach every time I tried to put the key in. I devised a novel and ingenious way to open it: sitting on the floor with my back to the door, my arm in the air over my head, stabbing at the lock with the key until I eventually hit pay dirt. Once inside, the room started spinning. I somehow managed to make my way to the shower, crawled inside, and promptly threw up.

The next morning, still drunk and nursing a raging hangover, we got on a small four-seater plane with an older couple from Texas and flew into Chichen Itza, landing in a field somewhere nearby. We were so excited at being there, we forgot how wasted we still were, and became intoxicated instead by all the death imagery that surrounded us on all sides. We marveled at the temple walls containing a mosaic of death's-head skulls, a huge ball court where losing meant certain death, and a Chacmool sacrificial altar that we took turns reclining on with our arms folded like mummies. Then we headed up to the top of the large, steep pyramid that was Chichen Itza's most prominent landmark. It was stiflingly hot and we were dressed in black. It was a miracle we didn't pass out or expire before we reached the peak, but we made it.

Before heading back down, Jeffrey pulled a miniature cardboard stand-up of Debbie Harry out of his rucksack that he'd brought all the way from home—a promotional item for Blondie's *Parallel Lines* album of Debbie in that iconic pose, hands on hips in her sleek white dress. He placed the tiny Debbie on top of the pyramid and took pictures of her. An artifact from the new world standing astride the old. I'm sure he was intending to send Debbie the photos. A lot of what he did was to impress her.

After a week of this, we arrived back in LA, hungover but not strung out, newly inspired and ready to head out on the road with the Gun Club.

On the Ledge

America had turned bad. Ronald Reagan had just been re-elected. The Olympics were coming to Los Angeles. Money was pouring into the city. All the things we loved about Hollywood, the dirt, decay, sleaze, and freedom, were being cleaned up and done away with. Old haunts were demolished and new buildings put up in their place. No-go areas were becoming gentrified. The existing population was being moved out. The authorities were busing the homeless, prostitutes, and other undesirables out of view in order to present this entirely false, superficial image of the city, making sure they were out of sight, if not mind, for the flood of tourists expected in the summer.

We were very disillusioned by the wave of nationalism in the country. It had even infected the underground music scene on the West Coast. You'd go to see a rockabilly band and they'd have an American flag, or even a Confederate one, on the stage behind them. It wasn't just other bands that did this. Terry also had an American flag towel in his bass drum as padding. To counter that, I hung a Native American one on my amp.

We headed out on tour, to experience for ourselves this strange American landscape that Jeffrey had written about on *The Las Vegas Story*. We hired my friend Marcy Blaustein as our tour manager, and Murray Mitchell, the Banshees' guitar tech, came along as a roadie and general journeyman. We drove cross-country in this Sprinter-style van that was painted blue. We used to call it the "Blue Whale." It was carpeted inside and customized with a loft-style bunk bed, video player, and TV. It comfortably held us all and our equipment. There was only one tiny window in the back, so it really felt as if we were cut off from everything, in the belly of a whale or locked in a space capsule. Terry and Amy, the Napalm Heiress, who was now Terry's girlfriend, rented a car and traveled separately. Sometimes I'd ride with them, just to escape everyone else for a while.

CB radio was all the rage at the time. When we got bored in the van, we'd screw around with our driver's CB and put Murray on the line. He had this thick London East End accent. We came up with an appropriate CB handle for him: Slimey Limey. He'd get on the radio and announce himself—"This is Slimey Limey, over"—then start talking about how stupid truck drivers were until he got a rise out of them. A barrage of threats from pissed-off truckers would come crackling over the radio: "We're gonna pull over at the next truck stop and kick your ass." Murray was always ready with another rejoinder: "Shut up, you stupid wanker."

We had a show in Lawrence, Kansas. After sound check, Jeffrey was whisked off to meet William Burroughs at his house. He arrived back at the venue right before the show, completely hammered and covered in mud. Burroughs had been drinking Coca-Cola and vodka. Jeffrey tried to keep up with him . . . and failed. His tolerance for substances, whether alcohol or drugs, was a fraction of his idol's. At some point, one of Burroughs's cats had gotten loose and jumped across a little creek next to the house. Jeffrey, drunk off his ass, tried to catch the cat and fell in the creek. He looked like he'd gone commando in a Vietnamese jungle.

Predictably, the show was awful. Well, we were great; Jeffrey was a mess. He would start on some rant between songs, in the middle of songs, whenever he felt like it. He ended up lying on the stage, on his stomach, blabbering incoherently, like an end-of-days Jim Morrison. I remember looking over, seeing him there with his pants riding down around his ass. We were playing in a big theater and the lighting engineer decided to have some fun at Jeffrey's expense by training the follow spot right on his butt crack. That made the show for me. We thought it was hilarious. I'm sure it wasn't for the audience.

In Cleveland, we had some special guests onstage. Bryan Gregory, whom I'd replaced in the Cramps, and Ike Knox, my replacement, both turned up at the show unannounced. Bryan looked even freakier than he had in the Cramps. He had this long black hair, wore contact lenses with silver mylar pupils, these tight-fitting low-rise leather pants (like something the East West Musical Instruments Company would make), and a jacket with no shirt underneath to show off his rake-thin, cut torso. Ike, whose birth name was Mike Metoff, was in fact Nick Knox's real-life cousin, so he had taken Knox as his Cramps name, in the style of the Ramones. But he didn't use it for long. He only lasted one tour, not even a year, and had recently been ousted. We were able to have an impromptu summit, there in Cleveland, of this very special and exclusive little fraternity of ex-Cramps guitarists, sharing horror stories and commiserating with each other about our respective exits from the band. It was only then I realized what a weird trip it had been being in the Cramps, a little cultish even. We had all escaped the cult.

Ike and Bryan both came on for the encore. We played the first song I ever learned, Bo Diddley's "Gunslinger," which, of course, was just one chord, so we couldn't screw it up even if we tried. We imagined Lux and Ivy having a fit seeing us up there all together, because in the Cramps, it was strictly verboten to play on anybody else's stage, and here we were flagrantly, even joyfully, violating the golden rule.

By the time we got to New York, Jeffrey was completely out of control. We played the Ritz in New York with the Dream Syndicate and Jeffrey pulled out a machete he'd bought somewhere on tour. People started freaking out. We were like, "Oh, it's just Jeffrey's sword." Nothing could really shock us when it came to Jeffrey's behavior at this point. He was obsessed with Japanese movies, samurai movies, and all things war. He was very big on war history. His favorite movie was *Apocalypse Now*. He would watch it constantly. When Jeffrey started putting on weight and took to wearing a bandana onstage, everyone would say, "Oh, he looks like Marlon Brando in *Apocalypse Now*"—and he did. It all sounded like fun and games unless you had to share a tour bus with "Colonel Kurtz" on a journey into his own heart of darkness.

The last show of the tour was in Buffalo, New York. Lydia Lunch co-headlined, doing one of her spoken-word performances. Before the show, Jeffrey found some kids near the venue to score from. Halfway through making the deal he realized he had nothing to pay with. "Wait, my money is in our van," he foolishly let it be known to the dealers. Then, even more foolishly, he took them to our van, where they watched him open his suitcase and take out a roll of money—the entire takings of our tour so far. He peeled off enough to buy his drugs, then put it back in the suitcase and came out of the van, all in plain sight.

The next thing we knew, the Blue Whale had been ransacked. They took all our instruments and equipment—apart from Patricia's bass guitar, which had gotten wedged between two seats—and all our suitcases too, just to make sure they got the one with all the cash. I lost two of the things most precious to me, my guitar and my journals. Patricia had her passport stolen. We were meant to be getting on a flight to Europe in less than a week, for the first dates on our European tour, in the Netherlands. It was an omen for the disaster waiting to happen.

Despite having a madman at the helm, the first few weeks of the European tour went off without a major hitch. Then we played the Hacienda in Manchester. We were late getting in and had to go straight to the venue to soundcheck instead of checking into the hotel first. Our van was broken into again. Fortunately, this time we were onstage, so our instruments didn't get stolen, but all our clothes did. The bigger loss was Terry's video camera and all the footage he'd shot on tour. Terry had taken on the role of band chronicler. He was crushed to lose everything. Somewhere deep inside, he probably blamed Jeffrey, even though this time it wasn't strictly his fault. But the chaos and drama that seemed to descend on us at every turn was beginning to grate on everybody. Everybody except Jeffrey, that is.

Mark E. Smith of the Fall was at the show that night. He was in the dressing room when we got offstage and the tour manager came in to break the bad news: "We got robbed again." Mark, being the Manchester character he is, offered to help. "I know every criminal in Manchester," he said. This was the first time we'd met him, but I had no doubt he really did know every criminal in Manchester, and probably Salford as well. "I'm going to get to the bottom of this," he assured us.

Somewhere between Manchester and Bristol, our tour manager went AWOL. Patricia said the last time she saw him was near the van, muttering, "We *must* have soft toilet paper" over and over again. We had driven him over the edge. Things started falling apart.

Four days later, we played the first date of our European tour, in Paris, at this grand hall that held seventeen hundred people. The chemistry between the band onstage had never been better. The show was great. But the next day, Terry was nowhere to be found. He and Amy had snuck out of the hotel in the morning without telling anyone and bailed on us.

We found a pickup drummer who filled in for a couple of dates, this French rockabilly guy, but he didn't have any time to learn the set and his English was not so good. We begged our agent in England to find someone else. He sent over this guy called Desi, whose nickname was Desperate. He had been playing with Alison Moyet of Yazoo. He was a session guy but a quirky player, very raw and weird. He was a perfect fit for us. He learned the songs very quickly and was able to roll with us when we improvised.

The band could have easily continued on in this configuration, but we were exhausted. It wasn't even that there were factions in the band. Nobody wanted to talk to anybody else anymore. We all just kept to ourselves. Terry going AWOL was the final straw. Patricia and I realized we were sick of Jeffrey too. Even worse, we had a whole bunch of dates booked to fulfill . . . in Australia.

It felt like déjà vu. An impending Australian tour. A band in revolt at its singer. But this time, Patricia and I were the ones ready to bail. We were sick of Jeffrey and didn't want to be around him anymore. He was obnoxious. And drunk. All the time. We were tired of being beholden to his bad business decisions, and beholden to him personally also. It was partly the cliché of the backing band being resentful at being ignored while the singer gets all the spotlight. We wanted to be ourselves, make our own decisions, and we figured we'd have a better musical life without him.

The Gun Club were firmly established in Europe, even playing the same-size venues as my previous band, the Cramps. We could have kept the group going indefinitely but couldn't see the point. We knew we were all going to end up hating each other even more than we already did. I went to speak to Jeffrey and suggested we break up the band and all move on. I appealed to his ego, telling him we'd be like the Birthday Party, a band we both loved, who had split two years earlier, leaving a small but perfect catalog of music. Nick Cave and Mick Harvey had since formed the Bad Seeds. Rowland S. Howard was playing with Crime & the City Solution. The Birthday Party's legacy had been preserved. "People love the Gun Club," I told Jeffrey. "They think we're a magical entity. We should go out on a high point rather than compromise the standard we've held ourselves to."

Jeffrey didn't put up a fight or disagree. "Sure, you're right," he said. There was no high drama. It was apparent, even to him, that the band had run its course. Of course, as the main songwriter and leader, Jeffrey also knew he had more options to start a new project than we did—he could do anything he wanted. Artistically, it may have been wise to break up the group; financially, it was another terrible business decision, especially for Patricia and me. But at least it was a decision we'd made ourselves. A gamble we were willing to take.

We played two final shows at Dingwalls in Camden to make up for all the money we weren't going to make on the Australian tour.

We were popular enough in London that they both sold out. One of those nights, Jeffrey and I took some acid; Patricia did some mushrooms. It was a small club; people were falling all over the stage. At one point, I turned to Jeffrey and said, "My strings are turning into *rope*." We were so out of our minds and free-form that we decided to play a cover of "The Twist."

Jeffrey spotted this young Japanese girl in the crowd and made a play for her. Her name was Romi Mori. She was a rock photographer for a Japanese magazine. She had been in bands in Japan, playing covers of the Runaways. Jeffrey was smitten. They moved in together almost immediately.

London was happening at the time, musically, and we knew we didn't want to go back to the States. We were so disillusioned with the horrible wave of nationalism that had taken hold in our home country under Reagan. We decided to stay in the UK and try to make a go of it. We became part of a community of ex-pat musicians living there already. Lydia Lunch was in London with Jim Thirlwell, living in the mews house Marc Almond had abandoned because Soft Cell fans kept turning up outside and terrorizing him. Marcy decided to stay in London also. She said she'd help and be our manager. Billy Chainsaw, a large, friendly bear of a man from Birmingham who worked for the Banshees and ran their fan club, offered us space in his flat in White City. Patricia and Marcy rented rooms from him. I slept on the couch.

We said we were breaking up. Really, we were just firing Jeffrey. The Gun Club as it was then—me, Patricia, and Desi Desperate—simply carried on without him as an entirely different entity. We roped in Murray Mitchell, who had been one of our tour crew, as guitarist. For Patricia and me, the reasoning was pretty simple and uncomplicated: We get along, we both have black hair—of course we should have a band together! Marcy came up with our new name: Fur Bible. It was surreal, blasphemous, obscene, and sounded like a word-virus from the mind of William Burroughs. I took to it straightaway.

All we needed now was a front man. Patricia and I knew just the person—Tex Perkins. We'd both met him on the Gun Club's Australian tour a year earlier. He was a real character and we'd been charmed by him. At the time, he was known as Tex Deadly and fronted a band called the Dum Dums. Since then, Tex, Spencer P. Jones of the Johnnys, and Kim Salmon of the Scientists had been playing in their occasional supergroup, the Beasts of Bourbon, whose stock in trade was a messy, dissolute country-blues with Tex's menacing voice front and center.

I wrote Tex in Australia, told him that the Gun Club was no more, Patricia and I were starting a new band, and he *must* come to London immediately to join us. Tex was so excited that he reconvened the Beasts of Bourbon to play a show just to make enough money to buy a plane ticket. The Gun Club had a Dutch booking agent, Willem Vinema, who said he would also contribute toward Tex's flight if the Fur Bible debuted at a music festival he was putting together in the Netherlands.

Being young, naive, and not having traveled outside Australia before, when Tex arrived and went through UK customs, he did the number one thing you must never ever do as a traveling musician flying under the radar at a port of entry: He told them he was a singer in a band. As he was wearing a coat made of monkey fur, they didn't have any reason to disbelieve him and detained him in the airport to make further inquiries.

Willem, who was waiting in the arrivals lounge for Tex, was called to run interference. At that point, things went from bad to worse.

The customs officer decided to inspect Tex's suitcase. It sprang open, scattering its contents all over the floor. The only thing inside it was doll parts. He was carrying a suitcase full of disembodied heads, arms, legs, and torsos. That and the monkey-fur coat were probably reason enough to refuse him entry, but realizing they had a wild one on their hands, the customs officers began pressing Tex as to whether he might be a drug user also. Tex started to sweat. His hopes of getting into the country to join his new bandmates were crumbling by the second. They put a big ugly stamp in his passport and prepared to deport him back to where he came from—not Australia but the last country he had traveled through on his journey to the UK, which happened to be a stopover in the Philippines. So that's where he was sent back to, without a penny in his pocket or a return trip to Australia.

Amazingly, even after all of this, Willem still put so much stock in the potential for our group, despite the fact we had no material and had never played a show together, that he was committed to trying to help Tex get back to Europe. In the meantime, he offered the rest of us a proposition. "Have you ever heard of the Legendary Stardust Cowboy?" said Willem. "Because I've booked a tour of the Netherlands for him and he needs a backup band." Of course we've heard of the Legendary Stardust Cowboy, we said, he's . . . legendary.

I'd seen him as a kid on *Rowan & Martin's Laugh-In*, the TV appearance with which he'd first found fame, along with so many other odd fellows who didn't fit the record industry mold, like Wild Man Fischer and Tiny Tim. Since then, "Paralyzed," the song the Legendary Stardust Cowboy had performed on the show—although to describe it as a "song" is questionable—had garnered a reputation as the worst record ever made. Despite that, the Ledge's reputation was secured, for him and for me, when David Bowie gave him the seal of approval by revealing he was part-inspiration behind Ziggy

Stardust. We didn't need any further persuading to take the gig as his band. I was elated; the Ledge did not disappoint.

Not even Lux Interior or Jeffrey Lee Pierce would prepare me for performing with the Ledge, which was more like flying by the seat of my pants than anything I'd ever experienced as a musician. The Ledge had no traditional sense of melody, rhythm, or anything else. He lived entirely in his own world, musical or otherwise.

He was very naive, very sweet, and absolutely sincere in everything he did. He was a regular guy from Lubbock, Texas, who believed in space exploration and the power of Frank Sinatra, and had somehow developed this character, the Legendary Stardust Cowboy, which he completely believed in and inhabited. The Legendary Stardust Cowboy wasn't an alter ego; it *was* him. I had a lot of admiration for that.

It was like he had walked out of the woods into a civilization he had no understanding of and was not equipped to function within. He was less Ziggy Stardust than the Man Who Fell to Earth. He had this one goal, one task, to spread the word of the Legendary Stardust Cowboy, and was single-minded in pursuing it. It was as if when he had found fame and notoriety, it was something he had expected all his life. He didn't see that what he did was offbeat in any way. And after meeting him, I didn't see it as offbeat either. Perverse, maybe. He was the real deal. The outsider's outsider.

He brought over a copy of his album for us to learn the songs from, and we learned them as much as they could be learned. He knew the songs by heart but had no way to instruct us how to play them. And we could not tell him how to follow us or when to come in either. That was not going to happen. The songs became free-form rockabilly jams, which we were able to elongate or truncate at will depending on the Ledge's whims while performing them. If he decided to embark on a monologue mid-song about outer space, we went with him. It wasn't that far removed from performing with Jeffrey.

After a few shows, we realized he did the exact same thing every night, like an autistic person would. He was strangely professional in that respect. He would regularly do a striptease partway through the set, coyly taking off his buckskin fringe jacket, one arm at a time, and swinging it around his head like a lariat. Then his chaps would fly off, leaving him wearing nothing but flesh-colored, high-waisted underwear and cowboy boots with spurs. Girls in the audience screamed as he shimmied, jerked, and high-kicked his way around the stage, happy as a clam, staggering like a toddler in a diaper, with a delirious smile pasted across his face.

The Ledge's childlike insanity was infectious. Soon, I found myself stripping down to my tighty-whities onstage also. It felt strangely liberating, playing guitar almost naked in public, stripped of any pose or pretension. Patricia's contribution to this madcap atmosphere was to transform herself from goth ice queen to country-and-western drag queen with a giant blond Dolly Parton wig and dark sunglasses.

All of this went down a storm with the audience. Every show was sold out. The Ledge got an insane amount of press, reviews in every Dutch newspaper and cover stories in their Sunday magazines. It was like he was Bruce Springsteen or something. It was a crazy, weird phenomenon, totally unexpected, even to Willem the promoter, who had tried to organize some buzz around the shows but was shocked at how it had taken off.

I got stopped going back into the UK myself at the end of our tour with the Ledge. I'd been staying there on a tourist visa, leaving the country every six months to renew it. I never bothered getting a work visa. This time when I presented my passport, they said, "You're with a band." How did they know? My passport. Fortunately, I wasn't wearing a monkey-fur coat. All that happened is I got sent back to Amsterdam, where I stayed with a friend for a while, put my passport in the washing machine, then applied for a "clean" one at the US embassy.

Tex finally made it back to the UK, around the same time as me, via a flight to the Netherlands and a ferry to Harwich. We started working on musical concepts for Fur Bible, which consisted of going out, getting very drunk, and trying to come up with songs. We got along very well, Tex and I. Too well, probably. We both felt weighed down by the expectation of living up to our former bands and that we'd be mining similar ground. We both wanted to break out of that mold. We decided to do the exact opposite of what was expected of us, something completely self-indulgent and experimental, using Captain Beefheart as our lodestar.

The Fur Bible was so free-form, though, that it wasn't long before we realized that, while we had no end of ideas, we also had no direction. Songs remained unformed and unfinished. Everyone was at odds musically. Eventually Tex got bored. "Nothing's happening, I'm leaving," he told me one day. It didn't come as much of a surprise. "I can't blame you. Go!" I said. And he did.

Now we were a band without a singer. "Why don't you do it?" Patricia suggested. That was the absolute worst thing she could have said to me. I'll drink arsenic, anything, I thought, just don't ask me to be the singer in our band. But I also knew if we were going to make this work, I didn't have a choice. Knowing I had extreme reservations about being a front man, Patricia was very supportive. She suggested I go see this voice coach who was working with Dave Vanian from the Damned. Every week, I'd turn up for my weekly lesson and always bump into the person before me: Kevin Rowland of Dexys Midnight Runners. Fuck, I'd think, she's been listening to the voice of an angel, and now this croaker comes in.

I had no confidence in myself whatsoever as a vocalist. And confidence, a good vocal coach will tell you, is half the battle won. That's what I came away with from those lessons, that being confident would mask any deficiencies in my singing. I was wrong. It couldn't hide that I didn't have a voice—my voice. But I soldiered on, determined to make a go of it anyway.

It helped that there was nothing but goodwill around us. We had come, collectively, from such a lauded musical pedigree that everybody was willing to give us the benefit of the doubt, sight unseen. Marcy got us a record deal with New Rose, the French label the Cramps had moved to after leaving IRS. New Rose had also released the first Gun Club album, *Fire of Love*. Jim Thirlwell agreed to produce us. We tracked our debut EP at Pete Townshend's Eel Pie Studios in Soho, where Siouxsie and the Banshees had recorded their last album, *Hyaena*.

Jim was very patient but also really pushed me, and I needed that more than anything else. I still hadn't settled on a vocal style. "You have to make a decision about how you want to perform," Jim said, "and commit to it." Commitment wasn't in my nature. Those recordings were proof. We cut three tracks. I sang on one, spoke/sang on the next, and screamed on the last.

If I wasn't happy with my voice, the music at least felt like it was heading in the right direction. I was very enamored with the arty musical expressionism of emerging post-no-wave groups like Swans and Sonic Youth and the ways they were using sound, which connected with the way I had always played guitar. Fur Bible took elements of that approach. We were abrasive and heavy. Our image was heavy too—heavily gothic. We went large on the eyeliner and Aqua

Net. It was too gothic for me. It felt like we were pandering, trying too hard to fit in with the mode of the moment. As a front man, I felt like I was fronting.

Siouxsie and the Banshees hired us and the Scientists, whom they'd first seen playing with the Gun Club, as opening acts for a two-month UK tour. Before that, we did one last short European run with the Ledge and then a show with Sonic Youth at ULU in London. Our EP had just come out and that was meant to be our big London showcase. Everyone was making a big deal about it and how important it was to play a good show because all the writers from the UK rock weeklies were going to be there to review it. Our friends and peers, including the Bad Seeds, had come down to see us also. Of course, given the weight of expectation, Murphy's Law dictated that everything that could go wrong did go wrong for that one show. The front-of-house sound totally fucked up. The PA was ringing with feedback throughout, but not the kind of feedback we wanted. We soldiered through, but it sounded like a big mess.

As soon as we got back to the dressing room, Marcy started in on telling us what a terrible show we played. It was the last thing I wanted to hear. I suffered in silence, seeing red, but must have looked like I was going to explode because suddenly, out of nowhere, somebody took my hand, led me into a neighboring room, and said, "Just sit here for a while." I looked up and saw this very pretty, angelic redhead leaning over me. Oh, I thought, it's Anita Lane, Nick Cave's girlfriend. I knew who she was, but we'd never met. She was so empathetic and kind to me. From that moment on, we became fast friends.

We muddled through the tour with Siouxsie, but our hearts weren't in it, even though it was a blast to support them at the Royal Albert

Hall. Patricia and I decided to call it quits and move on. We played one final tour of the Netherlands in March 1986, to pay back our Dutch promoter, Willem, for all his faith and financial support in us when we'd started.

By this time, Patricia had met Andrew Eldritch and he'd asked her to join his new incarnation of the Sisters of Mercy. I was left at a loose end. Our UK promoter, Richard Thomas, helped me find a place to stay by introducing me to Marcia Schofield. She had played in an early-'80s New York post-punk band called Khmer Rouge and had just been hired by Mark E. Smith to play keyboards in the Fall. Marcia and her boyfriend had a spare room in their squat near Holloway Road. Barry Myers, aka Scratchy, who was the DJ for the Clash, also had a room there. I moved in with them but still needed a way to make ends meet.

I became king of the odd jobs. Diamanda Galas had just moved to London to record *The Divine Punishment,* her first album for Mute. I'd met her briefly a year or so earlier when Marc Almond insisted we go see her. So we went, Marc, Lydia Lunch, Jim Thirlwell, Billy Chainsaw, and I. She was very impressive, and very frightening. Offstage, she seemed nice but I didn't know her really. Somebody told me she needed her flat painted in London. They said, "Can you paint a flat?" I said, "Of course I can paint it." I had no idea how to paint a flat; I just wanted the job. I met Diamanda again, and we got talking. I was a young gay guy, and her brother, Dmitri, a playwright, was extremely ill with AIDS at the time. She talked a lot about him. I already had friends who'd died of AIDS, and we bonded over that.

I started painting her apartment. "I want it glossy white." Those were her only instructions. Whatever I didn't know about house painting, I knew enough that gloss paint doesn't really adhere. But I thought, Who am I to argue with Diamanda Galas? If that's what Diamanda wants, that's what Diamanda gets. I painted the entire place gloss white—walls, doors, everything. It took me a couple of days. She took one look at it and said, "There's too much *glare*. We have to paint it again. Paint it matte." I dutifully painted the entire place again.

After that, I kind of became her assistant for a minute and started running errands for her. She'd say to me, "While you're out, can you go to this bookstore and get all these opera songbooks I need?" Or, "All my electronic equipment is arriving in the cargo area of Heathrow Airport. Can you go and pick that up?" Diamanda was the diva. I didn't want to say no. At the same time, she was so distraught over her brother, and though she was keeping up a good front and working, I could feel the immense sadness inside. I wanted to support her any way I could and be a good friend.

I managed to get a steady gig working at a T-shirt factory in London, Pop World, that manufactured merchandise for bands. It was full of other rock 'n' roll misfits. Nigel Lewis from the Meteors also worked there. I was put in charge of the shrink-wrap machine and had to gather up and box the freshly wrapped packages that came out the other side. It was soul-destroying . . . and nasal-destroying. I inhaled plastic all day.

One day, I was at the end of the shrink-wrap machine when out of it came a Cramps T-shirt—with my face on it—a band shot of the "Goo Goo Muck" single cover. That was it for me. I've got to quit this job, I thought. I need to start making music again. I didn't know what exactly I wanted to do. I just knew I didn't want to front my own band again.

While working at Pop World, I kept in with the music crowd in London. One of the regular party spots was a houseboat on Chelsea Wharf, home to two sisters, Chris and Cec Johnston, whose father owned Johnston's Paint in Manchester. I'd met them through Jessamy Calkin. Chris played keyboards in new-wave industrial band

Dormannu with her boyfriend, Simeon. They both lived on the boat. A lot of the people who used to hang out there were associated with the Mute record label, like the Bad Seeds, who would often stay there when they were in town.

One night, I was at the houseboat, sitting around the dinner table, drinking and talking with a small group that included Mick Harvey and his wife, Katy. Mick was Nick Cave's right-hand man in the Bad Seeds and the group's de facto musical director. I didn't know him all that well, but I'd seen the Bad Seeds play when they came to LA a few years earlier, and had hung out with Nick and Blixa—although, at the time, Nick was closer with Jeffrey than me. The band were living between London and Berlin.

"I heard Fur Bible split up," Mick said. I told him we had, and that I wasn't sure what I was going to do next. "Well . . . ," he said, "Barry Adamson's leaving the Bad Seeds." Mick, who had been playing guitar alongside Blixa, was going to switch to take on Barry's role and play bass. "We have a month of shows to play in Europe and we're looking for a second guitarist to take my spot. Do you want to fill in? We're rehearsing in Berlin."

Just like that, without any forethought on my part, I was offered the opportunity to join Nick Cave and the Bad Seeds. It was like being headhunted by Lux and Ivy all over again. What did I have to lose? Mick didn't even demand a finger.

Bad Seed

Berlin smelled like freedom. A breath of fresh air compared to London, which had begun to feel small and claustrophobic, despite being twice the size and population. The pop culture, the music scene, and the way everything was dictated by the music press—who was cool, what was worthy, and what was not—had started to irritate me. The class system in Britain made me feel uncomfortable; the casual and ever-present racism unnerved me.

I got called "Paki" a lot in London. One time, I was on a tube platform in North London and some crusty punk with a dog on a string passed by, looked me up and down, and sneered, "*Paki* in a leather jacket." They didn't have any concept of what a Mexican was. I just looked brown to them, had black hair, and the only way they could identify me racially was what they already knew of, as a member of the Pakistani population in England.

I became more and more self-conscious, even paranoid, about whether I talked too loud in the subway, about my American accent, my look, which was full "goth junkie" even though I wasn't doing drugs. It all fed into existing issues I had and exacerbated my low self-esteem. I was drinking a lot, blacking out, having no recollection of getting back to my flat. Or waking up in bed with someone, having no idea of how I got there or who they were. It was time for a change.

I got to Berlin and immediately felt I could be myself again and relax. The pressure was off. The music scene there did not have the relentless obsession with style. It was trendy but more innocent and freewheeling. I knew immediately why Iggy and Bowie, my musical heroes, had moved there, and why the records they made in the city sounded so beautifully desolate and wasted. That was the vibe, and it was intoxicating.

One of my first nights out in Berlin, I rehearsed with the band, then we all went drinking at one of the many places that catered to the army of night crawlers in the city, made up of the artistically inclined and the flotsam and jetsam of street characters who surrounded them. For some reason, I brought my guitar with me to the bar. When we left, close to dawn, Nick dropped me off in the cab at Yorckstrasse, where I was staying at Bad Seeds drummer Thomas Wydler's apartment.

In my inebriated state, I didn't realize until it was too late, and the cab had disappeared, that I'd left my guitar in the trunk. Fuck. Idiot, I thought. Someone at Thomas's apartment suggested calling the taxi company. They told us, "We take our lost and found to the police. Call them." To my amazement, they had my guitar. Someone had turned it in. Wow, I thought, people in Berlin are so nice and *honest*. I can't imagine this would happen in New York or London. I'm going to *move* here.

I couch surfed for the first few months, staying at an apartment on Paul-Linke-Ufer in Kreuzberg with a friend of Thomas Wydler's,

Maria Zastrow. She had moved to Berlin from Austria in her teens and landed a job bartending at an underground haunt called Risiko. A gregarious and enthusiastic concertgoer and music fan, Maria had an encyclopedic knowledge of all things rock 'n' roll but swore allegiance, above all else, to the King, Elvis Presley. She was a well-known face on the Berlin scene, a face you couldn't forget once you'd seen it. She was James Dean as a girl, intense and intensely beautiful, all chiseled cheekbones, square jaw, and sculpted eyebrows, topped with a perfectly combed jet-black pompadour. Her androgynous look was accentuated by a preference for wearing men's printed button-up shirts and jeans with thick belts and large heavy metal buckles. Maria took me around to all the best spots to search for good second-hand clothes and introduced me to Black & White hair wax, for maximum hold and shine. Maria had cut and styled Nick Cave's hair for the video to "The Singer" and the still from it that graced the cover of the Bad Seeds' covers album, *Kicking Against the Pricks.* We all took inspiration and fashion tips from Maria's impeccable sense of style.

There wasn't a whole lot of rehearsal time before the Bad Seeds went on tour. I learned the songs from the records and winged it. They used a lot of odd timings I wasn't used to. That was the biggest challenge, as well as working out where I fit in within a group unlike any I'd been in—larger-than-life personalities, alpha males all.

I wasn't the only new recruit to the Bad Seeds for that tour. Roland Wolf, a friend of Blixa's who had been playing with Neubauten, was brought in to play piano and organ. He was an affable and extremely intelligent chap, with a curled lip that suggested a slight dismissiveness, and the ability to moan in impeccable English. We bonded as new inductees in the gang.

It felt like, rather than any special talent, I had been cast in the band by Nick. We had all been cast. He had already assigned me a role that seemed to suggest I would always remain slightly out of sync with everyone else. He'd designed a foldout poster for a special tour single that featured photos and mini profiles of each band member. Mine was labeled "The Misfit."

Even though we barely knew each other at the time, he saw in me a quality similar to the one that had drawn Lux and Ivy, a quality I was not even sure of myself. A like-mindedness of aesthetics and personality secured my place in the Bad Seeds. That, and an affinity for the darkness in the songs, which was something I had been drawn to, over and over, whether through the Cramps or the Gun Club. Nick was expressing something similar but very different. His was an idiosyncratic and very Australian view of American roots music, specifically blues and country, an outsider's view of the culture combined with a true love of and identification with the music. The Bad Seeds didn't hide their influences, they flaunted them—which, coming to music as a fan originally, I loved and felt simpatico with. I already felt like an outsider in my own country anyway.

In this poster, Nick used this one photo of me that he'd found and really liked. I was wearing a ruffled shirt open to the waist, with one nipple peeking out, looking askance through hair that fell over one eye. "You look really sexy, crazy, and weird in this," he told me. I took it as a compliment.

The Bad Seeds, at the time, were very into dressing up. Greasy hair and dirty suits, that was the look. A '50s jazz lounge-lizard junkie kind of vibe. Just as I'd done with the Cramps, I came up with my own take on that. I was obsessed with *Touch of Evil* at the time, the Orson Welles film starring Marlene Dietrich and Janet Leigh, and Charlton Heston, in a bad fake tan, playing a Mexican cop in a corrupt border town. The villains of the piece were a pencil-mustached

Mexican mobster, Uncle Joe Grandi, and these murderous butch lesbians with slicked-back Elvis hair. My Bad Seeds look became a cross between those two: a killer lesbian Mexican mobster.

I started wearing my suit all the time. All you needed was two or three of them and your outfit was picked out. There was not a lot of fussing going on. A good shirt, good shoes, good hair—and you're off. That was a prerequisite to be a Bad Seed at the time. Slick and slightly disheveled, we fit the vibe of the city perfectly. Berlin was the kind of place where you could wear anything you wanted. No one looked twice at you, except for the old people, who seemed to fix everyone with perpetual scowls.

Surrounded by misfits and miscreants, it didn't take long for me to slip back into old habits. Two weeks into my tenure playing with the Bad Seeds, to be exact. The ninth date of my first tour with the band, we played the Élysée Montmartre in Paris. We had the next day off. Some of the band members announced they were going out to try to score. Bored, I followed them. It didn't seem like a big deal.

Finding drugs and drug dealers in a strange city is never as easy as it seems. After a few hours of eyeballing every shady-looking character on the street without success, everybody decided to take a cab back to the hotel, empty-handed. Except Simon Bonney (from Crime & the City Solution, who was doing lights for the group) and I. We took the metro instead. Walking down into the subway, we saw this guy loitering. He had "dealer" written all over him. We loitered too, giving him the hairy eyeball to see if he would play ball. He approached, beckoned us to follow. We scored a bunch of heroin.

Back at the hotel, temptation got the better of me. What the hell, I thought, just a little sniff for old times' sake. Knowing full well that just a little was never enough. I hadn't done heroin in a while. Maybe not since Jeffrey and I had gone to Mexico to clean up, three years earlier. As soon as I felt that intense rush, it all came back. Instantly. The familiarity. This is what's been missing from my life all along, I thought. This is who I am. This is how I want to feel. Nothing. Problem solved. Heroin is so insidious in that way. I was hooked again. Stupid me.

In Hamburg, after a show at Grosse Freiheit 36 and a further session of after-hours drinking, Roland and I returned to our shared hotel room. Before turning in, we decided a nightcap was in order. As we sat and chatted, to our astonishment, the mattress on one of the beds started raising itself up. A rather haughty punk girl emerged from underneath it, briskly got to her feet, and cursed us in German while heading for the door. We looked on in silence. Only afterward did we realize she had hidden herself in the room hoping to spring herself on a bigger, badder Bad Seed than us but had mistakenly secreted herself in the wrong room. Roland and I couldn't sleep for laughing that night, amazed by the zealousness of Nick's fans and relieved we didn't end up as a sweetmeat for one of them.

When we hit London, the Bad Seeds were playing to two thousand people at the Town & Country Club. The Gun Club were supporting them. Thinking my tenure with the Bad Seeds was going to end after that one tour, I'd agreed to join them onstage and play with Jeffrey again. I guess he'd gotten tired of wanting to be solo. Nothing was really happening for Jeffrey. He knew re-forming the Gun Club would be a winning proposition. It wasn't so much that we re-formed the band as I joined the Jeffrey Lee Pierce Band—a three-piece he'd put together with Romi Mori on bass and Nick Sanderson from Clock

DVA on drums—and we changed the name back to the Gun Club. That one-off felt good enough that I agreed to do a European tour with them immediately after the Bad Seeds tour.

By the time I returned to Berlin at the beginning of 1987, Nick was locked into his own addiction living in a small upstairs room in Christoph Dreher's place at Dresdener Strasse 11 in Kreuzberg. His typewriter was set up on a desk against a wall. Above it was a huge painting by Berlin artist Friedrich Wall, of a green-and-yellow woman lying spread-eagled on a sea of red. It was dark, lurid, and strangely violent. Pinned up around it were several naked center-folds, as well as the vintage photograph of a Shirley Temple–like cherub that would be used on the cover of *And the Ass Saw the Angel*, the novel Nick spent most of his time writing at this very desk, which also held his precious gun—a real handgun that he often took with him out on the streets of Berlin. Sex and violence were his twin obsessions.

Anita Lane and Nick had split up by this time. Anita had returned to Melbourne, where she started seeing someone else. So did Nick, in Berlin. She was a photographer, younger than everyone else, sweet-natured, and completely enamored of Nick. Her name was Barbara but everyone called her Bunny—and Bunny was all she was known by. I didn't find out her real name until many years later. She was blond and model-beautiful, with a very athletic body, almost the antithesis of the partner you'd expect to be with Nick Cave, then the dark king of goth. Maybe that's exactly what he was looking for. Somebody to rescue him from the darkness.

A moment of lightness came when we appeared in the Wim Wenders film *Wings of Desire*. I was a full-time Bad Seed now, not just a fill-in guitarist for the tour. This was one of my first official duties.

We went into Hansa Studios to record a live version of "From Her to Eternity" that we were going to play against in the film. I was a huge fan of the David Bowie and Iggy Pop records made at Hansa, of course, but also all the Boney M. albums. Recording there was a dream come true.

We shot our scene in the ballroom of the Esplanade, this palatial bombed-out hotel in Potsdamer Platz, a beautiful ruin that was an appropriate setting for the beautiful ruins we all were. It was winter in Berlin, a particularly brutal winter even by Berlin standards. Even Berliners were complaining. You could feel the freeze inside the ballroom.

Wim Wenders was exceedingly cool, the opposite of a hotheaded movie director. His personality was like one of his movies, slow and mysterious. Every movement he made was very deliberate; it seemed as if he was gliding through the set. Before we started shooting, he gave a little speech, pointing up at the crane to introduce the cinematographer, Henri Alekan, who had shot most of Cocteau's movies. "Please know that you are gonna be part of an incredible piece of cinema, just by being photographed by him." It was very sweet of him and created a special mood on the set—that we were part of a happening, even though our role in the film was so small.

Later, he even came up and told me, "I was such a big fan of the Gun Club." He had seen us play at Club Lingerie when he was living in LA. It was amazing to hear that from somebody I considered such a great artist.

Jeffrey had a batch of new songs. He was very prolific at that time and healthy. He'd stopped drinking and had dropped a lot of weight, shedding pounds and pounds. He'd even bought an exercise machine, taken up jogging, and gotten into boxing. This was his new crazy obsession—fitness.

He was living with Romi and her roommate, Kayo, in a basement flat in West Kensington. A third Japanese girl, Yuko, who used to tour with the Gun Club and sell our merchandise, was always hanging out with them there also. They would endlessly watch Japanese movies on VHS, and the girls cooked Japanese food. Beyond the giddy fantasy of being taken care of by three Japanese women—which, being the only guy and the center of attention, Jeffrey embraced wholeheartedly—it was a very idyllic and inspiring situation for him. I don't think Jeffrey had experienced the stability of that kind of domestic life since he'd stopped living with his own family.

Jeffrey had always been obsessed by Japanese culture, especially anything related to samurai and the Pacific War, but through Romi his interest deepened. He began learning the language. He and Romi were playing and writing together a lot.

We'd recorded some demos with Tony Cohen earlier that year in London that were very raw and aggressive. Jeffrey titled the album *Mother Juno*, after the Roman goddess of marriage and childbirth who had been eaten alive by her father, Saturn, along with four of her siblings, then vomited out whole. We never discussed why he titled it that, just as there was never much premeditation or discussion among us about how to record the songs Jeffrey brought to the band. Nick Sanderson had been playing with Jeffrey for a year at that point. Romi had started by playing guitar in his band, then moved to bass. We all understood the concept of the Gun Club and knew what to do. We wanted to revisit the older energy of the band. Then Romi introduced Jeffrey to the Cocteau Twins. He'd never heard them before. He fell in love with that dreamy, swirly sound and decided it would be a good idea to mix that with the

Gun Club's hard-rocking approach to roots music. He also wanted Robin Guthrie from Cocteau Twins to produce us. Being a fan of the Gun Club, Robin readily agreed. Jeffrey wrote one song in particular, "Breaking Hands," to be produced in the style of the Cocteau Twins. We recorded at Hansa, but Robin didn't come to the tracking sessions. He sent Lincoln Fong, the engineer he used at his studio, to record us in Berlin, and the tapes were sent back to the UK for Robin to work with. The whole process was very workmanlike and disciplined, and free of the usual drama that came from working with Jeffrey.

The opposite held true for the Bad Seeds. There was always a certain amount of chaos around them. Almost as if Nick was inviting it or felt he needed to inject some additional disorder just to keep us all on our toes. There was another lady in his life around this time also, Jeanette Bleeker. It might not be right to call her a girlfriend, but he was involved with her, and she gradually assumed a manager/agent role and so became entwined in all our lives, whether we wanted that or not. Jeanette set up this mini touring festival for the Bad Seeds to headline, Kings of Independence, that was to feature a host of indie music luminaries. There was one date in Hamburg and another the next night in Bonn. The Swans, Butthole Surfers, the Fall, Crime & the City Solution, and Die Haut were also on the bill. There were early warning signs, at least for me, that this was destined to be a calamity. Nine months earlier, the Gun Club had played Knopf's Music Hall, the venue Jeanette had booked in Hamburg. We'd sold it out all by ourselves, so it didn't take much thought to realize that with six bands our size all playing, the whole thing was going to be a real mess.

We arrived in Hamburg a few days before and I bumped into Michael Gira from Swans at the production office. He was completely sweet and nice, and we chitchatted for a while and caught up.

Michael had been a huge fan of the Gun Club and credited seeing us as a teenager with the inspiration to form his own band. Then he walked into Jeanette's office and all you could hear was him screaming at the top of his lungs: "I can't believe you don't have any of this equipment!" He came out and said to me, all sweetness and light again, "Oh, you want to go get a drink?" It was hilarious. There was a great camaraderie among the bands, even though we all had this feeling of great dread and foreboding that the entire thing was going to be a disaster.

True to all fears and predictions, the concert was completely oversold. The venue held two and a half thousand. People were jammed inside to beyond capacity. And there were at least another thousand who couldn't get in. It was going to be a very long night. The show started at 9 p.m. The Bad Seeds didn't get onstage till 5 a.m. By that time, a riot had erupted outside; there were people lighting cars on fire and smashing store windows.

The next day, the whole crew and all the bands, other than the Fall and Butthole Surfers (who were already on tour together and had their own transportation), took a bus to Bonn. Everybody was raging drunk. Jarboe from Swans had this pink quilted sleep mask on, just trying to shut it all out. So Nick sat behind her, openly shooting up to get her goat. That was typical of Nick and his perverse sense of fun, if only to humor himself.

The second night was a calamity too. The after-party ended up back at my hotel room. People were fucking and shooting up. The police raided the hotel after Alexander Hacke from Neubauten started throwing glasses into the swimming pool. Somebody left a syringe in my room. The police arrested me. Somehow, I managed to convince them I was the cleanest-living rock star in the group and managed to get myself bailed out. None of this would bode well for the recording sessions we were about to begin three weeks later, at

Vielklang and Hansa Studios, for the next Bad Seeds album, *Tender Prey*. A darkness was closing in around the band.

Tony Cohen, who had worked with Nick since his days in Boys Next Door and the Birthday Party, was producing. He was hilarious and snarky. We hit it off immediately. He had a good read of not only me but my role in the band: the new outsider in the pack. I related to Tony as a weirdo kindred spirit.

He was a huge junkie at the time. Sometimes we'd come into the studio and find him still there from the night before, asleep under the mixing desk. To be fair, he also worked like a man possessed and seemed to have a bottomless bag of tricks, in the form of unconventional recording techniques, some of which seemed positively counterintuitive. Producers often record the sound of a studio, as well as individual players, to capture room atmosphere. Tony's unique way of doing this was to hang microphones out the window, recording what could be heard outside while the band played inside.

This was the first time I'd been in the studio to work on new material with the group. They had a very established way of working, centered around Nick and Mick Harvey. Because they had known each other since high school and played together for such a long time, they worked instinctively, almost as if tapping into a shared third mind.

The songs came from Nick, but Mick, the arranger and musical director for the group, did much of the work to realize them. He would give us direction but, within that, everything was very free. Once the song structure was pretty much down, they'd say, "Now, Kid, go do your Kid thing." And Blixa was going to do his thing. If something wasn't working, they were brutally honest, in a very blunt Australian way. But it was never caustic, and I was never made to feel bad about anything. It was more an encouragement to try again.

Much of the time, I played a lot of the straighter rhythm guitar parts. I was very much learning and taking cues from Blixa, whom I admired a lot. We had both established this expressionistic style of playing that came more from feeling than any adherence to musical structure or notation. Mine still came from a rock 'n' roll base; Blixa's came from wherever he came from, this very abstract, musique concrète approach to the guitar that was influenced by his work with Neubauten. He was a lot more musically adept than people gave him credit for. He could play very ornate things, bluesy stuff, as well as play in open tuning.

We were working at Hansa one night when Mick made this loop of himself beating on his bass with drumsticks. Immediately, you could hear something very cool was coming out of it. That song would turn into "The Mercy Seat," which was completed at sessions in London a few weeks later. I didn't get to play on it, sadly, but it was enough just to be around while it was being recorded. You knew something very special was happening.

We were living in the shadow of the Wall. Almost literally. Whether recording in Hansa Studios, living in Kreuzberg, or partying at debauched after-hours clubs and bars like Risiko or Ex'n'Pop, where sex was de rigueur and drugs were openly taken. The Wall provided cover for all manner of illicit activity, as if the closer you got, the more decadent the city became—a middle finger to the authoritarian presence beyond. And I was hanging out with the most notorious group of ex-pat outlaws in Berlin.

One big difference with the Bad Seeds from all the other bands I'd been in was that we always seemed surrounded by a large crowd of people. I called them the "Berlin 500." Anywhere we went—after-hours bars, backstage, even the studio control room—there they were, en masse, the same familiar faces. Scenesters, friends, grifters, drug dealers, and other assorted hangers-on. They reminded me of Stevie Nicks's entourage at Ocean Way, a cloud of people encircling and trailing us like smoke. Everyone was doing this strain of speed that was said to literally drive people insane. Life was a constant whirl of intoxication, staggering from studio to bar to loft and back again, always accompanied, never alone. Even as a stranger in Berlin, solitude was not an option.

At the same time, I'd been thrown into a new situation, a new culture. Even among a crowd, I felt separated. I was the Misfit, the only American in the band, definitely the only homosexual. The Bad Seeds were macho in the extreme. Both arty and macho at the same time. It was a strange mix. They were flamboyant and, when called for, Nick wore as much makeup as I did, but nobody was outwardly gay. Inwardly, though, I had my suspicions. I put a lot of pressure on myself to conform and fit in but bonded far more with the women around the group—Anita Lane; Mick Harvey's wife, Katy; and Bronwyn Adams, Simon Bonney's wife—feeling able to talk to and confide in them and let my guard down.

Within the band, it felt as if I was playing a role. I suppressed my own sexuality in order to conform. In Berlin, sex was gender-fluid, free, and anonymous—whatever you wanted it to be, in any combination. I became very unsexual in the sexiest city in the world. The drugs played their part in that, but it was also the time of AIDS, and I was very wary. In London, I would go to gay bars and pick up people. I didn't have relationships. I was getting blackout drunk and sleeping with people. I got very scared of that, and very scared of the consequences of gay sex in general. Drugs complicated our lives even further. When the *Tender Prey* sessions moved to London in the winter of 1987–1988, Nick got busted for possession of less than a gram of heroin.

I was caught between the devil and the deep blue sea. Between Nick Cave and Jeffrey Lee Pierce. Both immeasurably brilliant and tortured artists, both extremely fucked-up, high-maintenance individuals. Fortunately, Nick had Mick and Anita and a whole support system of friends around, like Jessamy Calkin, to care for him when the tipping point eventually came, which it almost certainly would.

Jeffrey had me. And I had Jeffrey. Whether I liked it or not. We had something of a codependent relationship. We needed each other. When Jeffrey was at his worst, I did my best to protect him. Particularly from the incursions of the British music press, who had the tenacity, instincts, and ruthlessness of the tabloids and had already gone to town to expose Nick's heroin addiction and paint him as a negative role model who posed a mortal danger to his fans.

Jeffrey was living with Romi in London. She was taking care of him, basically nursing him. He had started taking a lot of Valiums. Jeffrey would ricochet from near-sobriety to being totally messed up. I wouldn't see him for a few months and would never know which Jeffrey I would encounter next time we reconnected. Somehow, he had managed to get a Valium prescription from a doctor. He was out of it much of the time. One afternoon, a journalist from one of the weeklies came around; Jeffrey had just gotten up and was virtually incoherent. I made up a half-assed excuse to cover for him—"Oh, he's not feeling well"—the kind of thing no one who encountered him would ever believe. The Valium did him no favors. I'd have preferred to deal with him on junk. At least he'd have been more functional.

Jeffrey wanted to be looked after but constantly made it as hard as possible for anyone to take care of him. It was as if he was standing on a ledge, leaning, leaning, leaning, shifting his balance until he was about to fall, waiting to see if anyone was going to reach out and stop him. If I fall, will you catch me? Consciously or unconsciously, that was the game Jeffrey was engaged in with all the people in his life who loved and cared for him. It was exhausting being around that 24/7.

I was fucked up also and doing everything I could to keep myself together. We were both just trying to survive, riding the ups and downs, twists and turns. We had to negotiate each other's lives, attempting to maintain a career at the same time. We never knew what life was going to throw at us next. One minute everything would be all fucked up, some bad bit of business, shows that got canceled, tours that went awry. Then suddenly something good would happen. We'd make a good record that would give us fresh hope and new energy. All we knew is that we needed to keep moving, no matter what was going on, whether it was illness, drug addiction, frustration. Like the walking dead, we just kept moving forward. Our one saving grace, slither of hope, and shred of self-worth was in the music we made and performed together—and we held on to that for dear life.

I left Jeffrey to go on tour with the Bad Seeds in Australia. Nick was arrested on arrival at Melbourne Airport. This was a month after his bust in London. I went straight from there to playing a short US tour with the Gun Club, a week of dates on the East Coast followed by another week in the West. Around this time, we'd be playing a show, and Jeffrey would be out of sync with everybody else. We'd be screaming at him onstage: "You're playing the song at half speed!" He was insistent he wasn't. Something wasn't right.

In Los Angeles, Jeffrey went for a checkup and was diagnosed with cirrhosis. He kept saying he was really ill but wouldn't say what it was. He would talk about his various ailments so much we never knew what was real and what was imagined. As he became more aware of his physical health, he got more depressed. He had a very depressive, low opinion of life in general. He couldn't see any future for the band. He was worn out, just trying to keep the band going in London and push it to the next level. We all needed to work and make money to survive. The only way to work was to make music. All of that was weighing on Jeffrey as the band leader. I knew he wasn't reliable, but I believed in him and wanted something to happen. I was still going back and forth to Berlin, so I would just duck out. As long as I wasn't there, it wasn't my problem. Jeffrey wasn't my problem. I'd just wait and see what happened next. I was still playing with the Bad Seeds, so at least I was employed.

Nick and Anita left Berlin in the spring of '88 and returned to London. I wish I'd gone with them. The city had become grim, dark, and dank. Purgatory for most people, but a junkie's paradise.

I was sharing a storefront apartment in Neukölln with Martin Rabitz, a musician friend of my friend Maria. He was in a garage-punk band called the Hippriests, named after the Fall song. We had another roommate also—a giant rat that lived rent-free in a hole in the wall under the kitchen sink. Next door, a prostitute plied her trade. Day and night people would knock on the shop window. I'd open the door to these meek-looking men, dressed in a suit and tie, holding a bunch of flowers, who looked more than a little surprised to see me. "Ist Schatzi hier?" they'd stutter.

"Schatzi? Nein," I'd reply wearily, directing them next door. "Sie wollen das Nebenhaus."

When not trying to outwit the rat and shoo off the johns, I spent most of my days engaged in my full-time occupation, being a heroin addict.

The big lie about the drug "community" is that everybody is completely isolated from everyone else, deep into their own trips, inoculated from reality by their habits. In order to maintain using, you callus over your emotions one by one, like the veins that become dead and unusable the longer you shoot into them. You can even make excuses for tragedies—and I was as guilty of that as anybody else.

Nick's sweet-natured girlfriend, Bunny, OD'd and died. I didn't know her all that well, but I liked her a lot, and somewhere deep inside I felt the pain of her death. I didn't realize it then, but it brought back all the feelings of senselessness, frustration, and anger that had overwhelmed me when my cousin Theresa was murdered. She was there, and then, in an instant, she was gone. I don't think I ever truly got over that loss. It had fueled all my years of reckless behavior and drug-taking since then, of wanting to lose myself in myself, to walk on the ledge, as close to the precipice as possible, without ever falling. Maybe the resurgence of all these feelings, or the realization they had been living inside me all this time, made the reaction of others around me to Bunny's death seem that much more hurtful.

I had these two drug dealers, Katrin and Michela, who lived in Kreuzberg. Katrin was a butch lesbian who dressed in men's clothes, had greasy slicked-back hair, in that very Berlin way that only butch lesbians in Berlin can be. She was very Ratso Rizzo, a hip version of that. On that level, she was my type. They were everybody's drug dealers on the scene. I was horrified at their reaction to Bunny's death, which was to dismiss it out of hand. That it was her fault, no big deal. She was just another junkie out of her depth who paid the price. I don't think I'd ever been around people that mercenary before. It scared me.

I'd made the mistake of getting too familiar with Katrin and Michela. One time, I even ended up staying at their apartment on Skalitzer Strasse, near Kotbusser Tor, house-sitting for them while they were away. When I left to play some dates with the Gun Club in the Netherlands, I dropped the keys off with a friend of theirs. Soon after, somebody broke in and ransacked their apartment. I got the blame. Katrin and Michela were very paranoid—not surprisingly, given the nature of their business. So paranoid that they started putting out word I had set them up. My dealers were throwing shade at me. I was cut off from my main connection.

I met this girl, Kathleen Stewart, on the street, another of the many Australians who had pitched up in Berlin. She was a poet and part of the junkie crowd, as we all were. "I'm going home to Australia and checking in to rehab," she told me. "But I want to talk to you. Meet me tomorrow at the coffee shop."

Oh good, I thought, she's going to give me all her leftover drugs. But when I met her the next day, she pulled out all this literature for Narcotics Anonymous and handed it to me. What the fuck am I going to do with this? I wanted to say. But I took it and she left. Soon I would leave too, for London.

In a way, I was relieved to be back. I was over Berlin, over drugs. I wanted to quit. My friend Marcia Schofield took me in, like the Jewish mother she is. I stayed at her flat in Green Lanes, trying to wean myself off heroin. I registered as an addict and got a teaspoon of methadone a day. It was strangely comforting, like taking vitamins. What wasn't very comforting was all the weight I gained.

By the time I arrived in London, Nick and Anita had already checked themselves in to rehab. At the beginning of August, Nick had pleaded guilty to heroin possession and only escaped a prison sentence by agreeing to undergo treatment for drug addiction. They went to a residential treatment center in Somerset called Broadway Lodge.

One night, I got a call from Anita. "I'm breaking out of rehab," she said. "I'm hitchhiking back to London and want to see you." Anita was a free spirit but a willful free spirit. She felt incarcerated. If she was going to quit drugs, she wanted to do it on her own terms. "I'm going to NA," she said. "You have to come with me."

She took me to this church hall in Chelsea. There were all these clean-cut, well-to-do people sitting in a circle, all dressed and styled very nicely. These people all look so square, I thought. That night, somebody was celebrating five years clean. She was presented with a cake and everyone sang "Happy Birthday" to her. I thought it was some weird evangelical Jesus-freak scam and reacted against it violently.

"What is all this garbage?" I raged afterward. "These lying people." I thought the whole thing had been staged for my benefit. I was still in deep denial. Anita understood. She was so sweet and empathetic that she talked me down and around. "You have to keep going," she said. "Just give it a shot." So I did, because I liked Anita a lot and trusted her. She was my lifeline. I half wanted to kick, half wanted to kick against the pricks. But I did make the decision to wean myself slowly off drugs. Everybody was very supportive.

When Nick came out of rehab at the end of September, Anita, Jessamy, and I went to meet him off the train. The Bad Seeds were due to go on a monthlong European tour six days later. It felt like a recipe for disaster, an invitation to relapse. Anita and I found a tour manager who could help keep Nick on the straight and narrow while on the road, music industry veteran Rayner Jesson, who'd recently been through rehab himself. Newly clean ourselves, Anita and I were zealous in our desire to protect Nick's sobriety. "I think we need a separate dressing room for the sober people," Anita proposed. Mick Harvey was quick to puncture that notion in that very droll, cutting Australian way of his. "I spent all these years sitting in rooms with you guys shooting up and now you want a sober room? Forget it."

I was busier than I had been for a long time, and more clear-eyed also, doing back-to-back tours with the Bad Seeds and the Gun Club. I had always played as part of a group, then, as night follows day, eventually would come the realization, like the Peggy Lee song, "Is That All There Is"? I had reached that point with the Bad Seeds after *Tender Prey* and getting clean, tiring of the circus surrounding the band. Sobriety had given me a new perspective on my life and career. I had a hunger to express myself through something other than junk and felt the need to strike out on my own.

I met a guy, Ray Conroy, who offered to manage me as a solo artist. His brother, Michael, was the bass player for Modern English. Ray was managing Colourbox, the dance-pop band on 4AD who'd just had a massive dance hit with "Pump Up the Volume," as part of M/A/R/R/S. The idea was that I should do some dance rock also, and I agreed because, as was my wont, I was always interested in doing something that was completely against the grain of what was expected of me, or what I expected of myself.

I called on friends to put together a band for sessions to record an EP of three tracks I'd written. Robin Guthrie played bass and did some programming. Marcia, whom I was living with in Green Lanes, played keyboards; Murray Mitchell, from Fur Bible, changed his name to Mitch Hunter and played guitar; Barry Adamson played bass; and Ray's client, Steve Young from Colourbox, did some programming. This incredible Jamaican trumpet player, Eddie "Tan Tan" Thornton, who had played with Georgie Fame and the Blue Flames, the Beatles, Boney M., and Aswad, also came in to play on the record.

When Tan Tan arrived at the studio, he said, "Who is the singer?"

I said, "I am the singer."

"I see you onstage," he said. "You are like Mick Jagger."

"I don't think I'm really like Mick Jagger," I told him. I had an ego, of course, but that would be going a bit far.

Mindful of Jim Thirlwell's advice when he was producing Fur Bible, I picked a vocal style and stuck to it for all three tracks: half-sung, half-spoken, in a world-weary tone dripping with mordant wit, heavily influenced by Lou Reed's '70s albums, especially *Sally Can't Dance*, but also by Lee Hazlewood and my early punk and glam idols, David Johansen and Tom Verlaine.

The record came out on an independent label called Nightshift, run by Robin Guthrie's brother, Brian, but it didn't make an impact or get much attention at all. There was no follow-up. My solo career died a quiet death. It seemed like a failure, a repeat of my experience with Fur Bible, albeit more satisfying creatively and, really, the point where I began to establish my own voice.

I had always felt I was faking it as a musician, some guy grifting my way through who got lucky, that all the good things that came to me were a fluke. That was my own assessment of my career. I didn't feel I had what it took to be the leader of a band, that the bar was set way too high. In Jeffrey, Lux, and Nick, I had worked with three front men without peer. How could I compete? But I had also lost sight of why it was that Lux and Ivy had picked me for the Cramps, despite having little in the way of musical skill at the time—their recognition that I was a magical being, like them. At the time, their absolute faith in me inspired a faith in myself and my still-developing abilities that allowed me to deliver on the promise they had seen in me. Heroin made me forget all that and clouded my intuition. I was too busy indulging one demon and running from others, the most crippling of which, ironically, was my low self-esteem.

Even if my solo career wasn't to be, fortunately I still had the Bad Seeds to fall back on for now. In February 1989, the Bad Seeds headed out on a tour of the United States, much of it by bus. Film-maker Uli M. Shüppel joined us to make a documentary, *The Road to God Knows Where*, which plays like a German expressionist rock 'n' roll fever dream. When I look at it now, I can see that, despite being an established member of the band, I was a little bit apart, still the Misfit. The band were always around Nick and hung on his every word. I was not like that. Maybe, because we were clean and trying to stay that way, I was just trying to separate and find myself.

I moved into a house in Clapham Junction with Nick, Anita, and Evan English, another of the Australian ex-pat posse, who had cowritten and produced *Ghosts . . . of the Civil Dead*, which Nick had just starred in. Nick and I were drawn to each other but somehow never became that close, despite living under the same roof to-gether. We were both feeling our way, newly sober, and spent a lot of time watching TV, mainlining movies instead of drugs. We related to each other more through films and music and humor. When we weren't sitting in front of the TV, Nick would be up in the loft, writing on a piano. That's where he wrote most of the songs that would become the next Bad Seeds album, *The Good Son*.

I continued to attend the twelve-step meetings in Chelsea I'd been so dismissive of at first and started to make acquaintants there that drew me closer to the group. Chief among them was a scabrous Irishman with a riotous sense of humor, John Foley. He had grown up on a farm in Dublin with brothers and sisters who instilled in him a love of rock 'n' roll, country, and gospel, especially the music of Johnny Cash and Odetta. He left home and became an out-of-control enfant terrible on the post-punk scene in Dublin, notorious for making appearances at clubs in outlandish costumes. Feeling un-comfortable in the conventional gay scene, he turned himself into a beautiful monster of his own making. He moved to London, got so-ber, and became a costumer—or as he referred to himself, a "stitch bitch"—for music hall productions at the Players' Theatre in Covent Garden, while manning an antiques stall at Camden Market on the weekends. John took me out and about in London, introducing me to all kinds of folks in fashion, art, and music who were also in recovery. He was a huge fan of both the Cramps and the Gun Club but far from a sycophant—in fact, quite the opposite. In him, I felt as if I'd found another kindred spirit, somebody who could laugh uproariously at the dark absurdities of life. Our friendship was a great escape from the emotional heaviness of life at the Clapham House.

The cracks in Nick and Anita's already tempestuous on-off relationship started to become even more apparent when they both became sober. Getting clean, you suddenly reassess everything about your life and the situation you're in, work and personal relationships alike; there is no hiding or denying anything anymore. Nick, perhaps looking for a way out, became infatuated with a Brazilian fashion stylist named Viviane Carneiro, whom he met when the Bad Seeds toured Brazil in April.

We were playing São Paulo. It was the first time the Bad Seeds had played in Brazil. Nick was received like a star. The shows, which were recorded for broadcast on TV, were a big deal. The first time Vivi walked into the backstage area, she lit up the entire place. She had this very natural, warm beauty, was down-to-earth and very sweet. She threw a party for us at her house, and you could tell Nick was immediately enraptured by her. He stayed with Vivi in São Paulo for the rest of the month and left his heart there when we continued touring through Greece, Italy, and Japan.

Anita knew the writing was on the wall. Nick broke up with her soon after. She was devastated. I did my best to console her. "I feel so terrible," she told me. "Like there's a dead body somewhere, but I just can't find it."

Good Son

Jeffrey Lee Pierce was a challenge to my sobriety. We were playing a week of West Coast dates as the Gun Club in the United States, and Jeffrey was neither clean nor sober. He was drinking heavily. No longer the svelte, health-conscious figure of recent years, his weight had ballooned. He looked ill and it was clear to anyone who came to see us that he wasn't doing at all well. The *Los Angeles Times* wrote up a show in Long Beach and spent most of it reviewing Jeffrey's performance rather than the band's. "Like watching a junkie sweat for 80 minutes" was the phrase they used. There was nothing inaccurate about that.

Everything about the tour reminded me of the past. We were playing the exact same underground rock clubs as the last time we'd toured the States five years earlier, and the time before that, and the time before that. Nothing had changed. It didn't matter how popular or critically acclaimed we were in Europe or elsewhere, the indifference to the Gun Club in our home country would always cut us to the quick. It was hard to shake the feeling we were treading water as a band, slowly sinking. As the captain of the ship, Jeffrey was set adrift. He had hit a downward curve and seemed prepared to follow it, all the way to the bottom. I was a mess myself, but I'd worked hard to get clean, and stay clean, in the year I'd spent in London and was determined to remain that way. I felt powerless to help Jeffrey. But if nothing else, I could set an example for him to follow.

I'd had a conversation about Jeffrey with Romi in London just before the tour. She was quite distraught. "He seems so weird and sick all the time," she told me. "I don't know what's going on."

For all the years I'd been around Romi and on heroin myself with Jeffrey, I didn't want to come across as a hypocrite, but I was genuinely concerned and wanted her to be realistic about his situation. "He's sick because he's on heroin," I told her.

"Really?" she said. Romi didn't get it. When it came to drugs, she was very naive, maybe even blissfully ignorant. She knew Jeffrey took drugs but not what he took. She probably figured his behavior was due to a combination of pills and drinking. Jeffrey hid his heroin use from her—but badly.

"I *was* wondering," she told me. "He had a big bandage on his arm."

When she asked Jeffrey why, he told her he'd fallen in a rosebush—the kind of typical half-assed excuse a junkie would come up with.

"He did not fall in the rosebush," I told her. "He's trying to hide track marks."

And I kind of left it at that.

On West Coast runs, Jeffrey and I would often stay on in LA at the end of the tour. Our last date was at Club Lingerie on Sunset

Boulevard, where Brendan Mullen had moved after the Masque closed down. I took the opportunity to visit with friends and my family, whom I'd barely seen since I'd moved to Europe. It was also the first time I'd been sober in LA since my teenage years. I found a twelve-step community to join in Hollywood, where I was surprised and comforted to see several old friends, and made a few new ones. It was a support network of former junkies, made up almost entirely of rockers, freaks, and misfits. I had found my crowd again. Among them was this inordinately handsome character with a boyish face and a body that was chiseled and inked, like a tattooed Tom of Finland character. He had my attention. His name was Ron Athey.

Ron was working as an editor at the *LA Weekly*, dancing at Club Fuck!, and putting on his own "modern primitive" performance art pieces. He'd been involved in the punk scene since the early '80s and had formed an experimental performance art musical group, Premature Ejaculation, with Rozz Williams of Christian Death, but somehow we'd never crossed paths. We hit it off. Then almost immediately had sex. My sexless period ended right there. Followed by my a-lot-of-sex period. Or rather, a-lot-of-really-safe-sex, because Ron was living with HIV. He had been diagnosed three years earlier. He was up front about that when we first got together. "I'd never do anything to infect you," he told me. "Because you'd never want this to be your fate."

There was no cure for AIDS at the time. AZT, the first drug said to combat the disease, had been approved by the FDA two years earlier but was costly and controversial. Like all who had succumbed before them, those living with HIV continued to live in the shadow of death. At the time, it was not a question of "if" but "when" their time would come. Ron was not cowed by his condition. If anything, it made him fight harder for those afflicted. He was heavily involved with not only the recovery community but an emerging community for those with AIDS and HIV, supporting people like him, creating art that spoke to a life adapted to the demands of the virus, working out how to transcend and challenge those limitations.

Soon after we first got together, Ron insisted I get tested. To our relief, it came back negative. Somehow, through all the years of sharing needles and anonymous sexual encounters that had become the norm for me, I was one of the lucky ones. I'd lost so many friends to AIDS at that point.

Being with Ron changed my perspective on life in so many ways. He was such an amazing force of nature and larger-than-life character—extremely positive, charismatic, and energetic. Ron made me feel whole. He made me feel wanted and desired, something I hadn't felt in a long, long time. Intimacy was alien to me. Not physical intimacy, emotional intimacy. I didn't realize until then how much I'd suppressed my true self as a heroin addict, contorting myself into this asexual posture that was very unnatural and extremely silly.

I had a very different connection with Ron, both sexual and emotional. I'd been avoiding relationships for so long, for fear of letting people get close to me and then losing them entirely. It was only after entering therapy that I realized most of this stemmed from the connection I'd shared with my cousin Theresa and lost with her sudden death, an event I had never ever gotten over. I hadn't really grieved for Theresa, instead losing myself in life and numbing the pain through narcotics. With Ron, I allowed myself to be seduced into letting go. We had a torrid affair. I fell in love.

I stayed with Ron at his Craftsman house in Hollywood. He swept me off my feet during the summer months we were together but, when all my savings ran out, I crashed back down to earth. I needed to work and earn money. The Bad Seeds were on hiatus while Nick promoted his novel in Europe. Me and this girl, Sweet Pea, who became a fashion designer, decided to find the easiest, dumbest job we could. That job was telemarketing.

I can't say we really thought this through at all. We had no idea what we were getting into. Whatever the opposite of life-affirming is, that's what this was. Soul-crushing, maybe. At least, that's what it felt like. What made it even worse was we were tasked with selling time-share vacation homes in Florida. The entire job consisted of lying to old people to convince them to part with their money for something that was clearly worth less than what they were offered the privilege of paying for. I was on salary, but the real money in telemarketing is made on commission. It was a job tailor-made for expert liars. Lying didn't come naturally to me. I was completely ill-suited to the job and wasn't making a lot of sales.

Every morning, Sweet Pea would pick me up on her motorcycle and we'd head down to this nondescript office on Hollywood Boulevard to spend eight hours in a cubicle cold-calling people. We lasted two weeks and both quit. It was just the worst, generating the kind of bad karma that takes several lifetimes to pay off.

Fortunately, in October 1989, the Bad Seeds called me back into service again to record *The Good Son* in São Paulo. When it was time to leave Ron, it felt like a great wrenching.

Nick had fallen in love with Brazil, as well as falling in love with Vivi Carneiro. He wanted to record the new album there. Everything about the sessions for *The Good Son* was so much lighter than *Tender Prey*—the scene, the atmosphere, the whole environment around us. For a start, we weren't in Berlin, on heroin, and the Berlin 500 were ten thousand miles away.

Our downtime was spent on the beach rather than in bars. Although São Paulo could be heavy too. You'd see taxi drivers with their arm out the window and a gun in their hand, people chasing little kids who'd nabbed a purse. Crime was ever present and visible. It was a little bit frightening. There was a lawless feeling to the place, but it was also the kind of big city you could easily lose yourself in.

Nick was obsessed with *Pixote,* the Héctor Babenco movie set in São Paulo, about a street child caught between corrupt police and drug gangs. That dark, dangerous underworld held a fatal attraction for him. This time, it didn't seep into our lives or the record we were making, which sounded less brutalist, more expansive, and even life-affirming than anything else in the Bad Seeds catalog. Tony Cohen had been replaced by Victor Van Vugt, another member of the Australian mafia, who had been doing live sound for the Bad Seeds for years.

The sessions were disciplined. Nick was laser-focused. As a nod to our Brazilian hosts, he recorded a song in Portuguese, a traditional spiritual called "Foi Na Cruz," which would open the album. They brought in some Brazilian singers to provide backing vocals. Nick had a very particular idea of how he wanted them to perform the words. They kept telling him, "We can't sing it that way. If you know the language, you'd know that nobody would do it that way." So there was a little push and pull with that. Nick insisted and prevailed. One of the vocalists didn't react well to being told how to sing in his native language. "OK, then," he said, "I'll just pretend I'm *dead.*"

It was a revelation to me that you could go to a recording studio, not be stoned or drunk, and still be creative. Even so, I didn't feel I was contributing much. A running joke among the hired hands in the Bad Seeds went something like this: Someone would ask, "What did you do at the sessions today?" and we'd reply, "We sat around watching Mick Harvey play everything." Even Blixa was in on the joke. For the title track, he sat his guitar on his lap and Thomas

Wydler came over and played the strings with drumsticks. Afterward, Blixa announced with immense pride, "It is my *greatest* guitar part yet." I guess he thought he was taking his notoriously minimalist guitar playing to new heights.

Listening back now, I realize I'm on the record quite a lot, with prominent guitar parts on "The Ship Song" and "The Weeping Song," two of the strongest tracks on the record. When we moved from São Paulo to Berlin to mix the album, my mind was far away, back in LA, with Ron.

It was the end of Berlin as we knew it. A deluge of people in acid-wash jeans and mullet haircuts were coursing through the streets of Kreuzberg. The Ossis, the East Germans, had breached the Wall. There were thousands of them, stumbling along the streets, stunned and amazed, like visitors from an ancient past who had just touched down in modern times. They pressed their faces in wonder against the windows of the Turkish shops to peer at the delicacies inside.

Earlier that evening on November 9, 1989, utterly oblivious to our proximity to history, the Bad Seeds had reconvened at Tritonus Tonstudio in Berlin, overlooking the Spree, a block and a half from Oberbaumbrücke, a redbrick railway bridge with Gothic turrets, one of the seven border crossings between East and West Berlin, which opened that night for the first time in twenty-eight years.

We were overdubbing and mixing, putting the final touches to *The Good Son*, without any hint as to what was to transpire or how auspicious the date would become. I was distracted by a violent stomach flu and spent more time in the bathroom, doubled over the toilet bowl, than I did bent over my guitar in the studio. The Germans were glued to the TV in another room. They kept coming in and out of the control room, talking excitedly to each other. It all seemed very sudden. Like the dam just . . . broke. The Ossis couldn't believe it either.

The session was called around 4 a.m. and we all tumbled out of the studio in search of taxis to take us home. Berlin is a twenty-four-hour city but other than the twenty-four-hour party people spilling from bar to bar, the streets are mostly empty after midnight, save the odd vehicle. Not this night.

People were flooding into the West, some for the very first time in their lives—but cautious as cats on unfamiliar terrain, walking almost on tiptoes, as if they didn't know how long this strange breach in the usual order of things would last. They were stunned at this turn of events but discovering life with every step. People were throwing food off the back of trucks. It was both celebratory and strange.

The next morning, we rose to find Kreuzberg still awash with people. There were lines out the door and along the street at every bank and post office. It had been announced that they were going to give West German marks to everyone from the East.

I went to a party at my friend Maria Zastrow's house on Paul-Linke-Ufer. She burst through the door and gleefully announced, "Look, I found some East people and they're Elvis fans! I told them they have to come to my party." And she went straight over to the record player and blasted some Elvis for her guests.

It was as if we had unfinished business in Berlin that needed to be dealt with. A darkness had descended on the group, collectively and individually, during the recording of *Tender Prey* two years earlier. *The Good Son* was an album full of light and hope, even joy, reflecting both Nick's sobriety and his new relationship with Vivi. Almost the antithesis of the dark, brooding nihilism of *Tender Prey*. The sudden wave of optimism in Berlin seemed to reflect that also. It was the first time I had been there clean too. It was incredible to see Berlin in a whole different light and appreciate the relentless creativity and lust for life in the city, without the overwhelming anxiety hanging over me about having to find and obtain drugs. When I left, I felt as if I was able to close a chapter on my life, without carrying the pain back home with me.

The recovery community in LA was extremely social. Everybody was so gregarious and friendly and open, having barbecues and hanging out outside. I'd spent so long immersed in the claustrophobic gloom of London and Berlin that I'd either forgotten about, or become uninterested in, that aspect of life on the West Coast. Everyone seemed so alive. I felt invigorated and filled with hope just being in their presence and wanted to further involve myself in the community.

Ron always had a posse of girls around him. That's how I met Patty. She was also in recovery and a stripper. But not a recovering stripper because Patty still danced at a notorious spot, located a few blocks from LAX, called the Century Lounge, which, famously, had signage outside it that read LIVE NUDE NUDES. Who wouldn't want to work there?

Like Ron, Patty was a larger-than-life personality and a force of nature. She befriended me. She was Canadian but had lived in New York for a long time prior to landing in LA. It turned out that not only did we know a lot of the same people, but she and I had both been at a party Bradley Field had thrown at Lydia Lunch's loft on Delancey Street that time I'd caught the Greyhound bus to New York, ten years earlier. It felt like we were fated to meet.

Through Ron, I was also introduced to Hank Ditmar, a young, dynamic, and radical urban planner in his midthirties, who had been given the job of running Santa Monica Airport at age twenty-eight. He was a poet and music fan, very good friends with all the people around us, and also in recovery. His wife, Sarah, had contracted HIV/AIDS from her first husband. She was in the final stages of the disease and already in hospice care. Ron and I visited her and supported Hank. She died in November 1989 of complications related to AIDS, shortly after I got back from Berlin. I attended the funeral with Ron and kept in touch with Hank.

I had been talking about starting a new musical project. Hank suggested I go see a friend of his, Sally Norvell, perform at the Dresden Room in Los Feliz. "Oh, you've both been in Wim Wenders' films," he said. "You should meet up." Sally Norvell had played Nurse Bibs, the brassy blond, and slightly awkward, peepshow performer in *Paris, Texas*, and fronted a punk band called the Norvells in Austin, Texas. "She's kind of at loose ends with singing," said Hank. "She's performing standards at this bar but wants to do some original music."

I went to see Sally one night during her residency at the Dresden, which was this bizarre restaurant-lounge bar at the edge of Hollywood whose decor was (and still is) a 1960s version of the year 2001. She was performing with the house entertainment, the piano duo Marty & Elayne, who were like a lounge act from the '50s. They would be surrounded by piles of sheet music and took requests of any standard you wanted to hear.

Sally's set completely bowled me over. She performed a version of "Ev'ry Time We Say Goodbye" by Cole Porter, transforming this incredibly sad love song about the end of a relationship into a song of mourning for the generational loss from AIDS. It wasn't heavy-handed at all; she did it in very subtle ways, just through her performance, intonation, and bearing. She was doing what people might consider schmaltzy jazz but had somehow turned it into this theatrical performance of beauty and tragedy. Listening to her voice reminded me of all the friends I'd already lost to this terrible disease.

If somebody wrote some songs for her, I thought, it would be absolutely devastating. I'd already decided that person should be me. We spoke after the show, hit it off immediately, and decided to collaborate, right then and there. Because of the nature of our meeting, and the nature of the times, our first live performance was a benefit concert for a friend of mine, Joseph Fleury, who was very ill with AIDS. He was the manager of Sparks and the Mumps. Kristian Hoffman was putting together the benefit to raise funds for Joseph's medical bills.

Sally and I wrote a song especially for the event, "Lullaby," our own paean to lost souls and those left behind. I wrote these very simple lyrics, channeling my emotions about Ron and Hank and the death of Hank's wife, Sarah, all still fresh in my mind. The music was inspired by this bootleg I'd heard of John Lee Hooker, where he's just banging on the body of his guitar, with an occasional *chung* when he hits the strings. The song started with that idea of a very basic primal rhythm, then built into a crescendo with Sally doing her torch singing. My old roommate Chase Holiday played organ and drums. We made a few songs like that. We didn't have a direction so much as we had an idea, an emotion, and a mission, to address AIDS—not just the people stricken by it, but the survivors. We decided to turn that into a band, a pure collaboration between Sally and myself, that we named Congo Norvell. In LA, we became known as the group that played the AIDS benefits.

In May, I got a call from Mick Harvey to tell me the Bad Seeds were going on tour and he was moving back onto guitar. It was his way of saying I wasn't going with them, and my services weren't needed anymore. That was another of Mick's roles in the Bad Seeds—the hiring and firing. We're still good friends to this day, though, so he's an expert firer.

Instead of playing with the Bad Seeds, I went back to Europe to record with the Gun Club again in Brussels. In the time since I last saw him, Jeffrey had traveled to Vietnam and returned saying he'd been bitten by some rare bug in the jungle. It was the kind of exotic story we'd come to expect from him, an illness worthy of Indiana Jones or one of the real-life adventurers he admired. In his fantasy life, he had caught an exotic tropical disease. Maybe it was a story Jeffrey needed to believe. He was incredibly sick and in failing health from the worsening cirrhosis and his failure to curb his addictions. The more ill he got, the more depressed he became.

We made a record called *Pastoral Hide & Seek*. It was a good record but a dark time, and I was still trying to keep my distance from everyone else, especially Jeffrey, to avoid falling down a deep, dark hole myself. I played on the record but was hardly involved in the creative aspect of it, leaving all that to Jeffrey.

The Bad Seeds, who constantly toured and recorded, had been my dependable steady gig for the last few years. Despite his personal issues, Nick was driven and ambitious in a way that Jeffrey never was. Jeffrey was currently AWOL in London, doing whatever Jeffrey needed to do. Now that I couldn't fall back on music, I needed to find another way to make money and support myself.

After dipping my toe into telemarketing, I got another job more suited to my skills: selling overpriced designer jeans and leather jackets at a store on Rodeo Drive in Beverly Hills. Same deal, different scam. One day, Bruce Springsteen came into the store. I was excited—not that it was Bruce Springsteen, but because I spied an opportunity to sell him an expensive leather jacket and get a commission on the sale. I guess the telemarketing had revealed a ruthless streak in me after all. As the Boss browsed, I kept a keen eye on him, waiting for my chance to slide in and make the sale. I was beaten to the punch by two high school kids who spotted him and got excited also, but for different reasons. "Look, it's Bruce Springsteen! Bruce Springsteen, I can't believe it!"

Bruce looked kind of annoyed at first, but when they approached, he was extremely friendly and started asking them which school they went to. That did it for me. Get out of here, I thought. Get off Bruce Springsteen . . . he's mine. At that point, commission be damned, I was ready to kick them all out. Then one of the kids called out, "Dad, come over here to meet Bruce Springsteen." The Boss was as gracious as could be to them, went over to say hello, and signed autographs. All my scheming came to naught when Bruce left without buying anything at all.

I quit shortly after. I didn't want to get any kind of job in an office or work on Rodeo Drive again. So I went back to school—massage school—and got certified as a massage therapist.

One day, Ron came to a decision: He didn't want to be in a relationship. It had been a very intense few months, capped by a sudden end. I was disappointed, but I understood his reasoning. He was a very sexually active person. The time limit on monogamy was up for him. I came away from the relationship a changed person, with a willingness to confront my own issues, as well as being much more open to considering the idea of entering a relationship. Even I couldn't have predicted what happened next.

Somehow, in my divorce with Ron, I got Patty. We decided to move in with each other and found a house on Benton Way. We were both in recovery, great friends, and the perfect support network for each other. Patty asked me to marry her. I'd always embraced the unconventional. We care for each other; what do I have to lose? I thought. There was only one place to make this union official, of course: Las Vegas. We figured we'd get married by a clown at Circus Circus. That proved not to be possible. The clowns at Circus Circus, we discovered, did not double as ordained ministers. Our fallback was Elvis, but that was way out of our price range, on a budget of nothing. We got married in some basement chapel called the Las Vegas Wedding Gardens. It had a "live" waterfall, but the garden was just a bunch of plastic vines stretched to their limits that looked as if they were about to snap. Not a good omen for a marriage.

Throughout my life, I had moved back and forth from being out, then back in the closet, then out again, depending on the circumstances and the group of people who surrounded me. Music had always been a neutral zone for me. I had adopted this rule somewhat arbitrarily, but it was something I sincerely believed at the time, that music was not something to be gendered or politicized. Being with Ron brought me to the realization of how AIDS, and the political and social unwillingness to even acknowledge the disease, had decimated an entire generation. It changed my thinking entirely: The personal *was* political. That idea found form, albeit in quite an abstract way, in Congo Norvell, which was the first group I had formed since the Gun Club, but also the first in which I had a stake, creatively and professionally. I had long ceded all control in the Gun Club to Jeffrey.

Congo Norvell's first show had been a benefit; its second was a memorial—in August 1990, at the Roxy in LA, for Gun Club bassist Rob Ritter, who had tragically died of a heroin overdose at the end of June 1990. Every band that Rob played in—the Bags, the Gun Club, and 45 Grave—were on the bill, as well as the Red Hot Chili Peppers, Thelonious Monster, the Nymphs, and the Weirdos. Rob was much loved in LA, and the music scene came out to bid him adieu. Jim Sclavunos joined Congo Norvell on drums that night.

I thought back to when Rob first joined the Gun Club and shared with me how he would make the hours of drudgery at his office job go quicker by putting a tea bag into a cup of extra-strong instant coffee to maximize his caffeine rush. It seemed so innocent then. Now I could see it as the budding addictive behavior we would both play out in our own way. Rob held his secrets close to his chest, especially when it came to his private life. I had no idea he was gay until after he died. We connected through music and that was all that mattered. Our individual sexual or narcotic habits had no bearing on our relationship within the band.

One afternoon, eight days before my birthday in late March 1993, I was at home preparing for a massage with a client, Jon Dee Graham, a musician who was married to Sally Norvell at the time. I got a call from my uncle. He told me my father had died. It was all very sudden and unexpected. Jon showed up just after I put down the phone. I was a mess, emotional and shell-shocked. I had spoken to my dad a few days earlier. He sounded fine. I just could not comprehend what had happened.

It turned out my father had left the house that morning to go to the auto shop. He was found sitting in his car at a stoplight with the engine still idling. The paramedics arrived. They couldn't revive him. They determined he'd had a heart attack and simply dropped dead.

The strangest thing was my mother had called me that week. "You need to talk to your dad," she said. "He's acting really weird."

"What do you mean?" I asked.

"He's really uncommunicative," she said.

My father had stopped taking his medication for high blood pressure and hypertension. He was moody and down, which was also very unlike him. She had tried to talk to him about her concerns. He brushed her off and said he was OK. She was not at all the kind of person to say something like this without good reason. It was totally out of character for her, just as there was something off about my father's behavior that she felt was out of his. My mother was fierce, but I could hear she was unnerved.

I gave my father a call. He sounded completely normal. "I'm OK, I'm fine," he assured me, and signed off saying he hoped he'd see me soon. I reported that back to my mom, even though it wasn't what she wanted to hear.

Afterward, I realized there was a five-alarm fire going off somewhere in the back of her mind, a premonition that something was not at all right, the way long-term couples are often in tune with their partners on an unconscious level. That's the only explanation I can come up with that makes sense. She felt this was serious enough that she needed to reach out to other family members to intervene.

The funeral was a big family affair. My father came from a large Mexican American family. He had a lot of brothers and nieces and nephews. They were all there. People were coming up to me, saying, "Were you close to your father?" It was such an odd question. "Yeah, we had a great relationship," I would tell them, not really understanding why I was being asked. Then it hit me. Weird. Gay. Musician. Son. In their eyes, I was the black sheep and didn't follow the path, so I couldn't possibly have been close to him.

The truth was I did have a great relationship with my father. Less than a year before, we had sat down and talked, having the kind of heart-to-heart, father-to-son conversation we'd never really had before. "I'm sorry I was a drug addict," I said. "I'm sorry if I was selfish and worried you guys." I told him all the things I saw in myself that I'd gotten from him, his general kindness and positive outlook on life. There was nothing mushy or sentimental about this. We talked it out and both knew where we stood, father and son on equal foot-ing. There were no issues there at all.

I would never have done that if I hadn't been in recovery. Part of the work I had to do was make amends to the people I had wronged, and admit I was at fault. I'm immensely thankful that the course of my life had brought me to that point of realization and reckoning at that time. But all the recovery could not help me answer one ques-tion: What had happened to my father?

Was he unhappy? Was he depressed? If so, there were no out-ward signs. He had worked the same job his entire life, as a welder at Stainless Steel Production. He had retired but kept himself busy at a community garden plot. That was his place for meditation and contemplation. If there was something wrong with his marriage to my mom, it wasn't apparent, and he never mentioned it. He was talkative—one of the reasons my mom felt his recent behavior was so odd—but he wouldn't really discuss his inner life. That's very much the culture of Mexican American families. We are very tight-knit, but those kinds of things are just not talked about. It reminded me of what happened after my cousin Theresa died. Everyone closed themselves off. There was no discussion about how it affected any-one. All the questions were left hanging in the air, unanswered. It was the same with my father's death.

Although I felt comfortable there were no unresolved issues be-tween us, his sudden passing, and the reasons for it, continued to weigh on me. I didn't recognize I was sinking into depression, that this was a coping mechanism giving me the excuse not to address what was happening to me in anything other than a surface way. I told myself I could handle it, that everything was under control. I was a disaster waiting to happen.

This Way to the End, My Friend

I was beginning to find my own musical identity in Congo Norvell. The lineup of the group was constantly shifting. That was a trick I'd picked up from the Bad Seeds. It kept things interesting and the music fresh. The core of the group remained Sally and me.

Kristian Hoffman, who was now living in LA, played keyboards and guitar with us. I loved the songs Kristian wrote for the Mumps, so I was overjoyed when he agreed to join the band. I would set up the mood and block out chords; Kristian came up with killer melodies for the choruses that gave room for Sally's voice to soar. We were a capable unit, finely tuned for high drama.

Mary Mullen was in a duo I admired called the Hesitations. She had a large acoustic contrabass that she often played with a bow, generating a deep, resonant growl. She also had a haunting voice that perfectly complemented Sally's. Jim Sclavunos, from Teenage Jesus and the Jerks, was our drummer for the first few years until he left to join the Bad Seeds. It was a nice little rock 'n' roll chamber group. My old friend ML Compton managed us.

At the end of 1991, we recorded our debut EP, *Lullabies*, with engineer Fred Drake. The lead track was the first song Sally and I had written together for Joseph Fleury's benefit, "Lullaby," which had set the tone for the group. When we played live, a young musician named Travis John Alford, an LA transplant from South Dakota, filled in sometimes on electric bass when Mary Mullen had other commitments.

Travis was this little leather-boy rock 'n' roller who was living with HIV. He had been part of the twelve-step group I'd joined when I first returned to LA, along with his boyfriend, Mark Haggard. I enjoyed their company. Mark was a tough-looking guy with an acne-scarred face and a bodybuilder's physique. He would scare everyone in sight, but he was a sweetie at heart, although very, very troubled. Sally and I figured he'd be the perfect tour manager, so we told him, "You have to come on tour with us."

We supported Nick Cave and the Bad Seeds on a few West Coast dates in August 1992. Mick Harvey agreed to produce some tracks for our debut album, *Music to Remember Him By*, which we recorded the following year in Echo Park and at Fred Drake's new studio, Rancho de la Luna, in Joshua Tree. Another LA musician, John Napier of Ethyl Meatplow, wanted to put the album out on his label, Basura!, which was distributed by the rap label Priority Records. It felt like things were happening for the group.

By this time, I'd also embarked on a new relationship with a friend of Kristian's, Patrick O'Leary. We met at a party Kristian threw for Arthur Brennan, part of the crew I'd met on my first trip to New York in 1979. Patrick was Arthur's roommate in New York. He worked in fashion and photography. We hit it off. He moved to LA, and we moved in together immediately. I threw myself into the relationship with Patrick and got very obsessive very quickly—perhaps as a reaction to how things had played out with Ron, but also because, deep down, the gnawing insecurity had returned after my father's death.

I still didn't know how to process grief and pull myself out of it. In a sense, I'd been grieving all my life: first for Theresa, then for all my friends who'd succumbed to AIDS along the way, now for my father. I subsumed myself to my new partner's desires. The community I had been part of for the last three years didn't interest Patrick, so I began to distance myself from my recovery group and stopped doing all the work that had helped me become whole again. Big mistake.

Congo Norvell was not really playing or recording enough for any of us to make a living. I continued doing massage therapy. A session musician on the scene in LA whom I knew fairly well introduced me to his wife, thinking we'd get along. She was also a massage therapist. She didn't know me. She didn't know my history. We became friendly.

One day, we were talking on the phone and, apropos of nothing, she said, "I just came back from New York and brought all this white heroin." China White was the purest smack you could get. In LA, all we'd ever get was black tar heroin. "I want to sell most of it," she said. Hearing this, something snapped inside me, as if I was the Manchurian candidate and she'd just activated my trigger. "I'm coming over," I said. "Right now." I hung up and drove straight over to her place in an autohypnotic trance. I couldn't have stopped myself even I wanted to. I was drawn inexorably toward my fate. "Show me the stuff," I ordered the second she opened the door.

First, I thought, I'll just sniff a little. This is the lie I told myself, even knowing I was already past the point of no return. Then, of course, it was maybe I'll just skin-pop a little. I tried to moderate my usage. That didn't last long. Soon I was full-blown using again.

Travis and Mark had relapsed also. They were in this weird cycle of using/not using, of seeing doctors and obtaining drugs for Travis, who was gradually getting sicker from the effects of AIDS, then abusing the pain medication with Mark and supplementing it with street drugs. It was all very sad and depressing. They were also sharing with me, so that became part of our relationship also. The circle was drawing closer. I was locked into a habit for the first time in three years—but on the sly. I didn't tell anybody, not even Patrick. It was my guilty secret—guilty, in that I was full of shame.

Jeffrey had been thrown out of England and arrived back in Los Angeles at the beginning of 1995 with nothing but his guitar and the clothes on his back. His mother, Margie, took him in at her apartment in West Hollywood.

Jeffrey, being Jeffrey, didn't just get deported for some mundane reason like losing his passport or overstaying his visa. No, that was far too easy. The story came secondhand to me long after the fact, by which time it had already passed into legend.

Back on heroin, and a wreck, Jeffrey had become a handful and impossible to be around. He was very belligerent and unreasonable, according to Romi. She couldn't take it anymore. Feeling she was distancing herself from him, Jeffrey started playing mind games with Romi to get back at her. He told her their Japanese roommate was in love with him and they were having an affair. Romi didn't know what to believe. Tested to her limit, she sought solace in an affair with Nick Sanderson. Jeffrey found out. The relationship ended. Romi stayed with Nick, whom she would later marry and have a son with. Jeffrey, distraught, started drinking even more heavily than usual and spending much of his time at a pub that was local to his West Kensington flat. He transferred his affections to a girl he'd see in there. A misguided attempt to woo her included reading aloud an erotic story he'd written about a young Japanese girl—the only problem being the girl he was sweet on was already taken by another, and her boyfriend, in the pub also, didn't take too kindly to Jeffrey sharing his most perverted erotic fantasies aloud. There was an altercation. Jeffrey was thrown out of the pub on his ear. He went home to fetch a samurai sword that Chris Stein had given him a few months earlier, returned to the pub, and burst through the doors, swinging the sword around his head like *Yojimbo*. Jeffrey was quickly wrestled to the ground by the landlord. The police were called, and he was arrested, charged, and bailed out, then deported.

In LA, Jeffrey took to hanging out at the Viper Room, which was walking distance from his mother's condo. He was back on heroin and drinking heavily. Johnny Depp, who co-owned the Viper Room, was a huge fan of the Gun Club. The place had lost some of its luster after River Phoenix had OD'd there two years earlier but was still a hangout for local musicians, many of whom knew and looked up to Jeffrey. He was never short of someone to buy him a drink or supply him with drugs. I kept my distance, partly because I didn't want Jeffrey to know I was using too.

Congo Norvell recorded a new album. There was a lot of excitement around the group in LA. Priority Records decided to take a bigger stake in John Napier's label, Basura!, which had released our previous album. We were effectively signed to Priority now, meaning we'd benefit from an increased marketing budget and a much larger back-office operation supporting us.

In June, we went out on a two-week tour in Germany with Little Annie and a short run on the East Coast when we got back to the United States. Bill Bronson from Swans joined us on bass, and Hoagie Hill from the Blue Daisies played keyboards. Back in LA, we set about recording the album with Joe Chiccarelli, who had produced records for my idol, Frank Zappa, and our friend Mark Eitzel's band, American Music Club.

Sally and I wrote a song for the record called "November (The Ballad of Mark and Travis)," about the hopelessness of the situation our friends found themselves in—their relationship facing an expiration date sooner than the pharmaceutical drugs they were taking, living on the edge with a predetermined future rushing toward them. Sally sang the lyrics both as impassioned outside observer and internal monologue. "Thirty looks so old from here," she sang, expressing the awful tragedy that Travis was living with, knowing he would not see out his twenties.

The record turned out so well, we were filled with optimism for its release later that year. We titled it *The Dope, the Lies, the Vaseline*, which was nothing if not an honest summation of my life at the time.

My relationship with Patrick was going through a rough patch. We were arguing a lot and acting very poorly toward each other. It became so antagonistic that I started having affairs with other people behind his back—but not so secretly that he didn't find out who I was cheating on him with. Then Patrick would sleep with the same people, just to spite me. We were locked into this cycle of maximizing our hurt. It could only end in tears. I was acting out, as if telling him, If you want bad, I'll be really, really bad; I'll show you what bad is. My behavior was that cold. I figured if I could make him leave, it would save me from telling him to leave. When Patrick did eventually find out I was using, he ran for the hills.

In retrospect, I was really projecting my own self-loathing onto the relationship, and the shame I felt for doing dope and lying to him about it. The fucking was just sweet relief from my pain, another short-term fix that only made me feel even worse about myself.

If I was doing badly, Jeffrey was doing worse. He wasn't really playing or doing any music at the time. He was just drinking his life away at the Viper Room, day in, day out. One of the Viper Room regulars was Mike Martt, the guitarist from Tex and the Horseheads, whom Jeffrey had produced when he was going out with their singer, Texacala Jones, in the very early days of the Gun Club.

Thinking it would be a more productive use of Jeffrey's time to be onstage at the Viper Room rather than channeling Bukowski at the bar, Mike put an all-star band together for him. It was Steve Jones of the Sex Pistols, Norwood Fisher from Fishbone, Clem Burke from Blondie, Keith Morris, and Mike himself. They rehearsed at Jeffrey's mom's condo and played a one-off show at the Viper Room in August 1995.

The show was successful enough that Mike called me and asked if I'd come play with them at another show. I knew Mike from recovery. He thought I was still sober. I didn't let on. He brought in the rhythm section who had been playing with Wayne Kramer of the MC5, drummer Brock Avery and bassist Randy Bradbury, who also played with second-generation LA punk band Pennywise. We did some rehearsals and played the show. Siouxsie Sioux and Budgie were in town and came to see us, as did everyone else in our hometown scene. The show was great. No matter how many times we went our separate ways, it always felt good to be back onstage with Jeffrey, playing songs we had worked on together and were part of the fabric of both our lives.

After that, in a very LA way, there started to be talk of taking the band on the road to "play the hits," so to speak. It was suggested we could make a lot of money from touring. Jeffrey and I spoke about it. He was dead set against the idea. He felt it was pandering, a nostalgia trip. I felt the same way, especially since it was somebody else's idea, not our own. Jeffrey was not in a state, physically or emotionally, to go out on a tour—and, if I was honest, neither was I. But we did play one more show together that month.

Travis John Alford had begun work on an album of his own music. He was an extremely talented songwriter, very magical and unique. He was well read and heavily influenced by Jean Genet. I thought he was a great artist who had a lot to give but, sadly, it seemed he would literally not live to fulfill his promise. He was getting sicker and sicker. It felt like the album was the only thing anchoring him to the world. Sally and I had a lot of concern and empathy for the situation he was in. He became a kind of project for us—really for all his musician friends in LA, who were rallying around him and contributing to the record to make sure it got completed. Dee from L7 and Carla Bozulich were also very much involved in this. We set up a benefit show at the Dragonfly Bar on Santa Monica Boulevard, hoping to raise enough money to finish it. Jeffrey and I played with the band Mike had put together at that event too. And we did raise the funds, but Travis died shortly afterward, on December 18, 1996. The album, *Lucky Pierre*, was released posthumously on World Domination, a label run by his manager, Laurel Stearns, who had also been a great champion of Travis and his music.

The day before Travis passed, I reunited again with Jeffrey to perform as the Gun Club at another benefit, an annual event thrown by

Pleasant and our friend Iris Berry, who were calling themselves the Ringling Sisters. What I didn't know then was that it would be the last show we would play together.

Randy Bradbury was going on tour with Pennywise, so we found another bass player, who, true to the history of Gun Club, was a woman. Her name was Elizabeth Montague. She was sweet around Jeffrey, very attentive, and committed to learning the songs. We rehearsed again at his mother's apartment because he wouldn't have been able to get it together to rehearse anywhere else.

I hadn't seen Jeffrey in a few months. He had left LA for Japan after the benefit for Travis. I was shocked by the change in his physical appearance in just a short period of time. He was very bloated. Even his head seemed as if it was twice the size. At the show, he wore all black: a leather trench coat, sweater, jeans, shades, and a black beret, looking like a cross between a Nazi officer and a French philosopher. It was pure Jeffrey Lee Pierce showmanship.

A few days after that, Keith Morris and Mike Martt got hold of me. Jeffrey was incoherent. They could tell there was something very wrong with him. They were trying to stage an intervention. They eventually convinced him to go and get checked out at a hospital.

I was in no shape to help and needed an intervention myself. Somehow, possibly due to the combined shock of Travis's death and Jeffrey's rapid deterioration in health, I made the decision to kick. I was staying at my mom's house over Christmas. I went cold turkey. It was brutal; I was vomiting. My mom was very concerned. I told her I had the flu, but I think she knew it was more than that. We didn't really discuss it, just like we'd never spoken about my sexuality. My parents accepted, and they knew. They just never wanted to talk about it.

In the New Year, Sally and I decided to clear out of LA and take our chances in New York. Priority Records had decided they didn't want to put our album out. They dropped their entire roster of rock acts, including us, to focus on rap, but they would not give us back the record so we could release it elsewhere. We'd become very disillusioned with the music scene in Los Angeles and felt we needed a clean break.

The previous summer, we'd played a show in New York at the Mercury Lounge, with the Contortions and this great new band Jonathan Fire*Eater. The music scene in the East Village, which was centered around a lot of new makeshift clubs and basement bars, seemed vibrant and happening. We rented a truck, packed all of our belongings into it, and hired Travis's partner, Mark, to drive us cross-country. Mark was still on a cocktail of pharmaceuticals. He had all these bottles of pills that he would try to refill on the road, arguing with pharmacists in weird small towns to honor his prescriptions. We all partook. I had come off the smack but was still drinking. Somehow, we didn't crash on the way.

Once settled in New York, we put a new version of Congo Norvell together: Jim Sclavunos, who was between Bad Seeds records, rejoined; Paul Wallfisch, a multi-instrumentalist with Little Annie who'd already played on the unreleased album we'd recorded for Priority; and bass player Brian Emrich, whom everyone called Bugsy. Occasionally, Phil Puleo from Cop Shoot Cop and Swans would sit in, and Liz Corcoran, a British musician, played viola. The band sounded great. We started writing material for a new album, mindful that Priority might still have some kind of legal claim over it.

I got a call from Jeffrey. He was living in Salt Lake City. His mother couldn't deal with him anymore and had thrown him out. His friends had tried to get him into rehab, but he refused. He'd been living with his father, whom he'd been estranged from for most of his life, in Las Cruces, Mexico, then moved to Utah. Henry Rollins had agreed to publish a memoir by Jeffrey. It was another of those situations where one of Jeffrey's friends who was genuinely in awe of his talent and brilliance wanted to offer an opportunity that would help keep him focused and creative. Henry, who'd always been one of the most disciplined and driven people any of us knew in LA, was trying to keep Jeffrey on a strict deadline. He had isolated himself in Utah and, to his credit, was writing a lot.

We started talking, maybe once a week, while he was working on the book. He would read passages out to me on the phone. It all sounded like prime Jeffrey Lee Pierce and the wild, unfettered creativity that was the hallmark of his best songwriting—a lot of free association, a collision of mad concepts, people, and ideas that had no business being thrown together. There were riffs on Isaac Hayes, conspiracy theories, and receiving transmissions from Tokyo Tower. It was all very Burroughs-ian—hilarious, in a very dark way. We were laughing a lot. It felt like it used to be. He sounded like his old self. So much so that we started talking about playing again. I told him about the situation I had set up in New York and enthused about the musicians we were playing with. "You should come to New York, we can do something here," I said, with one proviso. "If you feel up to it." I was still conscious that his health was extremely fragile. I had no idea how fragile.

Maybe a week later, I missed a call from Jeffrey. It took me a few days to call him back. When I did, his mother, Margie, answered the phone. "Oh," she said on hearing my voice, "I guess you heard." She didn't have to say anything; I already knew. "Did Jeffrey die?" I said, not quite believing what I already knew to be true. He had died the day before, of a massive brain hemorrhage, and keeled over in the bathroom.

I came off the call completely and utterly shell-shocked. It felt like the ground had been pulled out from under me. I was suspended—in disbelief, in grief—not knowing which way to turn.

I flew to Los Angeles for the funeral. I'd only just gotten to New York, had been there less than a month and was still finding my feet, and now Jeffrey was pulling me back again. I still hate going to funerals. I do go, to be supportive for family and friends left behind, but it continues to be extremely traumatic for me.

When I got back to New York, I was a mess. Jeffrey had died a few days after my birthday. My father had died around the same time two years earlier. I hadn't yet stopped grieving for him, and now I had to grieve again. It was more than I could take. I wanted to stuff that feeling deep down inside and not feel that way ever again. There was only way I could think of to do that. I started using heavily again.

Congo Norvell were playing out a lot more. We recorded a new album and found a small label in New York to release it, Jetset Records. The title of the record was *Abnormals Anonymous*. I was selling books on the street for a bookseller named Arthur Nersesian, a New York character who, at the time, was writing his first novel, this great book called *The Fuck-Up*. He'd employed another fuckup—me—to work at his booth on Astor Place in the East Village. The work suited me. At least I wasn't working in an office or a factory. It was a means to an end, a way to get by, pay rent, with money left over for dope.

Patty was very worried about me. She had moved to New York a year or so before I did. I had left our apartment in Silverlake when I got together with Patrick, but we stayed close and remained married. Knowing me and my ways better than anyone, she intuitively knew I was using; but, really, everybody knew I was using. I was blowing off rehearsals, not fooling anybody, even though I thought I was fooling everybody. The usual junkie game.

A friend of mine, John Foley, whom I'd gotten clean with the first time in London, stopped by the booth one day. "Come back to our side, lamb," he told me in his lovely Irish accent. "You've got to come back." He meant it and I took it that way. Just those few words were a potent reminder of the path I'd been on, and how I had strayed. What I didn't know was that this had all been orchestrated by Patty. She desperately wanted me to kick and had enjoined all my friends to help.

One day, Jim Sclavunos sat me down. "We know what you're doing," he said. "You're fucking up. It's not good. You're too old." That last part really hit a nerve. I'd turned thirty-seven that year. I felt much older, prematurely aged by all the wasted years of getting high. Junk time shrinks your day to two positions on the clock: time to fix, and time to fix again. So focused are you on the routine that days, months, years speed by without you even noticing. So maybe it was true? Maybe I had gotten old and not even noticed. Jim's words rang through my head over and over like a mantra, or a curse. The message stuck. I'm a fuckup and I'm fucking up.

We have a great new record. The label loves it. The band love it. And I'm surrounded by cool people who care for me. I have an amazing opportunity ahead of me. Don't blow it. Not this time, not again. This is what I told myself. There was the strongest fight against this inside me—a voice speaking against my true will, encouraging me instead to continue on my path to self-destruction. It spoke for me but didn't seem part of me, like Linda Blair in *The Exorcist*. However, miraculously, I listened to my better angels.

I knew that if I made the decision to quit, I was going to have to stick to it this time. This wasn't just about me.

October 22, 1997, is a date indelibly printed on my mind, as precious to me as my own birthday. The day I got clean and never looked back.

He Walked In

Sometimes we meet people by chance who change the course of our life immeasurably. What may seem like small, seemingly insignificant steps we take at the instigation and encouragement of others can have vast consequences for ourselves. This is life as chaos theory.

I often wonder how things might have turned out if I hadn't met Jeffrey Lee Pierce. Would I have ever picked up a guitar? Or would I have continued pursuing my first choice of a career and gone to college to study journalism? If so, would I still be writing about music rather than making it? The only thing that matters, that I can even be sure of, is that I met Jeffrey, and that chance meeting opened a wealth of opportunity for me that continues to this day.

Jeffrey was my alter ego and opposite number, my counsel and my inspiration, my antagonist and irritant. We were different in so many ways but somehow the same. His faults were mine also; his demons, my demons. Our paths ran in parallel, then diverged, but remained forever connected.

The strange individual I first met in line outside the Whisky a Go Go at the Pere Ubu gig was a nerdy music fan. The one that emerged from the songs and the music we began making together a few months later was entirely different: a vengeful, blasphemous orator—part preacher, shaman, and orisha, part provocateur and trickster. People, including even some who played in the Gun Club over the years, thought Jeffrey's persona was all a put-on and a pose. They wrote him off as a performer, even as they appreciated the genius of his songwriting. I knew different. I realized that Jeffrey invoked and inhabited these characters as a way to help him live and tell his story. They were as real to him as anything else in his life.

He had a personality that was so fragmented, it was a puzzle to everyone who encountered him. I knew many different Jeffreys. I didn't really think of it as schizophrenia or anything. I just thought, This is how he works, this is how he gets by and expresses himself and his connection to worlds both imaginary and real. He wanted people to feel something, possibly because he felt everything at an intensity that would have driven others mad—and may have done the same to him. Jeffrey was extremely sensitive. The imagery that emerged from him, through his lyrics and writing, veered from one extreme to the other. It was brutal and beautiful, soft and abrasive. He could turn on a dime from singing about sea creatures and blue coral to rape and murder. He embraced the dark and pursued the light.

That was the thread running through all the art, music, literature, and culture we discovered and obsessed over together: the darkness and the light, the merging of the two to make a full spectrum of emotion and experience.

Through all the ups and downs we both went through, the only constant in both our lives for so many years was our friendship. I was with him at the very first Gun Club show, and the very last. Those seventeen years shaped the course of my life to date. Now that he is no longer here, that is something I take great solace in—as well as the fact that he is so loved and revered, and that his songwriting has been so inspirational to so many people, as he was to me also.

For the longest time, Jeffrey had more belief in me than I had in myself. He said, "You can do this" over and over again until I finally heard it myself and realized that I could, that there was nobody, other than me, stopping me from doing anything I set my mind to. He saw something in me and brought it out. In some ways, he probably got more than he bargained for. He didn't figure I would take him seriously, pick up a guitar, learn how to play it, and form a band with him. That I would jump when he said jump. We leapt together into the unknown, and somehow found our footing.

And now that more years have passed than he was in my life, I don't see his death as a hindrance to our relationship. Jeffrey is always with me. He even comes to me in dreams.

I was in my mom's kitchen in my childhood home in La Puente, standing near the Bakelite phone fixed to the yellow wall, when Jeffrey walked in. An electrical cord was coiled around his hands. He wasn't alone. Brian Eno was standing next to him. "Eno wants to work with us," Jeffrey said breathlessly. "Are you game?"

"Of course," I said. "It's Brian Eno." In truth, I was more excited to see Jeffrey. It didn't feel odd or creepy, even though I knew he'd been dead for some years.

We chatted excitedly for some time, catching up and riffing on old stories. Then Jeffrey walked from the living room into the hallway, his eyes scanning the long driveway outside the front door. The white car he and Eno had arrived in was no longer there. He became flustered and perplexed. "It's all right, you can stay here," I told him.

"No," he said. "I have to leave. I need to go find Eno and the car."

I was sad to see him go and made him promise to return. Then I made him promise a few more times, realizing this was a visitation from the spirit realm and that he could come and go as he pleased, but I could not.

I watched as he walked out of the house and down Ahern Drive. I was just glad to have seen my old friend again.

Acknowledgments

This book has had many "authors" working behind the scenes to bring it from the mind to the page. Not least, my cowriter, Chris Campion, who stuck with me from beginning to end, helped me find my voice, and shaped and structured my story, pulling things out of me I didn't expect. Matthew Hamilton at the Hamilton Agency, quite simply the finest agent a "Kid" could have, who recognized the promise in the manuscript. Ben Schafer, whose great enthusiasm and support for the book, and belief in my story, made it more real than I could have imagined; and the whole team at Hachette Books—Fred Francis, Carrie Napolitano, Zachary Polendo, Ashley Kiedrowski—who gently guided me through the process of dressing and socializing the book so it was ready to show itself off proudly to the world. Susan VanHecke, whose sensitive and diligent copyediting chiseled and honed the text into final shape.

I've been fortunate to both meet and befriend many immensely talented people who have a "magic eye" for capturing life in images, and feel blessed they pointed their cameras in my direction, if only for a frame. Thank you to Marcy Blaustein, who captured me at my best in the incredible image that graces the cover of this book, and for being the designated driver to all those early shows we attended together; great soul mates Donna Santisi and Theresa Kereakes, chroniclers of my youth as an LA punk (and that of so many others); my Gun Club bandmate Romi Mori, who crystallized the chaos of our time on the road into so many elegant images; the inimitable and brilliant Danny Fields, Ramones manager and so much more, for immortalizing "the Prez" on celluloid; friends for life Jessamy Calkin and Paul Zone, who were there when it mattered; and the deans of photography: Anton Corbijn, Jens Jurgensen, Ed Colver, David Arnoff, Lilian Lohberg, Richard Dumas, David Jacklin, Herman Nijhof, Liz Seidman. And an extra-special thanks to my sweet sister, Ruth Mayer, for preserving the family photo albums with all their precious memories.

Too many of my nearest and dearest, longtime friends, and acquaintances left this planet before publication, and I think of them daily. My big sister, Barbara Tristan, Anita Lane, Chuck Fulton, Miss Mercy, Hank Dittmar, and the mighty Mark Lanegan—I miss and love you.

The initial idea to write my life came out of the extensive interviews my great friend Jonathan Toubin sat me down to do for his website, New York Night Train. Inspired, I started writing stories myself under the tutelage of Lynn Stearns, at her ace memoir workshops at the Writer's Center in Bethesda, Maryland. Whenever writing became uncomfortable, I could always count on my booking agents, Todd Cote at Leafy Green and Buzz at U-Turn Touring, to send me out on the road again; and Larry Hardy at In the Red Records, who put out as many records as I could make with an unwavering enthusiasm and support. Through it all, my husband, Ryan Hill, held down the fort, endured my self-doubt, reinforced my place in the world, and told me I could really do it. Ryan, you are dazzling.

Flea and Bobby Gillespie were two of the first to read the manuscript, and I thank them greatly for their exuberant and heartfelt feedback. The inestimably brilliant and perceptive Jon Savage got it, felt it, and nailed it more perfectly than I could ever have imagined in the incredible introduction he wrote for this book.

To Jeffrey Lee Pierce, Lux Interior, Poison Ivy, and Nick Cave, who saw something in me I didn't know I had, welcomed me into their world, and helped nurture and hone my talent. As a musician, I am one chord strumming in a void without all my fellow lifer players: long-suffering Gun Clubbers Terry Graham, Patricia Morrison, Romi Mori, and Nick Sanderson, with whom I recorded and played some of the best; dearly departed fellow Cramps Nick Knox and Bryan Gregory; Brit Fur Biblers Murray Mitchell and Desi Desperate; the very Bad Seeds Mick Harvey, Blixa Bargeld, Barry Adamson, Thomas Wydler—and Roland Wolf, who is greatly missed; the "girls" of the Knoxville Girls, Bob Bert, Jerry Teel, Jack Martin, and Barry London; Congo Norvell, the band I formed with the great torch singer Sally Norvell, which wouldn't have been complete without the incredible talents of Jim Sclavunos, Kristian Hoffman, and XX; and my band, the Pink Monkey Birds, who have stayed loyal and true throughout: Jorge Velez, Jesse Roberts, Kiki Solis, Ron Miller, Mark Cisneros, James Can't, and the very great Jack Martin.

Everyone I've ever known has been a major player and changed the course of my life, in ways big and small. Among those I cherish greatly are my "bestie" from New York, Lydia Lunch; my husband, Ryan Hill, whom I'm thanking again because I can't thank him enough; my wife, Patty Powers; lovers of the past who are still with me every day, especially Ron Athey; and friends for life Chase

Holiday, Howie Pyro, Marina Lutz, Mark Eitzel, Jody Robello, and Little Annie.

To all I have mentioned here, and those I have not, each and every one of you shines gold rays into the world, and I'm honored to bask in their glow.

And last but definitely not least, a huge thanks to all the twelve-steppers, for helping a guy out.